THE FAERY
TEACHINGS

Revised and Updated

Orion Foxwood

Cover Art
Martin Bridge

Internal Illustrations
Andrew Goldys

R.J. Stewart
Books

COPYRIGHT

Orion Foxwood © 2007

Cover artwork by Martin Bridge
Internal images by Andrew Goldys

Designed and typeset in Sylfaen
by Jenny Stracke Roanoke, VA

Revised and reprinted
in the USA © 2007

A catalog record for this book is available
from the Library of Congress.

ISBN: 978-0-9791402-2-8

R.J. Stewart Books
P.O. Box 802
Arcata, CA 95518
www.rjstewart.net

And they are older, far older than the human imagination
and even the ancient stones can envision...

WINDOW

We are fallen angels who've forgotten how to fly...
can't find the window laying underneath
the curtain of our minds.

Funny, fallen angels tripping daily on
our wings; we should laugh...
running into moments we don't see what they could bring.

While I was dreaming this, there were people living it.
This has gone on long enough, this ignorant surrender.
You can fly high as you want.
Find the window and remember.

Last night, I was dreaming of a world
I've never known ... so fine.
Fearless, giving people that would never stop the love.

While I was dreaming this, there were people living it.
This has gone on long enough, this ignorant surrender.
You can fly high as you want.
Find the window and remember.

The window's waiting to be opened.
Draw back the curtain and you'll see
open up your mind
then you're sure to find
waiting all this time
It's inside you

*From song entitled "Window" with lyrics and music
written by Ginger Doss performed by Dreamtrybe.
COPYRIGHT © 1996 Glass Umbrella Music/ASCAP*

A Note to the Reader

This book is a compilation of folkloric practices from oral lore, inspired poetry, contemporary practices, as well as some historical lore and practices documented through academic research. *It is not intended to be a scholarly document.* Rather, it is intended to be a practical one that presents a body of practices and lore that, in some form, extends from our distant past to the present time and will continue into the unknown future.

The best audience for *The Faery Teachings* includes practitioners of folk, magical, and earth-based spirituality and traditions, and those persons who are curious about modern and old Faery lore. It is also aimed at anyone who cares about our planet and all of the beings who dwell on, in, and around her.

My true prayer is that the reader will find spiritual insight for themselves and a motivation to heal the damage that humanity has made to our beloved earth and the world of nature. In these actions, we can rest assured that we humans will find our true spiritual nature.

The lore, techniques and exercises in this book, if applied, can produce profound changes in paradigm and perception. Only you, the reader can determine the appropriate pace for their application and your readiness for their effects. The most balanced effects are produced by following the instructions given and using them only within the context of the book and by using sound moral and personal judgment. The full responsibility for the effects rests solely on you, the reader and user.

To the Artists

This book would not have been complete without the extraordinary vision of two very talented artists. The cover art is the work of Martin Bridge, while the black and white artistic drawings were created by Andrew Goldys. As you can see, both of these men are truly gifted at capturing the haunting and alluring qualities of the Fay and their realm. I am so grateful to these inspired and talented gentlemen for their devotion and contribution to this book.

DEDICATION

Mateo Wildcat,
my human lover, life partner, friend and soul mate.

R.J. Stewart,
cherished friend, mentor, role-model and publisher.

Dolores Ashcroft-Nowicki,
cherished friend, mentor and advisor.

Lady Circe,
my Queen Mother, friend and "guide beyond the veil."

Brigh,
my Faery Lover and Queen.

Moonridge,
the sacred land that guided the foundations of this book.

Mellina Foxwood,
who made Moonridge possible.

Betty Jean,
my human mother who gifted me with the Second Sight.

The Old Gods, Faery people and the Ancestors; for they
are the vision, inspiration and purpose for this book.
Your ancient ways shall pass to yet another
generation of humanity.

And, to all seers, Faery doctors and Faery lore
researchers who have walked the hidden paths
of Faery and opened the way for all seekers.

ACKNOWLEDGMENTS

Sherrie McCain-Kistler,
for your loving and generous support of this reprint
and the ongoing Seership work.

Jhim Midgett, cherished friend and co-walker,
for your love and constant support.

Martin Bridge and Andrew Goldys,
talented visionary artists and friends.

Sibyl Foxwood,
great friend and the best book fetch a seer
and Faery researcher could have.

Foxwood Temple,
my spiritual family.

Anthony Restivo,
my original publisher and dear friend.

Jenny Stracke,
chief editor extraordinaire and her incredible
editorial group - Atalanta Foxwood, Sibyl Foxwood,
and Jhim Midgett.

Nuinn Foxwood and Darone Foxwood,
for your technical expertise in getting the artwork to
the page and for creating the cairn that opens every chapter.

Lady Ceres Moonspinner,
friend and wise inspirer.

FOREWORD

BY

R.J. STEWART

Greetings! You are about to read a fascinating and spiritually transformative book. I have read it, and found many riches therein. As a teacher and writer of the Faery/Fairy and UnderWorld traditions for many years, I feel some strong affinities with the material in this book, and recognize and respect many connections to my own work. But, dear reader, do not think for one minute that this is a book that repeats material found in other books, for it definitely is not! I have found many highly original and creative ideas, methods, discussions, and practical examples in these chapters and, most important of all, I also found insight and inspiration: rare commodities indeed in these dreary days of hack fairy books and clone authorship to screw a buck or two out of the unsuspecting public.

Orion Foxwood bases his faery magic in the folkloric roots of his native land of the fringes of Appalachia, and in the folkloric magic that surrounded him in early life. To this he adds material that he received from his own teachers, which (to me) is an amalgam of Welsh Brythonic tradition with other pagan sources. The result of this alchemical brew, this Cauldron of Inspiration, is the book that you now hold in your hands.

But there is more: it is clear to me as a contacted Initiate, that Orion works directly with Faery and UnderWorld inner spiritual contacts. This is essential, otherwise a book on such subjects is nothing more than romantic speculation at best, or cut and paste journalism at worst. So, when you read this book and when you work with the practical material it proposes (and I urge strongly you to do this), you are receiving from and sharing with someone who has the experience, the knowledge and the faery inner contacts. Without the contacts, all texts on spiritual matters are arid soul-less shells. With the inner contacts, a book such as this can offer much to the reader. Why? Not through mere information, but in living consciousness. So read it, enjoy and, above all, Do It.

Good wishes to you all,
R.J. Stewart
www.dreampower.com

An Author's Note

Many wonderful and challenging events have occurred since the release of first edition of *The Faery Teachings* by Muse Press in 2003. In addition to these events, the author (like the reader) is always growing and refining his material to better capture the meaning and essence of the teachings. All of these things have shaped the revisions in updates in this edition of the book. The reader will note the following changes in this revised and updated edition:

- The use of the upper, middle and lower world; or star, stone and sea worlds to describe the threefold nature of spirit and its realms. These terms are more consistent with the folklore across Celtic and other cultures where the Faery teachings appear. The use of the Welsh terms is not as pronounced as they were in the first edition.

- The consistent use of the term "walker" to describe the threefold life, the tripartite aspects or dynamics of the soul. This change simply reflects a refining in the use of the terms on the author's part.

- The removal of the chapter (#15) on the vision keys and the vision key cards themselves. These cards (or "keys" as I call them) are nine beautifully illustrated representations of major spirit contacts in Faery Seership and they lay out a design for creation, destruction, regeneration, magic and initiatory transformation. They will be handled as a separate product that can be purchased through R.J. Stewart Books. The keys are very powerful tools in the practice of Faery Seership and should be treated as such. It is advised that serious students obtain these keys and work with them.

- The revision of the chapter on the Moonridge sanctuary to reflect the transition of this land into the hands of new ownership.

- Additional information has been added to Chapter 14 providing more information on the Faery marriage and the vision keys.

- The insertion of a new Chapter 15 that is more personal in nature and reveals some of the insights on this material from the author.

- The cover has also been refined by the artist, Martin Bridge.

THE FAERY TEACHINGS
TABLE OF CONTENTS

INTRODUCTION

BY
DOLORES ASHCROFT-NOWICKI

Mention the word Faery to most people, even some, I regret to say, who are involved in occult work, and they will raise their eyebrows and smile. Yet the link between Humankind and Faerie-kind goes back thousands of years. Some of our oldest myths and legends tell of a mysterious life-form, like us in form but far longer in life expectancy and youthfulness. They favour certain areas more than others: woodlands, forests and secluded hills and valleys, even certain countries, those of the Celtic world being the most populated, though they are to be seen (rarely it is true) in most European countries.

The reasons for their withdrawal from our world are many and varied, the most likely being, that they were harassed by the rapidly increasing number of humans and the destruction of their habitat. It could even be possible that the World of Faery might become totally removed from us. That is why this book is so important.

It is the work of a man whose whole life has been spent living in close proximity to Faerie. He understands that world as few people do, and has become a part of it to such an extent that there are times when one feels he is on the verge of slipping into it for good.

There are many "teachers" who keep their knowledge close, giving it out grudgingly in tiny bits. Orion gives with open hands and an open heart, willing to share all that he has gathered over many years. This book is the result of his life's work to date. It offers to those who have yet to discover that "other-world," a wealth of knowledge, information, teachings and forgotten Lore, much of which is given out for the first time. It offers to the true seeker a map of Faery, a way into that other-world that is so close and yet so far from us. At the same time it shows the reader that these two worlds have a common ground, a love of Mother Earth and Her children, human, faerie, animal, plant and mineral.

Between its pages lie spells and conjurations, belief systems and inner world journeys, poetry and tales of love between human and faerie. It is enthralling, gentle, terrible and instructive, what more can one ask of a book?

With this book you hold a gift in your hands, a Faery gift, but one that will not turn to dust in the morning.

Do I believe in Fairies? Most certainly. Why? Because I have seen them and I even took a photograph of one; not intentionally, it just happened. I do not have to justify my belief, I know they are as real in their world, as I am in mine. Read on, and you will find yourself ...

" ... looking out from magic casements, on to faerie lands forlorn"

– "Ode to a Nightingale," Keats.

Dolores Ashcroft-Nowicki, Jersey, UK – 2003

CHAPTER 1:
THE SACRED QUESTIONS

I have gone out and seen the lands of Faery
And have found sorrow and peace and beauty there,
And have not known one from the other, but found each
Lovely and gracious alike, delicate and fair.

"They art children of one mother, she that is called Longing,
Desire, Love," one told me: and another, "her secret name
Is Wisdom" and another, "They are not three but one."
And another, "Touch them not, seek them not,
    they are wind and flame."

I have come back from the hidden silent lands of Faery
And have forgotten the music and its ancient streams.
And now flame and wind and the long, grey, wandering
    and wave
And beauty and peace and sorrow are dreams within dreams.

— *"Dreams Within Dreams," Fiona MacLeod*

To understand the nature of the spiritual realms, we must first look at our inner world and how we translate life around and within us. Our human lives are comprised of interlocking, interpenetrating conditions of experience which act as domains of human experience. These domains are cognitive, affective, behavioral and spiritual. The *cognitive* domain includes how we think, our intellectual, data gathering and analytical functions and our basic cognitive framework. The *affective* domain includes how we feel and even how we intuit. The *behavioral* domain includes how we behave, act and socially interact with humans and other beings. These three domains act like the wheels inside a clock, each driving the other in a motion that produces an outer effect.

The *spiritual* domain includes the interaction between the previous three domains. It is the sum and source of the interaction between how we think, feel and express. It forms our basic world view about who we are, how we are, what the worlds around us and within us are, and how they interpenetrate each other. The exploration of the spiritual domain is not unlike exploring the intrapsychic processes of human thought and emotion, the social interaction processes of the family or other human clusters, or the biological processes of the human physical machine. Biology is for the biological. Sociology is for the social. Psychology and neurophysiology are for the mental and emotional processes. Spirituality is for the spiritual processes. Spirituality is a science that aims at understanding the spirit or essential nature of ourselves and the world around and beyond us. As William Gray, the renowned ritual magician, stated: "We are spiritual beings on a human path ..."

THE FOUR QUESTIONS

There seems to be four primary "sacred questions" that each of us, as human beings, seeks to answer in our spiritual quests:

- Who am I?

- What is it (the great "It," God, the Creator, etc.)?

- Why do I exist (what part of "It" am I / where do I fit into "It")?

- Where do I go when I die?

The quest to find the answers to these questions forms the very basis of our longing, as well as the spiritual and religious traditions that we have evolved to answer them. You may notice that religion and spirituality are presented as two distinct modes of the human quest. I feel, as many others do, that many religions have lost their original purpose and thus lack spirituality. An etymological analysis of the word religion and its root *religio* sheds true light on this assertion. *Religio* loosely translated means "to re-link." In a spiritual context, it refers to the re-linking of the human seeker to the greater pool of being. This being goes by many names: God, Goddess, Great Spirit, All-That-Is. Sadly, many of our current religious systems are more preoccupied with conformity, politics and economics than the true human quest for meaning and at-one-ment.

It seems that the quest for answers has never been more aggressive and needy as it is now. Daily, we are barraged with advertisements for a new meditation technique, a new crystal (straight from the shores of Atlantis, of course), a new pill or a new consciousness expanding technique to help us "find ourselves." Perhaps, we never lost ourselves in the first place. The longing we have is natural, healthy and seeks no redemption, but rather a context for self, a fabric or design to interpret life and express our spiritual nature. In my opinion, there is no need for new and improved techniques filled with complex psychobabble designed to overcompensate for a lack of substantive spiritual understanding. The truths we seek have never changed at their core. The folk traditions, such as the Faery Seership tradition of this book, hold the elegantly simple directions that we seek for a place in the spiritual landscape. The answer, as my teachers said, is "in your blood and in the land." Unfortunately, many of our orthodox religious practices, and even the neo-pagan traditions, have led us far away from the still voice that utters in the cave, which is that deep spiritual knowing within each one of us. These traditions appear more concerned with following the rules than unfolding "the knowing," a Virginian folk term for spiritual or intuitive wisdom. It is my sincere hope that this book will guide the reader into a re-awakening of their knowing and a validation of the wisdom that flows in their blood. Let us examine the spiritual quest in light of the four sacred questions.

WHO AM I?

Ultimately, the answer to the first question, "who am I," requires a tireless inner inventory of our vices, virtues, tools and tendencies. But, are we ready to really see what we find in the mirror of our soul? Are we ready to embrace and transmute the darkest elements of our nature? Many say "yes," but their actions say "no." Many humans shatter when confronted with their true nature. In the old Faery Seership tradition, when we integrate the human and Faery self with our Faery lover and the intelligence of other living creatures, we delve into the deeper voices of the land and develop the "tongue that cannot lie." For the seeker of the hidden paths of Faery, there is a warning: "do not tread this path lest ye have the pure heart of a child." Those who attempt to steal the "Faery gold" or grab onto the illusions of their fears and desperations will return to the outer world with mere straw. The Faery gold is the "pearl of great price," the vision of our being and the vision of the planet – "for in truth, they are one." In the Faery realms, that which you enter in with is what you find.

To truly look into who we are means to delve into the "River of Blood," that deep ancestral wellspring within us that contains the voices of our bloodline and all that we have experienced in our journeys through flesh, form and the inner worlds. Deeper and deeper we go, passing through the layers of voices within us until we approach the "voice of one," (Stewart) the "voice that utters creation" that speaks of "who we truly are." In this journey we also discover the living community that comprises our physical forms and that lives within our blood. For indeed our bodies, our blood and our life walk are *sacred* – and everything matters. We are, as we will explore in the following chapters, living communities within ourselves.

In the quest for an answer to the first question, we discover that our hardships and difficulties are the vice which presses the coal of thy potential to the diamond of thy becoming. Again, everything matters. A crucial aspect to answering this question is to understand that "we see the world from where we stand." This simple maxim reveals that the world comes together for us based on how we see it, or as my mother used to say "if you have a spot on your eyeglasses then the world looks spotty." Perhaps the most fundamental part of answering the first question is to discover how *we* see the world and the positions we have taken based on this perspective. A great deal of who we are is based on who we think we are and who or what we think the rest of the world is. If we are to reconstruct or strengthen a sense of who we are, we must take inventory and clean house. I once saw a bumper sticker that wisely stated "Insanity is doing the same thing over and over and expecting different results." Who we are is an inner consensus based on the views we have adopted from others, the life framework we have constructed based on our experiences, our species nature as human beings, and an old Faery mystery of "the voices in our blood" that often cry out for recognition and even redemption.

In our quest we must understand that *we are human beings.* We have a role within the species we were born into and our species has a role within the planetary being it was born into. Therefore, the Faery teachings instruct us to understand the role of humanity at the table of the larger being. In fact, the Faery teachings instruct us that we are a living being within another living being playing out an aspect of itself. However, our free will, passion and awareness of mortality defines human experience as distinct. As we shall discover, free will is not free in cost or in independence. If it were truly free, I suspect that we as a species would have self-destructed some time ago. The Faery teachings give us an understanding of the sacred role of humanity and a remembrance of our individual roles within the collective role of the human species.

WHAT IS IT (THE GREAT "IT," GOD, THE CREATOR, ETC.)?

To answer this question, we must have already built a solid foundation in the answer to the first question. Otherwise, we will be trapped in the path of illusion. Are we ready to approach "God," (what we in my tradition call the Ancient One) on its terms? Are we ready for a direct experience of it, not on the basis of our consensus realities about how it should be or what our books say it is, but in its world and in its chosen form? If the Great Creator created all things, then it is logical that it created us. Know that there is no part of the created that does not contain an essence of the Creator. For example, in art we can glimpse into the soul of the artist through their expression of the art. As the inscription states over the reputed entry point to the Oracle of Delphi, "Know Thyself." This kernel of deep wisdom teaches that the knowledge of our self is the knowledge of the Creator or at least some aspect of it. We *are* the portals to the gods. Again, we see the world from where we stand. To understand the greater god, we must understand the lesser god or the god or goddess in miniature – our self.

The Faery Seership tradition, if nothing else, is about direct experience of the creative intelligences. It is not a tradition filled with dogma, "thou shalts..." or instructions that should compel blind belief. It is about direct experience, first through yourself, through your ancestry, through your Faery allies, through the great planetary being, and then through reaching out into the stars to the living flame of creation itself. It is recognized that, though we are an aspect of the creator, the creator is not anthropomorphic, or human-like. It is the source and sum intelligence of all beings. We approach this vast being, the Ancient One, through its outpouring states of life, creation and expression, and then follow these inwardly like Theseus in the Labyrinth laying string to traverse the labyrinth.

Faery Seership is a nature-based mystical tradition, though it is not nature as she appears which we seek, but the essential truth at the basis of natural processes. For us, nature herself is the Grand Grimoire, the Living Bible or Word of God. Encoded within the life processes of nature are the very truths of creation, regeneration and transformation of material lead into spiritual gold. The form that the Ancient One reveals, in this tradition, is dependent on the eyes that see it. The Ancient One is cruel and vindictive if that is what you desire of it. In its purest state, I have found it to be creative, powerful, honest, curious, profound and all meaningful. I invite you to discover it for yourself. However, it is advisable that you answer question number one to the best of your ability and, as my mother would say, "wipe your glasses." To truly practice the Faery Seership tradition, you must be ready to cast your suffering off of your altar and replace it with the heart of a child that abounds with unquenchable curiosity and innocence. When you do this, all of life becomes a workshop of discovery served by every experience you will have. I advise you to see the living magic of life and milk truth and joy out of each moment.

WHY DO I EXIST
(WHAT PART OF "IT" AM I / WHERE DO I FIT INTO "IT")?

The more we explore and understand the nature of self and the Ancient One, the more answers to this question begin to surface. The "why" is the essential purpose of the Native American ritual practice of the vision quest. It is standard practice in Native American spirituality that one must first purify themselves and only then approach nature and wait for their vision or purpose for being to be revealed. In the Faery Seership tradition, we would say that the seeker does not only seek their purpose for being (existing) but also seeks the purpose for the type of being they are (the role of humanity and their role within humanity). A primary distinction in the spiritual practices of the folkloric Faery Seership tradition is that, in this tradition, we (the seers) do not see spirituality as something which *you do*; it is something that *you are*. Neither do we seek spiritual knowing only for the good of ourselves as many other traditions do. Rather, we seek to fulfill our roles on behalf of all of creation, seen and unseen, human and non-human.

As we extend the focus of our seeking beyond the finite point of ourselves to the infinite expanded sense of our lives intertwined with other states of being, our role unfolds and reveals itself to us. Faery Seership is a tradition of remembrance. It involves re-membering the parts of us wrenched apart by our fractured post-industrial mindset. It also involves a retrieval of lost knowledge hidden in the deep recesses of our mind and in the memory of our blood. It involves walking through the flaming door that purges the impure and illuminates the inner sanctum of our longing to reveal what was there all along.

The classic movie, *The Wizard of Oz*, demonstrates this for us. Dorothy had to experience the trials along the yellow brick road only to realize she carried the power all along. Dorothy, like all of us, had to leave the comfort of what was real for her in Kansas to journey the strange and mystical realms of Oz, and to return home with vision. The Faery Seership tradition teaches that each of us must travel beyond the hedge to see life in its chthonic, creative modes and then grasp our vision as the winds of change move it past and through us. This is reminiscent of the northern god Odin who hangs upon the Yggdrasil (the tree of life), sacrificed by himself to himself to receive the secrets of life. Even before the sacrifice, he had to drink of the well of memories guarded by the Fates. In many traditions, the Faery are the Fatua, the fates who stand at the gate of becoming and weave destiny into the hearts of humanity.

The answer to "why do we exist" is encoded into our very gifts and propensities. A part of the answer sits in the tool caddy that we carry through this life. If you are unaware of these gifts, work with the Faery visions may surface your memory. The Faery teachings tell us that each one of us is born to redeem the blood of our ancestors. Though this may sound Christian to you, it is in fact a much more ancient mystical teaching. As you will note in reading the subsequent chapters of this book, the Faery teachings have a necromantic aspect to them. They work with the spirits of the ancestors in a very direct, experiential and daily way. The power of redemption is an often misunderstood at best, or ignored at worst, aspect of the inner teachings. In short, each of us is born to purify and redeem the vices of our ancestors by carrying forward the best in our bloodlines. We are the embodiment of what has preceded us – it is in our blood. These are some of the voices, crying out for redemption, that often lead us to chemical dependency and other maladies that seek to silence the voices in our blood. In Faery Seership, we listen and respond to the need for transmutation. We were born for this. We also do this for humanity and, in the later phases of our spiritual growth, we do it for other living creatures. Needless to say, a sound moral basis must grow concurrent with our spiritual development so we may anchor the best of our power into this and other worlds. This means to truly take your place in the sacred circle of life and be responsible for it.

My visions in the Faery realms have suggested that we humans are at a crossroad in our development. This crossroad is an intersection between who we are as a species intellectually, emotionally, socially and spiritually and who we are eco-logically within both the inner and outer living landscape of creation. We humans have been given centuries to explore the far reaches of our power in this world. If, however, we are to survive for centuries to come, we will have to learn a new technology that integrates our physical sciences into a co-creative, balanced approach to creating and destroying. This will be a regenerative science that integrates the human species into a balanced relationship with other living creatures. There is significant work in this direction already underway by such new pioneers as Machaelle Small Wright and the Perelandra project. Ms. Wright has tapped into the ancient Faery Seership tradition through a scientific approach she calls "co-creative science." These are techniques to aid human partnerships with nature and its intelligences. Her work bears a close resemblance to Faery Seership, in which the goal is the Faery marriage, the final incorporation of humanity into the topology of the sacred land.

People are remembering and their divine discontent is awakening them in the night demanding answers. The ultimate answers can no longer be fed to us. We must experience them. If you are ready for experiences, tread the Faery way and dwell at the edge of remembrance.

WHERE DO I GO WHEN I DIE?

Really, a more mystical quest is about where are we going while we are in physical form. If we achieve answering that, then the questions of "after life" are answered. The concept of what it means to be alive is redefined in the Faery Seership tradition. For us, there is no death. There is only embodied and disembodied, incarnate or disincarnate. The concept of what it means to be alive is no longer confined to the realm of physical form. In this tradition, we encounter many types of beings who once resided in physical form as well as many who have not and never will. Trust me; these beings are very much alive. As you discover the mechanisms that move your soul into form, many mysteries of life's processes at the physical and non-physical levels are revealed. In a nutshell, the answer to this final question is *you continue living.*

Faery Seership walks the hidden paths between seen and unseen. This constant experience in the otherworld de-mystifies the afterworld and death. Once you have eaten the fruits of Faery, you cannot return to the way you were. Life is changed and the wondrous vision of creation fills every aspect of your being like honey in a honeycomb.

THE FAERY WAYS: A NATURE-BASED TRADITION

The Faery Seership tradition offers many challenges to the skeptical, left-brained analyst. Such a person may wonder how a modern human being with all the technology afforded to us could believe in such practices. I have many thoughts for this person to consider. If all life processes are energetic and chemical and there is no consciousness behind the design, then how and why does consciousness come about in the first place? Are we humans merely chemicals thinking about chemicals? Our ancestors believed that spirits were responsible for many illnesses that seemed to come out of the air. With the advent of microscopes, we realized that indeed there were living, conscious beings connected with illness which we term germs, viruses and bacteria. If our human awareness is so much more evolved than these, then why can't we conquer and heal viruses such as the common cold? And, why does our life depend on microbes and bacteria which live in our bodies and without "whom" we would perish? How is it that a brief look at ecology and biospheres reveals that all life is so intertwined that the eradication of one species sets off a domino effect? We should wonder which of the species currently endangered by humans will, if made extinct, bring about the extinction of humanity. It is logical to surmise that this being (plant, animal, insect or other) is perhaps the most powerful force in the human world. If there is no life after death, then are countless millions of religious and spiritual humans spanning over thousands of years, who pray and acknowledge spiritual intelligence, simply ignorant and fear driven buffoons? How do we explain the precarious, delicate balance of the planet earth on its axis, poised ever-so-perfectly in relationship with the sun and other planets, while dodging impact with the countless billions of stars, planets and other physical forms passing us in space?

Faery Seership is founded in the folklore and practices of the common folk; the farmer, the hunter, the people who somehow survived the harshness of weather and disease without modern science. In *The Fairy Faith in Celtic Countries*, W.Y. Evans-Wentz gives us these thoughts to consider:

Instead of Nature, men in cities (and paradoxically some conventionalized men in the country) have civilization, and culture. Are city-dwellers like these, Nature's unnatural children, who grind out their lives in an unceasing struggle for wealth and power, social position, and even for bread, fit to judge Nature's natural children who believe in fairies? Are they right in not believing in an invisible world which they cannot conceive, which if it exists, they ... even though they be scientists ... are through environment and temperament alike incapable of knowing? Or is the country-dweller, the sometimes unpractical, and unsuccessful, the dreaming and uncivilized peasant right? These questions ought to arouse in the mind of anthropologists very serious reflection, world-wide in its scope.

THE PATH

You began your path at the point of your existence. I invite you to open the way between your expression and your being, your intelligence and your soul, your humanity and the realm of enchantment. This book offers a combination of traditional and historical lore and techniques combined with practical approaches developed by me through direct Faery contact. Behold and embrace the Faery Teachings. I am a carrier of the Faery Seership tradition and share with you these honored teachings in hopes that you may find your place in the sacred circle.

CHAPTER 2:
THE FAERY SEERSHIP TRADITION

In the hollows of quiet places we may meet, the quiet places where is neither moon nor sun, but only the amber lights and pale gold that comes from the hills of the heart. There, listen at times: there you will call, and I hear: there will I whisper, and that whispering will come to you as dew is gathered into the grass, at the rising of the moon.

— *"The Hour of Beauty," Fiona Macleod*

This evocative poem was written in 1895 by William Sharp under the pen name, Fiona Macleod. It speaks of the Faery seer's inspiration of the Faery realms. Along with Fiona Macleod, there were many turn-of-the-century Celtic revivalist poets who were mystics inspired by the Faery realms such as W.B. Yeats and George MacDonald. Each chapter of this book begins with words inspired by the Fair Folk and mediated to humanity by these and other anointed seers. Faery Seership is a poetic tradition filled with imagery that bubbles up from the wellspring of the underworld through the voices of our ancestors and the living light of the sacred land. Faery is indeed the underworld, or more appropriately the inner world of soul life in humanity, the planet, and the spaces "betwixt and between." It is the realm of the ever-becoming and thus the ever-young.

AN INTRODUCTION TO THE TRADITION

The Faery Seership tradition covered in this book is a collection of lore, customs, techniques, magical practices and prohibitions which originated primarily among the tribes of Northern and Western Europe. Its root origins appear lost in the sands of time. It has been most popularized in its Celtic forms, though it is believed to have pre-Celtic, insular European roots. Some seers, including myself, believe that traditional witchcraft from insular Europe (especially Britain) is an amalgam of Roman, Strega and Saxon magic combined with more indigenous Gaelic or Cymraec Faery tradition. I leave the final analysis of this to the historians to battle out. What is clear, as evidenced by researchers such as W.Y. Evans-Wentz, is that Faery Seership can be found in various Celtic lands including Scotland, Ireland, Wales, Cornwall and Brittany. As R.J. Stewart, noted Faery seer points out "The Faery tradition is not exclusively Celtic, for it is also Norse, Germanic, Finnish, Lapp, Lithuanian and so forth." (Stewart)

I loosely use the word "tradition" to describe the Faery ways, as there is no orthodoxy among seers, only a collection of lore and practices with a common core that spans many countries and centuries. There are diverse streams of these teachings, encoded into the folk magic, practices, customs and tales that are still practiced in Europe, America and other countries that, though diverse in their expressions, resemble each other in their core beliefs. The practitioners of these ways are skilled artisans in their magical craft. Though sometimes they are referred to as witches, more often they are referred to as cunningmen or women, hedgewitches, conjurers, rootwomen and men (especially in American Southern folk magic), Faery seers and Faery doctors. The names change in different cultural and linguistic dialects, as does the general public view of them as beneficent or wicked. Faery Seership bears little resemblance to modern witchcraft and western mystery traditions that are more Masonic, Cabalistic, Hermetic, Alchemical or Enochian in origins. Faery Seership is a tradition all itself. The tradition does not involve elaborate rituals, invocations, evocations or even deities with anthropomorphic images. In fact, it does not involve worship of any type.

In many ways, what makes Faery Seership stand out as a mystical folk practice is that it centers on partnership with co-existing beings. This partnership involves mutual exchange and commitment that, for the human partner, results in gifts such as the second sight, the Faery touch, healing, "the tongue that cannot lie" and the ability to alter patterns in the inner world before they crystallize in the outer world (i.e. magic). If one examines texts documenting the legal proceedings of the Inquisition trials as well as reviews texts that describe so-called witch practices in England, Scotland, Wales, Ireland, and even Spain and Italy, one re-occurring allegation is that the accused "traffics with imps" or "suckles demons or spirits." It is my firm position that the inquisitors were well aware of some of the existing folk magic practices which traditionally involved the use of otherworld contacts such as ancestors (ghosts), Faery, elementals, nature spirits and ancient deity forms. This type of work embodies the essence of Faery practices.

There are core beliefs that appear across cultural variants of Faery Seership which include:

- A co-existing order of pre-human intelligent beings exists very close to human awareness *but is not dependent on it for their existence.*

- These beings live in subterranean and inner realms and are intertwined with human affairs, sharing a symbiotic relationship with humanity.

- These beings can engage in creative partnerships with humanity.

- These beings have their own rules, prohibitions and culture known within the tradition that must be abided by for a constructive relationship with them.

- These beings are actively involved with the natural processes and, in particular, planetary and natural balances.

- These beings are connected to locations on land or sea, such that they are sometimes referred to as *genii loci*, or the spirits of place.

- These beings live in a realm of existence along with other beings such as elementals, planetary beings such as giants, and the ancestral realm of humans.

- These beings are not immortal but exist for a considerably longer span of time than humans.

- These beings influence human concepts such as fertility, luck, fate, and health.

- These beings and humans have maintained relationships throughout time. Some of these beings maintain relationships with specific human families that have carried over many generations to modern day.

- These beings live in the "sacred land," which is the original vision of the planet earth, its surface and underworld intertwined into a sort of paradise.

In the stream of the Faery Seership tradition that I practice and which is the subject of this book, there are core practices that include:

- Use of traditional Faery lore, customs, prohibitions, and symbology

- Visionary techniques to move human awareness from the surface world to the under and innerworlds and then back again

- Mediation of inner power and life essence through the three worlds of existence to the beings of those realms

- Redemption of the blood, which works with ancestral contacts, and the role of our current existence in work that extends both forward and backward in human lifetimes

- Techniques for surfacing, or opening out, into the surface world "the vision of the dreamer," which is the original balanced vision of the planet
- Simple rites of healing and of honoring the Fair Folk which are tied to specific seasonal, lunar and solar changes; and which strengthen the bond between humanity and the People of Light
- Magical rites and practices to produce change (curses, blessings, healing and other magical practices) that involve humans partnering with:

  - *cousins* – inner Faery contacts

  - *co-walkers* – other inner contacts and the use of the "siths" or otherworld bodies

  - *fetches* and *familiars* – minor spirits deployed to gather things or assist the seer

- Development of the second sight that gives the gift of prophecy and the ability to interact with spirits

WHO ARE THE FAERY?

There is much conjecture on the etymology of "Faery" or "Fairy." In *An Encyclopedia of Fairies, Hobgoblins, Brownies, Bogies and Other Supernatural Creatures*, Katherine Briggs suggests:

> The word "fairy" itself is a late one, not used before medieval times and sometimes then with the meaning of mortal women who had acquired magical powers. The French *fai*, of which "fairy" is an extension, came originally from the Italian *fatae*, the fairy ladies who visited the household at births and pronounced the future of the baby, as the three fates used to. "Fairy" originally meant *fai-erie*, a state of enchantment, and was transferred from the object to the agent.

Other citations include: *fey*, an old French word meaning enchanted or bewitched; and *Fai* or *fee* or the Latin *Fata*, meaning fate. Robert Kirk, a seventeenth century Scottish Episcopalian minister, Faery seer and author asserts that:

> These siths or Fairies ... are said to be of middle nature, betwixt man and Angel, as were daemons thought to be of old: [are] of intelligent, Studious Spirits, and light change-able bodies like those called Astral somewhat of the nature of a condensed cloud, and best seen at twilight. These bodies are so pliable through the subtlety of the spirits that agitate them, that they can make them appear and disappear at pleasure. (*Kirk,* Stewart)

In the tradition, the word *Fay* is used as a noun to identify the people of the realm of enchantment. Therefore, the Faery beings are the Fay. A human can never be a Fay, though they may have many of the attributes of this other species. There are indeed humans who have virtues similar to the People of Light. This happens in the human world when a person spends a lot of time with another race or culture and internalizes some of the elements of that culture. In this case, it is an inter-species shift or adaptation. There is a phenomenon where Faery imprints on a human bloodline, a concept of great sacredness.

The word *fey*, in the tradition, is used as an adjective or description of another being or place. When we use this term, we are simply stating that something is very otherworldly or like unto the state of enchantment. For instance, a human may be *fey* but not a *Fay*. A Fay is a whole other species. Likewise a human cannot be a wolf but may be wolf-like. Again, there are many reasons that are explained in the tradition as to why a human may be fey or Faery-like.

In common with R.J. Stewart, I use "Faery" to denote the old tradition of contact and work with these sublime and powerful beings, rather than the post-renaissance concept of the diminutive fairy. The *Fay-erie* are the people of the realm of enchantment. In tradition, they were both feared and revered, as were their human counterpart seers and magic workers. The Faery are the "ever-living ones," the "People of Peace," "Bright People," "Good Neighbors" and many other localized names. Likewise, the term "little people" is a way of handling their awesome power. There is a tradition that you should never actually use the word Faery because it may call them and, being associated with fate and luck, might bring ill fortune. It is also a more hidden and sacred name. Therefore names like the "Good People" were coined. They were also called "the Fair Family" or "Fair Folk" to call their more beneficent attention as well as to note their color of "brilliant light." There is also an element within tradition that suggests that things are smaller and more powerful at their essential core and take on larger more complex patterns as they surface in the outerworlds. Therefore, the Fay are condensed and powerful underworld forces that are larger and more visually potent in the surface world.

There are many warnings in the old teachings about the names used to describe the types of Fay one should or should not traffic with. In *The Fairy Tradition in Britain*, Lewis Spence, another noted scholar and folklorist, instructs:

To mention the fairy name either individually or collectively was not permissible. The restriction upon doing so is un-doubtedly associated with the primitive belief that the name of a person or spirit is implicitly a part of the individual and that to know it presupposes a certain measure of power over him, especially in the case of supernatural beings. These, in general, exhibit irritation at human knowledge of their names, nor were fairies exceptions to this rule. The sobriquets given the fairies by the peasantry reveal a definite recognition of such belief, such expressions as the "Wee Folk" or "the Good Neighbors" affording examples of its existence.

There is an old Scottish rhyme that warns:

Gin ya ca' me imp or elf;
I rede ya look weel to yourself;
Gin ya ca' me fairy;

I'll wark ye muckle tarrie;
Gin guid neibour ya ca' me,
Then guid neighbor I will be,
But gin ye ca' me seelie wicht,
I'll be your freend baith day and nicht.

Likewise, Scottish streams of the tradition warn that there are *seelie* (good/beneficent) Fay and *unseelie* (bad/wicked) Fay in the old rhyme:

Meddle and mell wi' the fiends of hell (unseelie wichts),
An' a weirdless wicht ye'll be:
But tak an' len' wi' the fairy men,
Ye'll thrive until ye dee.

Robert Kirk, in his seminal work on the Gaelic Faery tradition, states:

Their bodies of congealed air are sometimes carried aloft, while others grovel in different shapes, and enter into any cranny or cleft of the earth where air enters, to their original dwellings. The earth being full of cavities and cells, and there being no place or creature but is supposed to have other animals, greater or lesser, living in, or upon it, as inhabitants; and there is no such thing as pure wilderness in the whole universe. (*Kirk*, Stewart)

The Fair Folk dwell in a liminal state or "betwixt and between." They are beings that are not crystallized as we "surface walkers" are, but are living in the state of ever-becoming. By this I mean they live in the plane of influences whereas humans live in the plane of effects. Humans become aware of the Fay through a number of means: 1) the second sight (either temporary or acquired through birth), 2) at in-between times when the veil between physical form and the etheric world is thin, 3) during near-death experiences when the physical body and the etheric body merge, 4) on power sites where the veil is thin, 5) during sleep or other states of consciousness when awareness enters a not awake/not asleep state (light trance), 6) when the mind is unfocused from the surface world during daydreaming or out of the corner of your eye, 7) at funerals or childbirths where the Fay or other types of inner world beings are involved in connecting or disconnecting the human souls from the physical form, and 8) in rare cases, under the influence of psychoactive herbs and mushrooms.

There are many different types of Fair Folk. For example, the trooping type is always traveling and moving along the Faery tracks (inner-world hidden pathways on and in the earth that are unlucky to cross). The solitary Faery tends to be more linked to the inner ecology of a specific place such as those linked to sacred wells or ancient stone sites, and who are inner guardians of an area. The Faery realms, not unlike the surface world where humans physically live, are inhabited with many types of beings. Traditionally, the Fair Folk are human size or larger, of powerful presence, beautiful in appearance and humanoid (though this form is likely more for our benefit). They are more like the Lordly Ones or Gentry of ancient tradition though there are some that are not as lovely in appearance; these have less interest in humanity. There are countless other types of beings that live within the Faery realms that are sometimes beautiful, sometimes frightening, and not always welcoming of humanity. Most Fay live in hives or clans with kings and queens or a similar structure. This social structure mimics humanity and, likely more for our benefit, works as an interface to translate certain energetic dynamics by using human patterns and symbols easily translated by human consciousness. The kings and queens are more like focal points where numerous, thousands even, of Fay coalesce into a colonial type of being with a central and extremely powerful intelligence.

HUMAN AND FAERY RELATIONS

Traditionally, the Fay are linked to fate, fortune, weather, fertility and the vitality of humans, plants and animals. This is consistent with their nature as living in the realms of the ever-young or ever-becoming where they are tied to patterns at their primal source, thus influencing their crystallization. They tend to speak the language and wear the apparel of the human location under which they live. There are many powerful truths to this concept that involves the interpenetration of their world and culture with ours through human burial sites. These "intraterrestrials" often mimic or integrate human traits that are associated with the internment of generations of human dead into the soil. The Fay merges with the blood of our ancestors in the grave through the decomposition process. As a result, the Fair folk and the human clan in that area become as one. As you can imagine, our current embalming and tomb sealing practices are anathemas to the Faery Seership tradition. These practices hinder the ancient alliance between humanity and the "power of place," which has a detrimental impact on the inner peace and "sense of belonging" in the human race. This is connected to the concept of the Faery Seership tradition also being a necromantic tradition, or one involving the spirits of the human dead. Basically, the interment and decomposition of human dead in a place over multiple generations strengthens the bonds between the powers of the spiritual beings, such as the Fay, of that place and their human counterparts.

The Fay are humanity's spiritual next-of-kin, second only to human ancestral beings. They are the underworld people and humans are the surface world people. There is an ancient bond of resonance between the two species. It is a teaching within the tradition that the concept of the changeling child, in which a human child is stolen away by the Faery and replaced with a soulless simulacrum, is propaganda designed by the emerging new religions to either demonize the Faeries or to blame them for childhood withering diseases not understood by the mainstream healers of the time. It originally spoke of an interchange between humans and the Fair Folk, wherein a type of intermarrying and even interbreeding took place; hence, the mysteries of the "Faery Blood."

The Fair Folk revitalize the natural surface world by carrying the essence of the first world (which is the original vision of the planet) or, as R.J. Stewart terms it, "the earth of light" out to the surface world thus in-spiriting it. In Gaelic Faery tradition this essence is called *toradh*, or *pith*, and is the essential nature or substance of all things in all levels of life. This essence is sometimes called "elf-fire," "witch-flame" or "virtue" and is intoxicating and vivifying. When a surface world being such as a human lacks toradh, they wither, fade and even die away from the world of form. When the flow of this substance in a specific area has been hindered by human efforts, the surface life of that area will wither and die, or there will be an environment of misfortune and "bad luck." This substance is at the core of traditional witchcraft and Faery magic. The Fair Folk travel pathways, or as we term them "hidden paths" or "hedge roads," from their inner world to our outer world and bring this essence out with them. There are many "Faery tales" of humans falling asleep on a Faery knoll (hill or burial site) or at the foot of a sacred tree and awakening in the Faery world. There they engage in drinking "spirits" with the Fair Folk and in joyous and bacchanalian dancing and partying that may end centuries later in human time. These stories tell of the intoxicating virtues of the Faery food that is the substance of their world – the toradh.

In an intimate relationship, humanity ensouls the Fair Folk with our "free-will" or individualized consciousness and they inspirit us with their collective, regenerative consciousness. This is the source teaching of the Christian belief that the Fair Folk are soulless. This superimposes a belief that only humans have a soul – a position that offers much room for debate. Tradition is clear that both species, human and Faery, are incomplete and when joined form a symbiotic relationship that empowers both with new capabilities. Linked with this teaching is the concept of the *co-walker*, or *sith* as it is termed in this tradition. This is an invisible self that lives in the otherworld and draws vitality and other innerworld contacts out to the human or other surface life form. The Fair Folk know each human by its sith as well as by its bloodline. Connecting with the Fair Folk re-energizes awareness of the link between the surface walking human and their "Faery self" or sith and expands the potentials for the human array of senses. Thus, the evolution of magical and psychical skills that result from this partnership.

The Fay are primarily, though not exclusively, hive beings that are as R.J. Stewart notes, "one step, one change of awareness, beyond humanity." The Faery races are our natural allies between the outer realm of manifest nature and the inner-realms of the ever-becoming states of transformation. The human and Faery races mirror and complete one another. The Faery need toradh to maintain a strong link with humanity as the surface world is not their usual realm of existence. Humanity, like all surface world beings (plant, animal etc.), are a vast source of essence. It requires a constant flow of essence to maintain physical form and the bodies or siths that result in physical form. In a partnership, or what is traditionally referred to as the "Faery marriage," the human and Fair One share essence and live through each other in their respective realms in a spiritual symbiosis. This is why there are legends of Faery beings cast as thieves that steal essence from milk, etc. In fact, witches were accused of doing the same through enchanted "taps" and feeding it to their imp, or breast-feeding the imp through incisions under the armpit area. These folk tales and Inquisition allegations are in fact remnants of an ancient tradition.

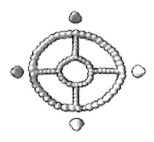

CHAPTER 3:
THE CORE TEACHINGS

Stand I at the crossroads, at the place between night and day;
And with my witch's finger, open I the Faery way.
Stand I at the crossroads, at the place between life and death;
And bless I now this holy place with my witch's breath.

– Orion Foxwood, 1992

This invocation was written through me by the Fair Folk to open the "hidden paths" that connect the physical realm (and its inhabitants) with the non-physical realms (and its inhabitants) at the thresholds of creation. It embodies a traditional concept that is basic to the Faery teachings: that the realm of the physical senses and another realm which lies just beyond them co-exist and interpenetrate each other. The connection between the two can be realized with a minor shift in awareness. The consecration of place, using the holy breath, taps into a deeper teaching connected to the Faery concept of "breathing for the land," which is a skill that develops when the practitioner reunites their outer awareness with the deepest being in the land, the "Dreamer."

The Dreamer is the "Lord of Light" within the land, or what is sometimes referred to as the "Star within the Stone," a concept dealt with more comprehensively later in this book. The basic teaching is that there is a living being, stellar in nature, which lives within the land and is embodied in the molten core of the planet. This being dreams forth all living things to the surface world, and the seer that attains unity with this being "dreams" or "breathes" for it, thus achieving prophetic ability and the ability to speak or breathe things into or out of being. Folk teachings of the tradition claim that this is one of the connections with witchcraft and the ability to cast a spelle or hex, which applies words of power. It is not unlike the biblical statement "In the beginning was the Word and the Word was with God and the Word was God." Ultimately, it is the Dreamer that calls the restless seeker to its discovery. In the process of delving deeper into the nature of the unseen realms, the Fay and the process of creation, the seeker discovers the answers to the sacred questions. But first, the seeker must "hear the call."

HEARING THE CALL

There is an impulse that sparks from deep within us and moves us to seek to answer the sacred questions. Suddenly, we find ourselves dissatisfied by what we have achieved, and searching for something with deeper meaning. It is as if a part of us is seeking while another part of ourselves is being sought. In the Faery work, it is this restlessness or wonder-lust for something intangible, unnamed but very real, which is the source of our inspiration. In brief moments of pondering it becomes clear that what we seek is not in material affairs, but in something richer, more elusive and much more personal. The tradition teaches us that the object of our desire is the indwelling point of divinity, our access point to fulfillment and unity with creation. We call this indweller the "Child of Promise" and it lives at the core of our being. It must be approached with the unstained heart or the seeker will be pixie-led into the dark woods of our fears.

This state of being cannot be reached without turning our awareness inward to the true "door of the temple." For indeed, it is through this door that we can reach for the Child of

Promise, the Dreamer and beyond. When we touch this core, the universe opens up to us. Faery teachings tell us that humans are mere surface walkers, incomplete and lacking inner unity. When we merge our outer human awareness with the Faery co-walker, we begin to come into true living and completeness. In fact, we fuse our outer awareness with the deeper nature of our own soul. For those who follow the hidden paths are aware that humans are shattered vessels seeking unification. We are aware that we must re-align our consciousness with the indwelling soul that lives in the original vision of this world. In doing so, we become complete and the Child of Promise is released from its confines to inflame the inner being with spiritual light and wisdom.

There was a time when humans lived closer to the land, sea and sky, and could hear the subtle voices that coursed through the elements. This kept us in touch with where we as humans existed within creation. We had customs and rites that aligned us to the patterns of life, death and regeneration and the beings involved therein. In fact, our concept of community was very different, and included beings seen and unseen, living in and on a sacred land that was an extension of our own identity. This way of living lends a deeper understanding to the travesty of forcing a race of people such as the Native Americans off of their ancestral land. These truths have not changed. Only our relationship, or lack thereof, has changed. We are fortunate to live in a time when we are becoming more restless, more apt to shake free the fetters that bind our spirits, and search again for our place upon the sacred land as a human species and as individuals.

The Basque peasants customarily opened their sharing of Faery tales with "this happened, sir/madam, in a time when all animals and all things could speak." I would change it to say "this happened in a time when all humans could hear." In the context of developing the Faery skills, I would alter this again by saying "this happened, sir/madam, in a time when we (humans) could hear all animals and things speak."

The development of modern human culture has enabled the capacity for science-based deductive thinking, while dwarfing the value of, and capacity for, intuitive deep knowing.

Faery Seership requires the ability to hear and see the unseen pulses that echo from states of creation, a place where the soul of every person and thing lives. It requires an imaging ability (also referred to as "imagination" or "visioning") that is attuned. Attuned means that the seer's mind has been trained so that it can receive impulses that are not confirmed or received by the five senses and can draw together image material from the deep mind to use as an interface or translation point for the contact. This requires one to broaden their view about how the imagination works and what it is. In Faery work, the central nervous system of the seer becomes an interface point for the Fay to imprint a contact which, through the attuned imagination, surfaces through a storehouse of images and concepts collected by the seer. This allows for cross-species interpretation of the contact. Without the traditional lore, customs, and prohibitions, the would-be Seer will lack the context to receive and interpret with any clarity communication from the secret commonwealth of the Fay.

During training, the novice seer discovers the nature and content of their own "mind-chatter" and the method by which they translate interaction with the inner thinking and feeling world into outer concrete reality. This process is called "approaching the voice." This "voice" is ultimately the source and sum of our purpose for being and is the embodiment of the Child of Promise and the Dreamer. It is the indwelling god/dess that knows, creates, destroys, transmutes and re-generates. But one cannot approach this awesome power without due preparation and discovery of the haunts in the house of the mind – again, the mind-chatter.

Before we can understand what the voice says to us, we must understand what we say to ourselves and accept as truth. These are the voices in the cave of our being that, until recognized and addressed, truly control our destiny. In the process of approaching the voice, we cross the "River of Blood" and traverse the thorn-thicket to approach the "Cave of Voices." This is the point within us where the impulses of the outer world that come at us and the impulses of the inner world that surface through us co-mingle, are interpreted and projected onto the screen of the senses to crystallize as our reality.

Anyone who has attempted meditation is well aware of the Cave of Voices when they close their eyes, approach stillness, and a cacophony of feelings, images and thoughts present themselves to be recognized and interpreted, many of which make no sense or seem like a hodge-podge of unrelated and frivolous mind-stuff. Both the River of Blood and the Cave of Voices are traditional images that refer to the stream of life that rushes up from the underworld into our consciousness.

If the seeker is to evolve the capacity for true seership, it will require a steadfast commitment to approach the River of Blood and the Cave of Voices with the ultimate intention of activating the deep awareness of the deeper workings of the mind and the creatures that dwell there. Again, the would-be seer courts truth and the journey to discover it as a passionate and constant commitment. In the deepest recesses of the Cave of Voices is "The Voice." This is the voice that calls us to remember who we are. It is the voice of the Dreamer in the Land. It presents us the sacred questions that become the fuel for our spiritual quest. It is the calling that stirs us into a restless seeking for answers. This call launches the spiritual quest that culminates in "hearing the voice," "receiving the vision," and "seeing the face of God." As tradition has told us, we cannot gaze directly upon the face of God (or the gods) or we would burn up in its glory. We must approach this face by looking for its reflection in the mirror of our soul – the indwelling deity, the Child of Promise.

To approach it, we move through layers of being, referred to by R.J. Stewart as the "conditions," and create the ritual magician's "stillness." Franz Hartman, in *Magic: Black and White*, asserts:

To be silent means that we must not allow any desire to speak in our heart, but only the voice of truth: because the truth is a jealous Goddess and suffers no rivals. He who selects wisdom for the bride of his soul must woo her with his whole heart and dismiss the concubines from the bridal chamber of his soul. He must clothe her in the purity of his affection and ornament her with the gold of his love, for wisdom is modest, she does not adorn herself but waits until she is adorned by her lover. She cannot be bought with money nor with promises, her love is only gained by acts of devotion. Science is the handmaiden of wisdom and he that makes love to the servant will be rejected by the mistress; but he who sacrifices his whole being to wisdom will be united with her.

DIVINE DISCONTENT / RESTLESSNESS

In accord with tradition, within each one of us is the Child of Promise trapped in the pillar of form. This Child, like its parent the Dreamer, contains our purpose for being. It is the source of the divine discontent that drives us to seek for answers. We, however, as seekers of the hidden paths, must first hear the calling of the Child. The call beckons us to re-member, to journey through the dark hidden paths only lit by the starlight of our hopes and dreams, to find it where it is held captive by the wicked queen, king or stepmother (so often discussed in fairy tales) and release it from bondage. We are modern Cinderellas, held captive by the wicked stepsisters embodied in consensus reality as set forth by religion, culture, science and industry. The sisters tell us we are unworthy, stupid, ugly and inherently flawed. Thus, we are restricted from attending the dance of life (the royal ball) that brings awareness of who and why we are.

However, the Faery Mothers from the realm of enchantment will always find us at the depth of our despair and discontent, and make the impossible possible. In fact, this is the crossroads of transformation, the hallowed place of initiation back into our true selves, as so many of us have experienced when, in the thralls of despair, a sudden clarity and strength surfaces and we are permanently changed. We are freed for a moment to attend the ball and find our Faery lover or "sovereign self" (the prince). But eventually the Faery magic must wear off; our personal magic takes over and we return for a moment to the old self, still carrying the inner seed of the Faery touch. Like eating the fruit of remembrance, once we have attended the dance we cannot forget, and by the potent power of magical memory we will become the sovereign of our inner kingdom. Once we traverse the realms of Faery magic, our spiritual feet remember so that when the Faery lover crosses into our world and comes back for us, we will be presented with the glass slipper of truth; it is a perfect fit and a queen (or king) is born.

This process describes the awakening of ancestral memory spurred by a restlessness for something greater, better, deeper and more meaningful. Divine discontent, if obeyed, leads us through a labyrinth of experiences that have a seed of familiarity in them. This familiarity is the sacred remembrance, the ancestral memory in our blood that tells us that we are exactly where we ought to be. Once we embrace divine discontent, we will never stop our search. The Faery quest differs from most religious doctrines that instruct the seeker on how to have an experience of God by following a set of dictates and through complete submission of personal will. In Faery Seership, the Voice is revealed to us by a process that involves:

- Extending awareness beyond the five senses into an energetic state of being (the siths or walkers).

- Experiencing the siths as the multiple states of being that co-exist and comprise the totality of who we are. These bodies are our vehicles for "walking" in this and other worlds.

- Experiencing a direct contact with, and relationship to, other states or modes of being that include the Faery and ancestral realms.

- Experience directly the state of active creation involving the fusion of spirit to soul, soul to form, and the regeneration of these cycles as they shift.

- Redefining what it means to be alive.

- Approaching deeper, more profound states of being that lead us to the eventual experience of the Voice, the Child and the Dreamer.

BASIC PHILOSOPHIES OF FAERY SEERSHIP

Life, as we know it, is made up of layers upon layers of expressions and processes. Upon and within everything are other beings, all of which are intertwined into a series of relationships that in turn comprise a large and sentient holism. This approach is akin to the Gaia concepts of ecological holism and derives from ancient tradition. There are many orders of life that create the greater planetary and, subsequently, the universal being. For most of us, we are affected by these beings and states of being but are totally unconscious or unaware of them. We are like tiny ships tossed about on the ocean of life thinking that manipulation of the outer world elements are our only oars and sails. Physical form is an outer surface reflection of deeper dynamics. The Faery seer works directly in the process of creation with the beings of creation. It is direct and non-ritualistic. It deals with few symbols, since the Fay are not symbolic of anything. They are living, intelligent, ancient and sentient beings, alive in a way that is even more profound than human existence.

In Faery Seership, life is depicted as involving three primary realms of existence, which for the purposes of this chapter are simply: the underworld, overworld, and surface world. The underworld powers are of ancestry, Faery and deep planetary beings which surface and flow out through us and other portals. The overworld powers are stellar/universal and move onto us, then through us and into the planet. The surface world powers (seen and unseen) flow across the surface of the planet or, like humans, "surface" from the underworld and interact with us. These fellow surface walkers may assist or hinder us in anchoring the unseen forces of the other worlds into form.

It is in our human best interest to share intelligence with these beings as opposed to the current human approach which is an attempt to impose our chosen intelligence framework (i.e. belief or disbelief, as opposed to simply existing or not existing) on these beings, thus only closing *our* perception and ability to co-exist, expand and refine our intelligence capacities.

The soul dynamic of human beings (or any other being) carries the inherent nature and individualized consciousness of that being. Though the soul expresses itself in the surface world, its origins are in the underworld. The soul of a human is its ultimate Faery, or enchanted, self. As such, we share a soul-based resonance with the denizens of the Fay. Therefore, a fully actualized soul must, for its own well-being, maintain contact with the underworld and its inherent inner-connections. When a human being is moved away from conscious contact with its soul, the human becomes confused, loses direction and becomes weakened and dispirited. When the human being maintains contact with the soul, it is balanced and powerful. Therefore, the underworld work of Faery Seership re-unifies outer awareness with inner soul-meaning and thus re-vivifies the human being. In Faery work, this contact occurs by working through the siths in visionary travel to the other worlds to explore the topology, working through the Faery co-walker to make inner contacts and open inner to outer-world pathways, and by fusing inner and outer awareness through constant work and alliance with the Faery, ancestral, and other realms. This part of the work requires a disengaging of the intellect, for the soul does not use intellectual capacities – it simply "knows." It has no need to understand exactly what it knows or why. Therefore, science will not free the soul, but direct experience will.

Faery Seership is unique in many ways. It does not involve any of the basic elements found in religions such as worship, focus on transcendent deities, or complex rituals. It is a folk tradition with simple concepts incorporated into everyday life. There are some basic over-arching qualities to the traditions that include:

A) *Emphasis on partnership and intimate relationship with, first, the spirits (the unseen company including Faery, ancestral, and other contacts) and, secondly, the deities (vast universal intelligences or regional powers), as opposed to objectified worship of them.*

These beings are not interested in being worshiped or placated. They are only interested in a partnership of mutual exchange for the growth of both humanity and their own species. Though there are many customs throughout Europe that involve ceremonies to appease localized nature spirits, the tradition teaches that this originally evolved from techniques developed by seers in partnership with the Fair Folk. In this work, humanity gains vision and spiritual well-being through their contact with the sacred land, and exchange with their spiritual cousins, the Faery. The Faery/human partnership involves an exchange of elements which completes each partner.

B) *Orally transmitted tradition comprised of lore, customs, rites and techniques interwoven with a communal paradigm.*

There are no grand grimoires or ancient texts with all of the teachings in them. In fact, the tradition, within its specific culture, differs between localities though it shares a common core. Often, there are customs specific to a family or line of seers that differ from any other body of Faery practices. The Faery Seership tradition covered in this book is drawn from several Celtic lines. The teachings are customarily transmitted from mother to daughter or father to son through stories, household practices and hunting, planting, and harvesting customs. However, some of the more advanced techniques are only shared by specialized seers, or Faery doctors, to those they wish to teach and bring into the practice. In this manner, there is an apprenticeship that may involve initiatory rites. Lore is often passed through ballads, rhymes, Fairy tales, myths and everyday practices. Often, specific localities have their own Faery beliefs and they are woven into the stories told around the hearth or campfire and shared by all of the locals.

C) *Work with the ancestral, Faery and other beings as intermediary spirits between humans and the universal creative forces.*

There is a belief in Faery Seership that we all must "make good" with as many of our ancestors as possible; because after death they dwell at the edge of the unseen and can bar our entry into the other worlds. Therefore, the tradition works with both the ancestors and the Fay as our closest of kin in the other world. They assist us in opening the way to work with the universal forces we may term as "gods" or "goddesses." It is important to understand that there are many Faery traditions where there are no deities, only the direct powers of nature with no anthropomorphized image or a deity image in a humanized form. Faery Seership involves a gradual opening inward of awareness and reconnection to the unseen forces, an attunement of the senses to the subtle forces of the inner, creative world. The human Seership student works to acquire a partnership with ancestral spirits and Faery beings wherein the human is the bridge of awareness into the outer or surface world of form for the spirit; and the spirit (Faery or ancestral) bridges human awareness inwardly to the realms of creation.

D) *Emphasis on the development of the second sight, called the Knowing, as a way of exchanging with the spirits and deities.*

Our physical eyes look outward onto the surface world of physical form, or what tradition calls the "land of stone and bone." The second-sighted person has the ability to look inward to what tradition calls "the blessed isles." The second sight looks beyond the world of form into the spiritual realms where the relationship with the world of physical form is ever-becoming or, as tradition calls it, ever-young. Hence, prophetic ability often comes with the second sight, but this is not a steadfast rule. For some people with "the sight," they have the ability to see and contact spirits, but do not see the future. Ultimately, humans see what we are trained to see, or rather restrained to see. In more agrarian cultures where the daily life is closer to the land, seasons and the invisible tides of life, there is a higher prevalence of the second sight. Perception is often about consensus reality. In these situations, the wider the consensus, the broader the reality. There is an inherent ability in all humans for the second sight, though it is particularly strong in certain family lines. These family lines produce the seers. Those with a weaker ability can work with Faery Seership, but do not become seers. A seer is a specific type of practitioner who is often sought after but rarely found. The second sight, as it is known in the Gaelic tradition, is called "the Veil" or "the Knowing" in the Southern American folk magic practices of my native Virginian culture.

E) *Emphasis on practical work that produces tangible results.*

Faery Seership is based on everyday folk practices wherein the mystical union with the inner world is not primarily for spiritual development. Rather, in its natural or cultural environment, the practices were aimed at healing of disease, divination of clan/family/individual destiny, ensurance of food supply (fertility of crops and food animals), and good fortune or luck.

This approach still holds true today. Direct work with the creative intelligences and tides of life inherent within the natural world will, by its nature, produce tangible changes in physical health, fertility and fortune. The missing element for modern, post-industrial humanity, which is primarily focused on resource productivity and development of the individual self, is a sense of connectedness, purpose and perpetuity. For most modern humans, nature and the spirit(ual) worlds are mysterious, dangerous, occult, distant and threatening. This is the trade-off for the mixed blessing of modern technology that gives us comforts and increased control over our personal environments. The cost for humanity is that we have built a self-imposed wall around ourselves, in our minds at least, that separates our species from the greater fabric of life. This approach leaves us empty and looking for that ever-present "something" missing from our lives. Working within the Faery tradition allows the human to reconnect with the land and basic principles of life and to glean visions of the inner pattern and workings of the natural world and where we, as humans, fit in. The Faery student strives to regenerate the natural world, through inter-species exchange and, in the final analysis, finds deep spirituality – not the other way around.

REDEFINING "ALIVE"

There is a great initial challenge for the seeker of the Faery ways to understand how something that often cannot be seen, measured, or contained can be real or "alive." This dilemma has evolved out of human dependency on hard science and the five senses. The sensory approach to reality suggests that if a thing cannot be felt, seen, heard, tasted, or smelled, then it is not real. This approach fails us in the most costly way when dealing with many poisonous gases and radiation that defies all of the senses, yet is deadly. Though sciences such as physics, biology, and chemistry have contributed immeasurably to our existence as a species, we must never forget who created these categorical approaches – humans. The universe did not send us a dictate that the human scientific schools of thought are complete within themselves. Most scientists will readily admit that we still know very little about the machinations of our universe and its origins. It is not necessary (or appropriate, for that matter) to discard the findings and thought processes of modern science. Rather, it is prudent for the student of the Faery ways to apply scientific approach and scientific research findings as additional windows into our miraculous natural world.

There are general mindsets that must be challenged and eventually discarded for a human to attain and sustain meaningful communication and partnership with the unseen company. A primary one involves redefining what we consider to be existence and "being alive." The Faery generally do not live in a crystallized state in the surface world. Their forms are composed of etheric, pre-physical substance. The old teachings instruct us that physical form is a vehicle for expression for those beings requiring it. It is not the central or only mode of life.

There are three primary modes of life in the Faery Seership tradition. The core of each of these terms is the relationship with form, flesh (*carna*) or embodiment:

- *Incarnate* – Orders of life that are comprised of physical substance in any pattern. These beings range from viral, cellular, and atomic levels to complex life forms such as plants (including bacteria) and animals. These forms of life are in measurable physical form, however minute. There are otherworld beings that form relationships with each other, which we term as "clusters," and bring forth physical form. These are elementals or, as Fiona Macleod terms them, "the little children of earth's delight." Elementals cross between incarnated, disincarnated and reincarnated form.

- *Discarnate* – Orders of life that have, at some point in their life process, moved through physical form and now live in a non-physical state of being. These beings are the expression of the soul nature of life forms that were once in physical form but now reside and live in non-physical form states. All ancestral beings, human and non-human, live in this state between reincarnation or "re-entry into form." Some beings move out of the surface world and never return, but live their lives through other beings living in a body.

- *Non-carnate* – Orders of life that have not entered into the band of physical form and may never. All incarnate beings have, in their pre-physical state, been non-carnate. The greater populaces of this mode include beings for whom physical form would be restricting and perhaps even deadly, and thus will never incarnate. Just as physical form dictates that there are certain environments that are not conducive and even deadly to our form, the surface world (or band of incarnation) isn't conducive for non-corporeal beings such as Faery and other orders of life.

In the Faery tradition, a being is not defined as existing or "alive" by its specific mode of life. It is considered to be alive if it has intelligence, pattern, and the ability to communicate. If it has intelligence, which all beings of form have, then it has the ability to communicate across intelligence types. As Machaelle Small Wright, in her brilliant Perelandra work asserts: "Intelligence is the organizing dynamic that provides the movement of soul through form," and "What all form has in common is its intelligence" (*Co-Creative Science*, Wright). Faery Seership acknowledges that all living beings have a soul, all patterns of life are forms, including physical and non-physical states, and all of these have intelligence and thus, the ability for inter-species communication. Further, Ms. Wright asserts:

One of the first problems we [humans] face when we attempt to establish a co-creative relationship with nature [in this case, the Faery nature intelligences] is the assumption that nature intelligence operates and has the same properties as our own intelligence. Generally, this happens because the only intelligence we are familiar with is human intelligence and we have been made to believe that the only existing intelligence is human intelligence.

However, Faery Seership differs with Ms. Wright in her assertion that:

When speaking about nature intelligence, these kinds of words do not refer to individual, independent beings within nature. This brings us to the issue of elves, fairies, gnomes and devic angels. Nature intelligence does not include these types of beings. It is a massive intelligence, a dynamic. It is not made up of individual life forms. This intelligence dynamic flows through form. It is not made up of these forms. One may, however, look at beings such as elves and devic angels as communication bridges between man and nature intelligence.

Contrary to Ms. Wright, Faery Seership asserts that there are individual beings in nature that are tied to the major functions of creation, destruction and regeneration. The Faery, like humans, are independent life forms with a function.

The Faery tradition teaches that there is no level of nature without beings living upon it. The Fair Folk are an example of beings living within a distinct mode of natural life. Perhaps, in concurrence with Ms. Wright, all life forms are communication bridges into and across form, utilized by one massive intelligence to explore and develop itself. Perhaps this intelligence is the creator itself. However, thousands of years of tradition supports that the denizens of the Faery realms are not only real, but perhaps more real than we humans can imagine.

The Faery student seeks to establish healthy relationships with associated orders of life in all three of these modes. By doing so, the student begins to understand the role and nature of each order of life, including humanity (discarnate and incarnate), and how they express a beautiful holism within and with each other to move the vision of planetary and universal being into fulfillment. Additionally, the belief in and fear of death fades from the human who experiences the Faery realms of enchantment – for indeed there is no death. There is only life changing forms.

CHAPTER 4:
THE WORLDS AND POWERS OF FAERY

The wind blows out of the gates of day,
The wind blows over the lonely of heart,
And the lonely of heart is withered away,
While the faeries dance in a place apart,
Shaking their milk-white feet in a ring,
Tossing their milk-white arms in the air:
For they hear the wind laugh, murmur and sing
Of a land where even the old are fair,
And even the wise are merry of tongue;
But I have heard a reed of Coolaney say,
'When the wind has laughed and murmured and sung,
The lonely heart is withered away!'

– "The Fairy Song," W.B Yeats

There are some basic images that form the framework for both the paradigm and techniques of the tradition. They are the Celtic Twilight, the three worlds, the Bilé and the Sacred Flame. This chapter will lay the foundation in understanding these images and their importance in Faery work. In addition, this chapter will explore the many powers and attributes connected with the Faery, including their association with the dead, childbirth, and fate.

CELTIC TWILIGHT (LIMINAL MAGIC)

W.B. Yeats, a turn of the century Celtic revivalist writer and poet, coined the term "Celtic Twilight" to describe the liminal, dream-like, "betwixt and between" state which is the source of all Faery inspiration and magic. Work with this other world is fundamental in the practices of Faery Seership.

Have you ever taken a walk through the woods at dusk or dawn just as darkness falls or the sun rises? It is a shadowed time when the world seems to slip into a different mode. At dusk, the encroaching darkness seems to receive the day into its bosom and tempt our eyelids to close and our motivations to slip into passion or repose. At dawn, the approaching light heralds possibilities, and taunts us to awaken and receive its play. These are moments when we stand at the threshold of possibilities. We stand at both initiation and closure, beginning and end. At these times, we tend to move into a sleepy, but not asleep mode as we move into and out of different states of consciousness. There is a feeling of "in-between-ness." In fact, the world around us expresses that feeling in form, as leaves are in the process of falling from the trees or flowers are in the process of blooming.

This same feeling is experienced through the seasons, especially spring and autumn, which are transition points into the two primary seasons of the Celtic mystical year – summer growth and winter repose. Each night as our consciousness falls into sleep we experience this same "in between" feeling. Each morning while we are waking, we also experience it. This is the liminal state that is betwixt and between. It is most often experienced at Beltane (May 1) and Hallowmas (October 31), though these fixed dates are really points in time when this process peaks. These are the two holy days when tradition says that the trooping Faeries are most active, drawing life inward at Hallowmas or outward at Beltane.

The Celtic Twilight is at once a state of consciousness and another place/another time, a "not place/not time" that is between the worlds of seen and unseen. It is the realm of enchantment and the working state of the Faery seer. This is the state of consciousness where the Fair Folk and other threshold beings live. At these times, our human awareness has not yet anchored itself in one place, but stands at the threshold between the inner and outer world. This is the optimum state for the Faery seer's work. Although sleep time or the dream space is also useful, they are more difficult for the seer to control. Use of the Twilight requires the seer to develop the following faculties:

- the ability to recognize the state when they are in it
- the ability to be comfortable working in this state
- techniques for entry and exit of the Twilight
- techniques for bridging contact from the outer world inwardly or the inner world outwardly
- knowledge of the terrain and denizens of the Twilight
- knowledge of the prohibitions and rules, as well as the consequences of violation

Movement from the outside world of humanity into the spirit world involves a specific trance state that we call a "rapture." It is a special trance state wherein the seer is neither conscious (to the outside world) nor unconscious, but rather a state between sleep and wakefulness, deep trance and alertness. Work with the rapture allows the seer to move into that hazy moment, and to "fly" beyond the hedge that marks the transition from the everyday outer world to the inner creative source world.

The Faery student who works with this liminal state will quickly learn that the Faery people never receded away from the natural world, as was believed. They only receded away from most humans because of our species' disrespect of the natural worlds and the Faery races. Their influence on humanity has never waned.

THE THREE WORLDS

A central part of both the overall Celtic mystical tradition and Faery Seership is the concept of "the three worlds." This philosophy categorizes life in its many expressions into three modes or dynamics. The terms used to describe them were provided to me through oral tradition and change between localities of origin, language or dialect, and the transmitting teacher or seer. However, their meanings seem to be relatively universal across the traditions of Celtic teachings, and the beliefs and practices of other indigenous people. The concept of the three worlds is relative and based on our human view of life from the vantage point of living on the earth's surface and seeing a realm above us, around us and under us. The three realms and their denizens are as follows:

- *The Star World*: The upper world, which is really the "around world," is symbolized by the sky. The tool that is used to work with the essence of this realm is fire, which embodies the shared essence between humanity and the gods. It is called the "white place" because it is made of the substance of the stars and is often known as *Gwynfyd (gwin'-vid)*. It is the original source world from which all things come and into which all will return. It is stellar in nature flowing into the land as our planet moves through the stars. It is the home of our spiritual lives. It is also influenced by our sun, which is the earth's stellar lover. The beings that dwell there are deities in the most universal sense. There are threshold beings that live at the edge of the under and upper worlds and mediate divine power. Humans can work with them, though it requires considerable preparation first, and even then we cannot approach them directly for their light cannot come through a dirty window. We must be very clean spiritually before we work with the Lords of Light. The light of Gwynfyd is the essence that feeds all things – the golden honey of Avalon that sustains the clan of peace. This realm is the source of the original vision of the sacred land. It is the spirit world.

- *The Stone World*: The surface or middle world is the earth plane, which is the world of physical form, is symbolized by the land and often known as *Ddaer (thay'-er)*. It is the surface world which embodies the impulses of the underworld. It is expressive and impermanent, and is best likened onto the wake of a ship. The "ship" is actually in the other two worlds. It is the home of our material lives. It is influenced by the other two worlds and the seasons of planetary change. We humans are well aware that there are many beings that inhabit this world with us, though we have distracted ourselves from understanding the true power of our neighbors (i.e. trees, plants, animals, weather formations, etc.). This realm is the state where the vision of the sacred land is to be made manifest. It forms through pressure and trials. It is the embodiment world.

- *The Sea World*: The underworld (in reality the "inner world") is symbolized by the ocean which connects the land and sky. The tool we work with to embody the essence of this realm is water. It is the boundary between our world and the sky world of the gods. This shadowy realm is illuminated by the stars within the land and is often known as *Annwn (ah-noon')*. The Fay live at the edge/hedgeway where ocean and land meet. The sea world is the land of the spirits and houses the summerlands which is the ancestral resting place of all discarnate beings. It can be terrifying because its nature is like a mirror that reflects back the contents of your soul into form and feeling. In the physical world, its power is embodied by the moon which governs tides of change and interconnectedness. Stellar beings (creative life force/toradh) fall into this underworld as serpents or dragons.

This serpent power becomes the vivifying essence of the star and stone worlds. Deep within the underworld, this power is acted upon by the Nar (beings who hold the designs for all manifested being) and elemental spirit functions which are the architects of form. They shape it and give it form (which may or may not be physical) as well as life, then surface it from the formation state (earth of light), also seen as the underworld or the "primordial ocean" to the stone world. It is primal, chthonic and transformative. The beings which dwell here are Faery, elementals, Nar, ancestors and deep planetary beings. It is the state wherein dwells the Dreamer who holds the vision of the sacred land. It is the soul world. Nearly all Faery work takes place within the waves of this world and the pathways between it and the realm of the stone world.

THE BILÉ (BEE'-LAY)

These three primary states of existence are unified by a central power which we call the Bilé. It is imaged as a sacred oak tree. It is the *axis mundi* that connects all things. In the American folk magic of the South, the name has become the "Billy Tree" or "kissing post." This is the unifying power and truth behind all things. It is the strand of the web that interconnects the three worlds and is manifest in our human form as the spine which connects the mind, heart and regenerative organs. The beings in all three worlds approach each other through following the path of this sacred tree. Any world or being that is not unified within the tree should not be worked with by humanity.

THE SACRED FLAME

There is also a holy formless flame that does not burn the pure and which travels the tree from the heights into the depths. It is embodied in us. This flame is toradh, pith or the inner sun that gives life and form to all things as it is issued forth from the stars into the Sea World and reflected into the surface world of stone. This holy flame is the shared essence, and thus Faery magic often uses fire to open and close entry points to the Faery realms. In addition, Faery works with the sacred flame as the essence of the stars.

THE VEIL AND THE SECOND SIGHT

Throughout the human cultures of the world are customs and lore that deal with certain people who have the gift to see into the spiritual realms. These people reputedly have the ability to see future events and communicate with deities, angels, Faeries, deceased humans and other beings that are otherwise not in communication with the average person.

This "second-sightedness" in American and European folk tradition is marked by the existence of a placental sheath covering the eyes of the newborn. In Jewish tradition this is termed the "caul." In American Southern folk tradition it is called "the veil."

Though few people are born with the veil, a certain amount of the sight can be developed by practicing the techniques taught by the seers, some of which are provided later in this book.

THE FAERY, THE DEAD AND HUMAN RELATIONS

Indigenous people who live and die on the same piece of land over many generations have a deep kinship with the inner ecology and Faery beings of that place. This is not to imply that meaningful relationships with the Fair Folk cannot be achieved when one lives a more transient life. It does imply that the relationship is considerably stronger when a seer lives on a specific land base and integrates themselves into the inner ecology of that area. This enhances the skills given by the Faery partners to the human.

There are several ways that generations of human life on a particular land area affects the relationship between humanity and the inner powers of the land.

- Consuming foods raised on a specific land area ensures that the humans of that location are composed of the essence of the place.

- Farming and other daily activities on a particular land area maintain contact with the power of the place, thereby integrating a human place into the ecology of the area.

- Each generation of humans born on the same area of land ensures that they are composed of the land, since they are born to parents who have consistently lived on and eaten the foods raised on that land.

- Each generation of humans who live and die on a familiar land area are interred into that land. In this way, the land receives them and they become a part of the land's physical substance through decay which feeds into the land and water of the area which, in turn, becomes food for the living.

- The Fair Folk also integrate into this substance and, thus, the human families, the land and Fay become one. This is why it is common for a human to see a Faery being wearing the clothing of the human past in a particular area. In the folk culture of some countries, when a person dies they are referred to as "living with the Faeries or becoming a Faery."

Most of us do not continue to live on the land or in the general area of our birth, though this is optimal for Faery work. Often, we move into many different land areas throughout our lives. This reduces the clarity and intensity of our relationship with the Faery realms. Until we bond with a specific land area, our work has some limitations. Understanding this concept should also increase one's understanding of the horrible effect of forcibly relocating indigenous people from their land of heritage. This action spiritually damages people as they loosen or weaken their inner contact – at least initially.

CHILDBIRTH AND DEATH

The Fay are believed to influence both childbirth and death. For example, in Welsh tradition we have *Bendith Y Mamau* or "the Mother's Blessing." Tradition tells us that they were termed blessed so that their kinder natures would be invoked and they would not harm or steal children during childbirth. They were also believed to be terrifying if not appeased. Likely, these Faery mothers were once ancient mother goddesses reduced to tutelary beings of ill intent by the new religion. There are many concerns and customs throughout Europe regarding the role of Faery wives in childbirth, sometimes as mid-wife, other times as thief. Tradition teaches that the lore regarding changeling children evolved during the post-Christian era to blame the Fair Folk (and demonize them) for stillbirths and infant mortality.

In the Gaelic tradition, we have the Washer of the Ford, a Faery woman who appears at the water-way under a bridge used for funeral processions. She is seen washing the deceased person's soul from their body. Some lore suggests that she is washing the sins from the slain. Fiona Macleod provides us with a hauntingly poetic account of the Washer:

There is a lonely stream afar in a lone dim land:
It hath dust for its shore it has, white bones bestrew
      the strand:
The only thing that liveth there is a naked leaping sword;
But I, who a seer am, have seen the whirling hand
      of the Washer of the Ford.

A shadowy shape of cloud and mist, of gloom and dust
      she stands, The Washer of the Ford:
She laughs, at times, and strews the dust through the
      hollow of her hands.

She counts the sins of all men there, and slays the
      red-stained horde-
The ghosts of all the sins of men must know the whirling
      sword of the Washer of the Ford.

She stops and laughs when in the dust she sees a
      writhing limb:
"Go back into the ford," she says, and hither and
      thither swim;

Then I shall wash you clean as snow, and shall take you
      by the hand,
And slay you here in the silence with this my whirling
      brand,
And trample you into the dust of this white windless sand.

This is the laughing word
Of the Washer of the Ford
Along that silent strand.

The Fay have a natural interdependency with humanity and thus they are our "cousins." They live at the gates of light and dark, life and death, generative and regenerative. Tradition tells us that they are active in affixing the human soul (the co-walker)

to the human form, as well as "un-hinging it into the death state."
There are hundreds of examples of Fay activity at childbirths,
death beds and funerals.

THE POWERS OF THE FAY

The Faery races have many powers and they can (and do) exert great influence over human life processes. The lore tells us
that these powers can help or harm humanity. My experience,
and that of other seers I know, is that if they do not like you,
they will not even approach you. Humanity has a great deal to
learn from our otherworld cousins. In fact, we have more to
learn from them than the other way around.

By their nature, the Faery people have magic but humans have
to acquire the art. The old lore tells us that magic, music and all
creative endeavors are gifts to humanity from the Faery. The
Fair Folk live in the realms of magic and are composed of its
essence. Humanity, however, lives in the realm of form which
reflects or embodies the outcomes of magic. For us, magic and
spiritual ways are something we must learn. For the Fay, it is
something that they simply are. Where humans are bound to a
degree by their physical form; the Fay are not and can change
their form at will. The Faery can affect human health, luck,
wealth and fate, and are involved in birth into and out of form,
since they live in the state of ever-becoming, hence ever-young.
They can blight or bless crops, grant wishes, prophesize and heal.
Of course, they can also use these powers banefully when offended by humans. Luckily, they are older and wiser than we
and are often very forgiving of our frail emotional natures. Most
Fay have a natural love for humanity. There are considerable
blessings that we humans receive in our work with the Fays.

- enhanced magical, healing and divinatory skills
- understanding of the inner workings of nature and how to
  apply this to regenerative magic for humanity, the land and
  other life systems

- the ability to shape-shift. This may not be used to change our physical form, but may change our whole internal world to bring forth power and vitality.

- a sense of purpose as we glean our species and individual roles in the unfolding vision of the Dreamer in the Land

- development of the second sight

- the ability to communicate with other forms of life

- the ability to affect the weather

Remember, these skills are developed in partnership with the Fay. They must not be used to the detriment of another being unless in self-defense. The repercussions of "bad washing," as baneful magic is called in the old ways, can make the concept of bad karma seem like a mere allergy attack. I do not advise any human to test this hypothesis.

CHAPTER 5:
FAERY GATEWAYS AND
THE REALMS OF ENCHANTMENT

How beautiful they are, the Lordly Ones
*   who dwell in the hills, in the hollow hills.*
The have faces like flowers and their breath is the wind
*   that blows over summer meadows,*
Filled with dewey clover.
Their limbs are whiter than shafts of moonshine:
They are more fleet than the March wind.
They laugh and are glad, and are terrible:
When their lances shake and glitter every
*   green reed quivers.*
How beautiful they are,
How beautiful the Lordly Ones in the hollow hills.

– Fiona Macleod

Fiona Macleod speaks to the incomprehensible beauty of the Lordly Ones of the high Faery clans. These beings may appear as male or female, but are in fact neither or both. Before exploring the types and temperaments of the Faery clans, it is important to map out the entry points and topology of the Faery realms. The information shared in this chapter is based on traditional lore. Of equal importance is the use of the siths which we use when traversing the realms of enchantment. The images for the entry into Faery are for visionary constructs. Traditional visionary images work like the tumblers in a lock. When they are combined in a sequence, they unlock doors to the inner Faery worlds. These images are very simple, but must not be underestimated in their power.

TRAVELING TO THE FAERY REALMS

There are a few basic mechanisms to open the doors to the Faery realms. All of these involve traditional practices in one form or another.

- *Use of traditional entry and exit points used in a guided imagery fashion*: These should be used weekly for a while until the land and the human attune to each other.

- *Developing the "second sight" (the ability to see and interpret spirit and spiritual influences) to see the hidden paths and the opening between the worlds*: This is more advanced and takes years to develop unless the student already has the second sight through birth and only needs the tradition to translate their experiences. The second sight is a core concept in the Celtic mystical experience.

- *Attuning the imagination through using traditional imagery until the student has developed their own visioning ability*: The student uses the traditional methods until they become more attuned to the feel and flow of the Twilight state (the trance specific state employed in Faery Seership) and can deviate from the vision and let it unfold naturally within them.

- *Developing a direct relationship with a piece of land by attuning to its sacred power and "inscape"*: This method begins by the human student developing a land-based site to open as a contact or interface point with the Faery.

- *Practices such as offerings, planting trees or sacred flower groves, building and activating cairns or sacred hills, and caring for graveyards, sacred trees, wells and springs to assist with developing a relationship:* When this method is used, the student should first choose certain traditional images to open the way. If the student uses any of these attunement methods coupled with the images, a deep and meaningful relationship should develop. The denizens of the otherworld notice our repeated offerings as sure as humans notice a flare. Their response will likely not be immediate. Rather, the human seeker will have to repeat the practice many times in order to build trust and to energize an opening.

- *The use of psychoactive plants as an ally:* I would be remiss to not mention this method, as it is a traditional Faery visionary technique. It is quite dangerous and should only be used with an extremely adept seer guiding the student. In short, it is *unnecessary and not recommended.* The damage to the human psyche can be irreparable. It is also important to note that these allies can be used without ingesting them. They can be carried in a pouch or placed on an altar or other sacred place and engaged during the visionary process. Their psychoactive properties are not as necessary as their energetic resonance. The use of hallucinogenic mushrooms is one of the more common practices of this type. Mushrooms are traditionally referred to as Faery homes and are entry points into "Faeryland." In my tradition, they are referred to as the "Roses of Annwn" for they are the flowers that blossom out of death. They are also linked to the regenerative, life-out-of-death aspects of Faery magic. They were used as a hallucinogen to move the senses and perceptions from the outer world of effects to the inner world of causation, a practice also known as "parting the sheath of Saturn," or "flying beyond the hedge" in a rapture.

Other forms include:

- using a magical word such as "*Boram...Boram...Boram*," a word used in Irish Faery tradition to open the Faery way

- straddling a bean stock or ragwort (also known as *Bucalauns*) which is sacred to the Faery, or

- wearing a magical cap or other enchanted item of clothing

These are the primary traditional forms of traveling to the Faery realms.

OPENINGS INTO THE FAERY REALM

Tradition gives us many visionary constructs for the seeker to use to shift into the rapture. These constructs are powerful images that have been used over centuries to signal deeper levels of consciousness to open themselves as gateways to the underworld. All of the examples used in vision, or the visionary process, can also be used in their actual locations, though this is not necessary.

For example, the entry point to an actual cave or the top of a cliff can be used as the place to locate yourself physically to begin a visionary process or it can be visualized in total. Do not actually enter the cave or sepulcher, or jump off a cliff for obvious reasons of physical safety or legality. In fact, it is not absolutely necessary to be at the physical location described in these images for the traveling process.

You do not take your physical form into the Faery realms. Rather, you use your sith through the action of visual inner constructs to travel through to the world beneath physical substance: the Faery realms. This following list of access points is not exhaustive, but gives you examples of material to use for your own visionary techniques. Just envision the images used to open the way. It is advised that, if a visionary construct is used to enter the otherworld, then it should also be used to return to the outerworld. Only after long periods of practice is it advised to

return by other means. It is also traditional practice to envision these portals closing or drawing back away from the physical world after the vision is completed and the traveling human has returned to outer life. This allows the opening to close and resume normal daily activity. Examples of traditional visionary images used as access points to enter the Faery world include:

- Your sith can enter a sepulcher, mound, cavern, well, cleft in a rock or a spring. The best time to enter by using an actual physical site is at Hallowmas or Beltane. These visionary constructs are the most powerful when used at these auspicious times. The visionary passage downward into the land, or into ancient stone, or in a sepulcher which is a house of death (an otherworld interface) is an important element in visionary process. This signals the mind to move beyond physical surface substance into a deeper stratum of life-becoming where the gates of life and death are one.

• Sometimes a ball, apple or wheel rolls out of the otherworld from a Faery being and the seeker follows it to the Faery realms. In this vision style, the contact is made by the otherworld first and the human takes hold of this and follows it inward.

• The image of a glass boat that crosses the etheric timeless ocean into Faery can be used. This is a very old image, often used to transport the souls of the dead to the otherworld. The boat is crystalline because it made of light, which crosses space and moves beyond time and matter.

• In Gaelic tradition, the seeker circles a grassy hill nine times counter-clockwise and upon completion of the rotation exclaims "open door, open" three times and the gates shall open. This is best done during a full moon. This technique uses a call from our world to the inner world to open, reveal itself, and permit us entry.

• Other openings include open graves, holes, rivers, marshes, lakes, springs and wells. Notice, many of the visionary elements involves passage into the land or through water that embodies astral or otherworld substance. The otherworld divorces from time and space and is fluidic in nature.

• The green "Faery mists" of eternal spring can be used to activate the shift into Faery. This technique raises the underworld to this world and attunes it. It literally involves envisioning a green glowing mist that rises from the land, which engulfs us and enchants the world around us.

• "Faery rings" (rings of mushrooms or patches of green grass) can be used. If you are lucky enough to have one made of physical substance, it is a wonderful access point. Again, this is the use of a natural gateway into the otherworld.

- Call to the seven doves of the goddess Rhiannon to transport you to the underworld. This old traditional technique calls on the seven notes of universal harmonics, as embodied in the seven doves, to open the seven sacred ways of the four directions, above, below and within.

- Climb a cliff to a high point and envision the wind taking you to the land beneath the mists (sometimes referred to as "beneath the cloud wheel"). Some seers believe that this may be the Wheel of Ezekiel discussed in biblical scripture. It involves flying or passing effortlessly outside or above the boundaries of form into the eternal movement of the stars which light the halls of Faery.

- Envision a journey beneath the ocean or to an island.

- Cross the "moon-bridge" which is to travel across the reflection made by the moon on the ocean or other bodies of water. If this is done with an actual body of water, the student is advised to have someone else present to prevent them from walking into the water. This technique uses the magically magnetic virtues of the moon's silver light to part the night sky and reveal the light that cannot be seen with the eye but only with the heart.

- Use of a fire, such as a candle, can lead you into the underworld as a "doorway of flame." Examples of this method will be given later in this book. This is a very traditional technique in Faery work and older forms of witchcraft where the light of fire marks the opening place between the worlds.

THE LANDSCAPE OF THE FAERY REALMS

There are many elements that are repeating themes in Faery tales, ballads and other forms of oral tradition that describe what Faeryland looks like and where it is located. These images tell us much about how the inner and underworld works, what it looks like, its location and its interpenetrating relationship with the surface world where the physical resides.

Examples of some traditional elements of the topology or landscape of the Faery realms and their implications include the following:

- *Rivers of wine and mead:* These are tides of light which move through the Faery realms, carrying the essential toradh of all things to the Faery races for their sustenance, as well as to the surface world where it becomes the orders of life as we humans know them. The concept of liquid rivers that flow with an intoxicating essence denotes the euphoric and flowing nature of the Faery realms which are nourished by living light.

- *Beneath the roaring of the ocean:* This image embodies the inner tidal quality of energy and astral substance, and captures the philosophy that the Faery realms are beneath the world of physical form and under the tides of time and matter. Since all life emerged from the ocean, the concept of "beneath the ocean" may refer to the pre-physical nature and location of Faery reality. The human traveler in the Faery world may hear the roaring of the surface world above them as they pass into the deeper strata of the source world within and below the surface world.

- *Across water to an island (this can be an ocean or river):* This image informs the seeker that traveling to the Faery realms requires movement of consciousness away from what is familiar to a place which stands apart, such as an island. The realms of Celtic magical tradition are sky, earth and sea. The sea connects the worlds and transmits their essence between the realms. Again, the Faery realms are in another place, betwixt and between, not sky, nor sea, nor earth, but another place indefinable. The Faery world is at the very basic nature of our surface life, but is in a state all its own.

- *Rivers of blood and water.* River images refer to tides and the movement of toradh through, into and between the other worlds and our own world. These two rivers embody the polarized nature of the universe (i.e. male/female, positive/negative, electric/magnetic). In this image, the poles are separate in the otherworld before they intertwine and create life as we know it. They are often referred to as two dragons or the streams of life that flow from the stars into and around the planet earth and rise again into the heavens. The human traveler may wade in these rivers at different times to seek their inner power and wisdom as they embody other natures beyond the polarity concept alone.

The topology of the Faery realms can also change based upon the direction from which you enter.

- *In the east, it is described as "beneath the cloud wheel" and is entered by climbing a cliff and envisioning jumping off:* The east is the place of the rising sun, the breath of life, creation, and the movement of the stars in the heavens. The cloud wheel embodies a cyclic opening at the place of beginnings that opens the gate to the otherworld between the rays of sunlight. It implies that life begins with movement and the Faery realms are in the state of the ever-becoming "word of life." The cloud wheel is often seen as the primordial pool of life with the Faery realms in an order of life that precedes even that. The use of flying in vision instructs human awareness to shift out of normal modes of perception into a place outside of the common rules of human life. When the human traveler encounters the cloud wheel, they have entered into the realms of the "wheel of fortune" which places things into natural order. Again, this image, like many of the others, suggests that these realms are in constant movement – constantly becoming.

- *In the South, it is the "land of summer and eternal youth":* The southern realms embody the place of living light which

is the quintessential essence of life. This light is the sunlight
that vivifies our planet as seen in the green world of living
plants. In this light all is new, ever-becoming and ever-young;
hence the Faery people are described as the "bright ones,"
"people of light" and the "immortal clan." The deeper the
seeker travels into the underworld and through the Faery
realms, the closer they come to the living light within substance as embodied in the "sun in the underworld," which is
the living earth. This light changes the surface world whenever it comes into contact with it. An example of this is a
volcano which is a surface phenomenon of the star, or sun,
that still burns at the center of our world. As R.J. Stewart
states "the nearest star is beneath our feet."

- *In the west, it is beneath the waves or on an island where it
  may be reached by the "moon-bridge":* The western realms
  embody the land of the waters of life which is the great ocean
  of energy from whence all things come and to which it all
  returns. This realm is governed by the luminary powers of
  the moon. Through its gravitational pull, the moon influences the tides of the ocean as well as all tides of life including not only a woman's menstrual cycle, but the ebbs and
  flows within your own life. This illustrates the cyclic and
  regenerative nature of life. In this vision, the moon opens a
  path in its relationship to water on earth that leads the seeker
  to the inner ocean below the substance of physical water.
  This path is embodied in the seeming path of light created
  by the moon's light cast onto the ocean, pond or lake water
  that forms the moon-bridge. The seeker crosses this moon-
  bridge to the Faery realm located in a world connected to
  humanity by a place between night and day where moonlight and shadow move apart and darkness reveals its mystic
  light. The Faery live in a place that eludes the invasive light
  of the sun and can only be encountered when the silver light
  of the moon creates a third place – not lit and not dark, but
  in between and hidden in a cloak of silence.

- *In the North, it is through a mound, cleft in a stone or deep fissure, or through the door which opens when the moons light strikes an enchanted stone*: The northern realms embody the land of stone, silence and ancestry. In Faery Seership, the north is the place of the ancient clan, of the stars as they flow into the earth. It also embodies the natural law of life. Thus, the ancient stones that remember the beginning of life on earth and the Faery realms are alive within the land of the "star within the stone." Again, the moon that governs the tides of life strikes a stone and causes it to part its substance to reveal an inner Faery world. Indeed, all physical substance is the portal to the enchantment that is its truer nature.

Though these images reflect some of the nature of the Faery realms, there are many more images that will surface that are specifically attuned to the inner world of the human seeker and the place of seeking. Regardless of the entry point or the topological elements which describe the lands of Faery, the would-be seer must understand the nature of the three realms of the Faery and Celtic tradition, for this is the very map of the realms used to navigate the states of existence. These realms are interconnected by invisible lines of power, resonance, inter-dependence and function described as "the hidden ways."

THE HIDDEN WAYS

The hidden (or secret) ways are like windows into the soul of the world and the topology of the inner realms. The soul of the world is the ever-becoming inner mind or vision of our planet and her living consciousness that is "the Dreamer in the Land." They connect the realms of Gwynfyd, Annwn, and Ddaer. Imagine a city and the many roads that lead into and out of it and you have a basic understanding of the concept. In the human body, these paths would be analogous to the tendrils of neurons that form the complex network of the nervous system which allows expression to be moved from the mind outward and experience to be perceived and fed inward to the mind. These paths lead into and out of the realm of the Dreamer carrying the toradh that gives life and being to the natural world. The Faery beings traverse these paths and are involved in weaving the unseen pattern between things, as well as holding open these paths as life-giving umbilical cords from the core of planetary being to its child – the surface world and nature as we know it.

These secret and enchanted paths were often alluded to in the witchcraft trials wherein the accused witch allegedly spirits away the substance and vitality in milk, or a man's potency or from crops leaving them empty, without life and useless. These allegations implicate the witch's knowledge and use of the hidden paths that join the seen and the unseen in a network of connections, resonance and inter-dependence. They also suggest that the Inquisitors were aware, to some degree, of the beliefs and practices of their local folk magic traditions. It is known within the inner circles of the old ways that the Faery tradition and traditional European witchcraft have always been intertwined, especially in crossroads magic and work with spirits. There are also other names for these secret paths such as ley lines, Faery paths, Faery trods, witch or Faery roads, and Faery tracks. Lore states that they begin in the other world, lead through this one, and then disappear again. A house dare not be built that interrupts the movement of power on these roads or bad luck, hauntings and illness can result. Magic is made where the hidden paths (the road of Faery) and the surface world (the path of humanity) cross. These paths occur through the substance of the earth in thousands of actual locations, but smaller ones occur everywhere on the planets surface. This is why the seer is able to open and work with them anywhere and anytime.

These paths begin in the inner world and lead outward, only to lead inward again. They feed life essence outward to sustain our world and carry experience inward. As long as they are active, life will continue in our world. Should they ever close, it will be the end of life as we know it. So, for those foolish human who think that the Faery have died and the hidden paths have closed because humanity has strayed away from their role in keeping the roads open and honoring the Faery ones, think twice. The paths are open, only not to us on a personal level. They can be again if we commit to re-energize them and seek the deeper companionship of the Elder race.

Many of the visions and techniques used in Faery Seership begin by experiencing or feeling the presence of the four hidden paths that lead in toward us from the unseen worlds. Envisioning this puts the human participant at the center of the magic crossroads where the ancient alliance is rekindled. For in truth, we always stand at the center of the paths, for they merge into us as four streams of life (air, fire, water and earth) which fall into the earth from the sun, moon and stars, and surface into the patterns that become all of who we are and what we may become. To open the hidden paths, we simple have to envision, feel and affirm them, and they are there. They always are because they have always been. One of the most basic components of Faery Seership training is the experience of the hidden paths.

VISION #1: Opening the Hidden Paths

This vision will help the human student begin to open out and attune to the constant presence of the hidden paths which exist just on the other side of form. It should be performed weekly until the student has the feeling of the hidden paths firmly ingrained.

a)   Draw your senses inward into yourself. Be aware of your presence here and now. Also be aware of the sounds and sensations around you, allowing them to pass through you unaffected, like water through a sieve. Close your eyes to draw your awareness inward.

b)   Be aware of your breathing which mimics the breath of the universe as it passes in and out of the void, creating and de-creating. Allow all cares of the human world to pass away from you and be left behind as you enter into the eternal communion of spirit.

c) Be aware of the sun above you that shines its radiance on the backdrop of the dark space. This is the star that dances in the infinity of night. Feel its presence as it radiates power onto the earth and all who dwell upon her. Be also aware of the sun within the earth that gives light to the mysterious underworld, the home of Faery, ancestral, deep planetary beings and your soul.

d) Now be aware of the fire that burns within your heart, for it is the center of your inner universe. Its light shines into all of the areas of your body and mind. Envision these three suns coming together in a light line connecting you to all above, below and within. This is the Bilé tree.

e) Be aware of the four directions. One is before you, with another behind you, and one is on each side. Traditionally, you face east with the south at your right, west at your back and north to your left, but this is not absolutely necessary.

f) Be aware that these directions extend from and into the other worlds (where, in fact, they were created), opening to and into you.

g) Be aware that you sit at the center of the crossroads, as the center-post of the universe. All of the powers of the four directions come together within you.

h) Feel the presence of the four paths that now open to you. There is a buzzing sound, like bees. Feel the electricity that travels up each of the four directions, co-mingling at the center. This is called "the hosting."

i) Be aware that a being forms in the center that tells you about the power of this place and begins to attune you to the sacred land. Spend a moment in communion with this being.

j) Now the *Genii Loci* has shared with you and the feeling of the four hidden paths is within your being. The being now flows back into the four directions and the paths draw back like a roll of carpet, back into their world.

k) Once the directions are no longer felt, open your awareness back into the physical world being aware of your body, the temperature, sounds and all the sensations that come to you. Open your eyes and let the feeling flow out into the room.

Once you have completed the vision, spend a few moments settling yourself. Gather your thoughts and, most importantly, your feelings of the experience. Record them in a journal as they form the foundation of your experiences in the Faery realms.

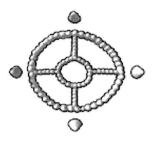

CHAPTER 6:
THE TRIBES OF THE FAERY RACES

Up the airy mountain,
Down the rushy glen,
We daren't go a-hunting
For fear of little men;
Wee folk, good folk,
Trooping all together;
Green jacket, red cap,
And white owl's feather!

— *"The Fairies," William Allingham*

All too often, when people speak of Faeries, they are refer-ring to the post-renaissance reconstructed images of gossamer-winged sprites, happily tip-toeing through the tulips. This image is completely out of sync with the older, traditional concepts of the Faery races. The Faery are, in fact, ancient pow-erful beings and humanity's spiritual next-of-kin. Traditionally, the Fay are human size or bigger, and inspire awe, reverence, terror and even lust when we are in their presence. They rarely inspire humanity with cuddly feelings, though they can bring both deep comfort and unimaginable levels of love, incomprehensible to humans. They are often described as beautiful and terrible at the same time, not unlike ancient lore describing angelic beings. In fact, they are often described as the angels within the earth. Perhaps they are beings of stellar origin, but then all of us are made of stardust. This may be the origin of the modern concept of Faery dust or glittering sand.

These holy creatures are the Elder Race, predating humanity and the physical world as we know it. Lore tells us that from the beginning of time humans have been in a relationship with them, learning all sciences, arts, crafts, the use of fire, poetry and song-smithing, metallurgy, magic and many other practices. There are many theories about the origins of the Faery races and belief in them. The Fay are often described as spirits of the dead who are caught betwixt and between, nature spirits, deities or an independent race, non-human in origin. In some traditions, they may be described as any of the above or a mix, since Faeryland is well populated with many types of creatures. There are three main theories to explain the origin of the belief in Faery spirits:

1) that they are the spirits of the human dead; 2) that they are elementary spirits – that is spirits of nature, the genii of mountain, flood, and forest; [and] 3) that belief in them is due to reminiscences of former peoples or aboriginal races which have been thrust into the more distant and less hospitable parts of a country by the superior weight of an invading stock. (*British,* Spence)

Faery Seership teaches that the Fay races are in fact all of these, depending on their tribe, location and the stratum of the Faery realms being accessed. W.Y. Evans-Wentz shares that, in Wales, they were described as "a real race of invisible or spiritual beings living in an invisible world all their own," or "beings half-way between something material and spiritual, who were rarely seen". Likewise, these beings are seen as more powerful and knowledgeable than the human race.

We find in most countries a popular belief in different classes of beings distinct from men, and from the higher orders of divinities. These beings (such as the Faery) are usually believed to inhabit the caverns of earth, or the depths of the waters, a region of their own. They generally excel mankind in power and in knowledge, and like them are subject to the inevitable laws of death, though after a prolonged period of existence. (*The World Guide*, Keightley)

Much of the lore on their origins has been watered with Christian mythos. However, if one peers deeply into the mystical implications of these legends, much insight can be gleaned. In Ireland, there are explicit beliefs that the Faery are fallen angels. In Scotland, they are an independent race or the dead. Katherine Briggs quotes Evan-Wentz, who recounts a story given to him by Alexander Carmichael:

The Proud Angel fomented a rebellion among the angels of heaven, where he had been a leading light. He declared that he would go and found a kingdom for himself. When going out at the door of heaven, the Proud Angel brought prickly lightening and biting lightening out of the doorstep with his heels. Many angels followed him – so many that at last the Son called out, "Father! Father! the city is being emptied!" whereupon the Father ordered that the gates of heaven and the gates of hell be closed. This was instantly done. And those who were in were in, and those who were out were out: while the hosts who had left heaven and had not reached hell flew into the holes in the earth, like the stormy petrels.

Lady Wilde provides us with a very insightful account of Faery origins in *Ancient Legends of Ireland, Vol. 1*:

The islanders, like all Irish, believe that the fairies are the fallen angels who were cast down by the Lord God out of heaven for their sinful pride. And some fell into the sea, and some on the dry land, and some fell down into hell, and the devil gives to these knowledge of power, and sends them to earth where they work much evil. But the fairies of the earth and the sea are mostly gentle and beautiful creatures, who will do no harm if they are let alone, and allowed to dance on the fairy raths in the moonlight to their own sweet music, undisturbed by the presence of mortals.

These beliefs tell us much about Fay origins. Likely, they are of stellar nature, born at the beginnings of our universe when there was an outpouring of light from the void, which fell into form. Does this infer that the gate of heaven is a black hole? Who knows for sure? I leave that to scientists and theologians to discover in their way, and no doubt battle out whose truth is truer. But the lore suggests that there are places or "planes of existence," as embodied in the images of land and sea and air, where these beings have dwelt since the origins of life. The teachings suggest that the life orders of the elementary kingdoms live within their elements which are, in fact, worlds in themselves. Again, this leads us back to the crossroads where multiple orders of life come together, co-mingle and create new living patterns, biospheres and orders of life. Perhaps the elementals and Faery beings not only live in these otherworld strata, but are a part of infusing these worlds with living vitality.

There are core elements to Faery lore that appear in all of the countries where Faery lore is prevalent. One such example is that there are two overarching orders of Fairies, a beneficent and a maleficent one.

Perhaps the most definite statement that such a differentiation was entertained in Scotland is to be found in Rev. Charles Rogers' *Scotland, Social and Domestic*, where it is said that 'the northern elves were of two classes, 'the gude fairies' and the 'wicked wichts' which were otherwise described as the 'Seelie Court' and the 'Unseelie Court', the word 'seelie' in this regard denoting 'reputable' or 'canny'. The members of the Seelie Court,' says Rogers, 'were the benefactors of mankind.' They supplied the poor and aged with bread, gave seed-corn to the industrious farmer and comforted those in despair. But the 'wicked wichts' inflicted harm and skaith upon mankind at large. (*Fairy Tradition*, Spence)

THE FAERY TRIBES / RACES

Not unlike our human world, there are many races and temperaments of the Fay. Since there are multiple levels in the Faery realms, there are multiple types of beings that live there, much as birds live within the air, fishes in the water, and humans on the land. There are different types of beings that surface in different locations on the earth's surface. There are some beings that never surface here and aggressively avoid doing so. Some Fay like humans, while others deplore them. Considering the damage that humanity has done to their handiwork (nature) and the misuse of the technologies given to humans by the Fay, who could blame them for being distrustful of us?

The poet and Faery seer, W.B. Yeats, coupled with other oral teachings has provided us with the following classifications of the Faery tribes: a) solitary, b) hive, c) trooping, d) stationary, e) domestic, and f) elemental. This provides the Faery student with a solid base of reference in understanding the clans. Each of these clans have differing roles in the natural, creative world, potential for partnership with human co-walkers, and legends about their customs. In *The Vanishing People: Fairy Lore and Legends*, Katherine Briggs provides two more general headings of the Fay: nature and house spirits. There are also other types best described as elementals. It is important to note that the Fay may not appear in human form at all. They may appear as an animal, human or any mix thereof. They can take an entirely foreign shape, even of a species of being that seems right out of a science fiction movie. They can also be seen as balls or streams of light or shadow. For many humans, they are only felt or heard but never seen. Do not limit yourself by traditional images of the Fay. They will appear in the manner and time they choose, not unlike cats. Following are some basic descriptions of the appearance and temperament of the Fay. These are general types, but may vary from country to country and between the areas of human contact and associated cultures.

TYPES OF FAERY

I have provided few examples of the European names for the different classes of Faery beings. My reasons for doing this are simple and practical: 1) there are varying names across different languages, cultures, countries and families for the same type of being (there are several fine examples of encyclopedias of Faery beings in print that have captured many of these names); 2) this book is intended to provide the reader with sound, historical and experiential Faery practices, not academic research; and 3) students of Faery Seership who are reading this book are located in many geographic land areas, all of which have Faery beings. The broad classifications fit any type of being anywhere the student lives. The living Faery tradition is about experiencing the beings within the land, not attempting to force European images on African American, Native American or any culturally-oriented beings. The Fay will present themselves as they wish to be seen in and on their land, with or without anthropomorphic elements. A true student experiences the beings on their terms. Therefore, these classes of Faery are descriptive, but not defining.

Traditionally, all of these beings are not classified as Faery, though they are Fay in that they live in the realms of enchantment. The trooping and hive types are the classical "High Faery" and "Lordly Ones." They tend to be human size or larger. The stationary type are often deified as local gods and goddesses because of their power. Although the elementals are often confused with the Faery, they are not an actual part of the folkloric tradition, though they are inexorably intertwined with form and its function. The elementals create and the Faery beings sustain.

Solitary

The solitary Fay are the least friendly of the Fay, with the only exception being the domestic house spirit often described as a brownie (*broonie*), and occasionally, the banshee which is linked to family lines. Yeats describes them as wearing red coats and being potentially aggressive towards humans. This type of garb is not as prevalent in America, though the beings are. Examples of the solitary type include the brownie, leprechaun, pooka, glaistig, bogeys and banshee. They are often ugly in appearance (by human standards) and avoid human contact.

Do not seek them out. When a human comes into contact with a solitary Fay (which is a rare occurrence indeed), the human may experience it as frightening and dangerous. If you have ever been in a wooded place that was visually beautiful but left you feeling unsafe and unwelcome, it is likely that you have encountered a solitary Fay. The solitary Fay experiences the human as an annoyance and not a threat. Sometimes the solitary Fay is the guardian of a place, especially if it has been abused by humanity in the past or is a sacred place specifically for the Fay. If they seek you, ask them their intent. They are honest and if asked a question directly, they will answer directly. Most of the Fay that unite with humanity are of the other types, especially the hive and trooping varieties.

Hive

The hive Fay are a type often employed in magical operations. In fact, they are the beings that swarm or "host" when the hidden paths are opened. A variant of this in Scottish tradition is called an "eddy of wights" or "the haunted wind." This wind is a cyclone of Faery beings that rises up from the underworld and sweeps across the planet, and is a reoccurring phenomenon in the folkloric traditions of many countries. If you have ever felt a wind sweep over you that left you unsettled and feeling like there was something more to the breeze than mere wind, you have probably been touched by the haunted Faery wind. There is no need for worry, however, as they tend to be gregarious and friendly toward humans.

These Fay move about in a collective like ants or bees, which are sacred in the tradition because of this similarity. Each Fay in a hive knows what all of the other hive beings know and experience. They are the high Fay or Lordly Ones organized in a courtly fashion with hierarchies. A queen usually rules the hierarchies, though there are occasional kings. These rulers are composite beings constructed of the totality of their court. When you encounter one of them, you have encountered a multitude of the Fay coalesced into one collective being, which also means that they are very powerful. When the hive being enters the physical world, humans experience it as the sound of buzzing, like a swarm of bees, or through the cold chill of the haunted wind. Many humans who have encountered hiving Fay report seeing a group of "Faery lights" in natural wooded areas or places with the reputation of being haunted.

Trooping

The trooping type is another class of Fay often employed in magical operations. Yeats describes them as wearing green coats. They can be friendly or dangerous to humans. They are called trooping because they are always moving, usually along the Faery tracks or ley lines, which are the hidden roads of the Fair Folk. They range in both size and temperament. There are many folk accounts of these Fay trooping from the sea to the land and back again. Visual sightings report a line of lights that appear to be moving in an orderly fashion.

When encountered, they can be baneful, causing sickness, or they can be blessed, bringing fertility. It is best not to test their temperament by disturbing them while they are trooping. They will let the human seeker know when and if they wish to communicate. They are always encountered when the hidden ways are opened, as they are always trooping on the myriad of Faery roads that lead into and out of our world, filling it with living light the way honey fills a honeycomb. These Fays are often connected with transporting the spirits of the dead to the otherworld, thus their connection with the human dead. All Fay are threshold beings living in between life and death, inner and outer expression, in that place we humans visit in the twilight time.

The trooping Fay are associated with the traditional vision of the "Faery rade," which occurs on the Celtic holidays of Hallowmas and Beltane when the veils between the worlds are thinnest. At Hallowmas, the gates open and these Faeries ride with the hosts of the dead across the land, drawing life inward. They gather the wandering souls of the dead leading them to the regenerative powers of the underworld. At Beltane, the gates open and the Fair Ones rise up through the ancient well, drawing life outward and weaving the green tapestry of life. Tradition teaches that the trooping Fay move their dwellings every season on the first Monday of the quarter, as marked by the Celtic Fire festivals, and this causes the turning of the seasons.

In Welsh tradition, the trooping Fay (specifically the Faery rade at Hallowmas) are often accompanied by *cwnn annwn*, or wish hounds, also known as Gabriel's hounds. These Faery hounds are also trooping Fay. They are white or black hounds with red tipped ears, and are often encountered in the otherworld, even in America. The "hell hounds," as they are often called, or "witch hounds" in the American South, are a re-occurring apparition in folk culture.

Stationary / Nature Spirits

Stationary beings or nature spirits can also be worked with in magic. In fact, traditional Faery Seership often involves a symbiosis between the seer and a stationary Fay, though there are other types of Fay that form the "marriage" as well, specifically the hive or trooping types. Stationary Fay are the inner guardians of a place. They are also called *genii loci*, or local spirits, and are tied to the power of a place. They do not change their dwelling places and are often referred to as a local haunt, or "hant" in American Southern folk tradition.

All places of power have *genii loci* connected with them. This type of being knows the inner topology, history and life of a place. If a human does not engage in a meaningful relationship with this being, all of the other "powers of place" will be closed off to them. Sometimes they are friendly to humans and sometimes not, but they are rarely dangerous in intent. The beings are usually connected in some way to sacred stones, waterways, trees, etc. Some of these beings guard and assist specific animals, trees and plants. They are a reoccurring element in local folklore, since humans often encounter them. They can be one powerful being or a family of beings that are the caretakers of a place. Places of great power tend to have one primary being with hosts of other less powerful beings that obey it.

All wooded and natural areas have nature spirits who care for the balance, harmony and integrity of a place. Some tend flowers, much like the image of the Fairy in Shakespeare's *A Midsummer Night's Dream*. They also include a broad range of beings, including mermaids, elves, kelpie, cavern people, wood wives, moss people and the stereotypical gauzy-winged sprite. These beings are inexorably intertwined with the life vitality of the woods, sea and all natural places of power.

Domesticated

These Fay are the friendliest to humans. They share intimately in the lives of the humans with whom they bond as "house spirits." They are akin to the *genii loci* for a home. They are often passed down through families and tend to be tied to specific homes or land areas. In most traditions, they cannot move when the human changes homes. However, there are ways to transport many of them, though not beyond the hemisphere of their birth. The most common of the domesticated type are the brownies. Traditionally, a call to a brownie is sent forth as an invitation to live within the home of the human, and a local nature spirit will come forward.

Occasionally, reported poltergeist activity (disruptive haunting) is, in fact, either angry or disturbed *genii loci*, or a brownie that needs to be acknowledged and integrated into the household. An area should be set aside for them in a corner of the home or under the stairs where offerings such as honey and cakes can be left undisturbed. They can be quite protective and helpful to a human friend and family. They often guard the home from fire, theft and other harm. During the Yule holiday, the domesticated Fay, known as a *lare* in southern European tradition, is fed and invited or, if it indwells a statue or other object, paraded through every room of the house and brought into the festivities. The link between the humans and their household Fay grows stronger as the human incorporates the Fay into their domestic life and rituals.

These Fay sometimes appear as apparitions of humans we have lost to physical death. If a being like this appears, ask it if it is indeed the spirit of dear dead Aunt Agnes or rather a Faery being wearing her form. Domesticated Fay often read our memories for a form to wear as garb, a form that is familiar and pleasing to us. However, it is important for the Faery student to understand that Faery Seership has a strong necromantic aspect as well. The spirit, which presents itself in a human form, may in fact be dear old Aunt Agnes or the spirit of another human who guards the place or the household. Ancestral spirits also live in the Faery realms and may choose to continue to link with humanity in a healthy or unhealthy way.

There are other spirit beings that are used as household guardians and fetches. A classic example of this is the mandragora or *alraun*, which is a type of fetish employed in traditional witchcraft. In summary, the *alraun* is the root of the European mandrake (*mandragora officinarum*), though several varieties of bryony can be used as well. The plant is used because of the powerful plant or Fay spirit in it. It is harvested in specific ways and at specific times to both encourage the assistance of the residing spirit and to avoid its fury for being harvested. Once collected, it is carved, then later dried, dressed and fed in specific manners. From then on it becomes a guardian and fetch for the human caretaker. This bond remains for life. The use of powerful roots or plant parts that house a Fay being as a familiar spirit is common in older forms of witchcraft and American conjure traditions.

Elementals

These beings are commonly employed in magical operations. They are not Faeries, though they are Fay. They are not a part of the traditional Faery lore, though most Faery practices, including Faery Seership, incorporate them in because, being "architects of form," they are a central part of the etheric and physical world interchange. Therefore, I will spend additional time explaining these mystical beings.

Katherine Briggs provides us with a concise explanation of the elementals and their relationship to nature:

> They are members of a very small class consisting of four: the four elementals, Gnomes, Sylphs, Salamanders, and "Nereads (or undines)," who belong to the four elements, Earth, Air, Fire and Water. Man and all mortal creatures are made up of these four elements, variously compounded, but the elementals were pure, each native to and compounded of its own element. (*Encyclopedia*, Briggs)

This was the hermetic and neo-platonic doctrine and all medieval science and medicine was founded on it. The first description of gnomes as the element of earth is to be found in Paracelsus' treatise *De Nymphis* published in 1658. In addition to the names of the being types, there are elemental rulers. These names are very helpful as focal points to work with the elementals who can be a bit rambunctious at times.

The elementals, Fiona Macleod's "little children of earth's delight," are powerful beings at the very root of substance itself. For all of life as we know it is composed of other life forms in keeping with Robert Kirk's assertion (and R.J. Stewart's interpretation) that "they [the seers] avouch that every Element and different state of being, has [in it] Animals resembling those of another Element." (*Kirk*, Stewart) Again, within each order of life in this world, there are other orders of life. These are the elementals. This teaching also points out that an elemental is only pure in its element when it is either created by a sorcerer, conjurer, witch or magician, or is found in the deep places of Annwn. Usually they have predominant elemental forces within their composition, with minor elements also present.

Elementals are intermediary beings between the inner outflowing dynamic of creation (the plane of forces) and the outer expressive dynamic (the plane of effects). Most humans confine their awareness to the surface world, which is the plane of effects or outcomes. The elementals are the beings which transmit, through their blessed bodies, the streams of power that incarnate our existence. Each elemental type is an agent of specific states of being and, as the name "elemental" implies, they are basic to all form. Their action and intelligence type is symbolically expressed by the use of the four elemental classifications of air, fire, water and earth, or the classical sylph, salamander, undine and gnome. These elemental types are, in fact, expressions of being and comprise whole conditions of life, often described as planes of existence.

The elemental beings exist within these elemental states or "sub-planes" of the etheric condition. Elementals activate (sylphs and salamanders) or fuse and anchor (undines and gnomes) spiritual energy into specific pre-defined patterns which culminate in what we think of as form. There are elemental forms on all planes of existence, though one or more types may be more primary in each plane (e.g. gnomes on the earth plane). We humans, as surface walkers, tend to experience elementals by their effects and rarely in their actual life being. By this I mean that it is rare for a human to interact with an elemental purely on the basis of two life forms in exchange. Usually, we humans interact through our five senses with the effects of the elemental (i.e. solidity, fluidity, etc.). A primary effect of Faery Seership is to move humanity away from this shallow mode of interrelating with elemental life forms.

The following illustrates just some of the effects of elementals in our world:

Elemental Name	Name Meaning	Effects on the Material World	Ruler
Sylph	Sylphe: being with gauzy wings	Motion, extension, opening of ways, breath, and life	Paralda
Salamander	Sa(o)lam (fire), Andros (man): man of fire	Warmth, vivification, and illumination	Djinn
Undine	Undina: creature of the waves	Pattern, depth, harmony and ensoulment	Necksa
Gnome	Gnoma: knowing one	Crystallization, embodiment, deterioration, decay and regeneration	Ghob

Elementals are hardly "cutesy critters." They are powerful and sacred beings. Some of the more dynamic ones (sylphs and salamanders) can be playful, but also dangerous. Undines can be evocative and deeply touching emotionally as they exude their potent magnetic powers. Gnomes are not cookie-making elves or happy-go-lucky munchkins. They tend to be evasive, somber and all-knowing about physical life. They, like all of the elementals, are engaged in magic in the names of their rulers. It is rare that any of the elementals present themselves to humanity in an anthropomorphic form. For example, American gnomes tend to appear as moving shadows, sometimes human-shaped and sized, which flow through the woods and are often perceived out of the corner of one's eye. The elementals can be called down the hidden paths, as seen in many modern magical practices such as "calling the quarters," or they can be sought in their natural environments where the element embodies their effect.

Sylphs tend to be prevalent in high places such as mountains and high buildings, or in a hosting as a tornado, dust devil or cyclone. Salamanders tend to live in deserts, volcanoes, lightening, electrical currents and ley lines. Undines live in water ways such as rivers, oceans, creeks, wells and springs. Gnomes live in the mountains, mounds, crypts, stones, graveyards and heavily wooded areas.

Elementals comprise the form and life essence (toradh) of all things, including the human condition. Note that I have used the word condition instead of species. This is to help the reader make a leap from perceiving each living being as a distinctive life form which is individuated and separate to perceiving each being as a condition of the one being cast onto the fabric of form. Human beings are a state or condition of the Ancient One acting a certain way in a certain form, an experience which we call "human." In fact, humans, like all creatures, are made up of the very same essence and universal intelligence as everything else. When we truly embrace that fact, we (as humans) have begun our return to the family of creation.

A human being is composed of a collective state of elemental beings. At the point of insemination during the procreative act of sexual union between a man and woman, the human soul (or the soul of any being born into physical form) which is about to incarnate, sends out a sound or call which sets the pattern for an elemental hosting or vortex. This is a call to action for the appropriate elementals to cluster and form a pattern that becomes the vessel (or baby) matched to its soul needs. The elementals, in the course of creating or clustering form, imprint themselves on each form. This creates a resonance within the form with the elementals and an interdependence between the human soul with the elementals. Because of this, all beings in physical form have a kindredship with the elementals and thus, they can be called and worked with in magic, as "like attracts like." The elements within call to the four streams of life: the elementals.

Larvae

There are many other types of beings in the otherworld, including human ancestors, which we will address in a later chapter. Most of these originate from human consciousness, for we have been given the ability to project forth otherworld life from our being. Thus, we can also create elementals and other beings from ourselves. Unfortunately, there is another class of not-so-pleasant beings called "larvae," which are vampiric in nature and do not find their origins in the natural worlds. They are solely created by humans. These beings are not of the Faery races, though they live in the same stratum of life, and the Faery student *will* encounter them, rest assured. Forewarned is forearmed.

The term "larvae" appears in both modern theosophical tradition and ancient Roman occult tradition. The concept, however, appears in cultures all over the world as vampires or beings that feed on the life essence of humans and other animals. Larvae are life forms created by humans and ensouled with emotional energy which are uncontrolled and have no other purpose than to survive. Humans usually create them unintentionally when they project emotional outbursts of energy. This energy becomes a life form that is always hungry and feeds off of toradh. They look like worms or maggots in the otherworld. They attach themselves onto people when the host either enters into an environment where they live or breed, or when the host is the target of intense emotional projections from another person over a period of time. Sometimes humans pick them up in sexual relationships that involve intercourse and orgasm. They are spiritual infections and are why the magical practitioner needs to be very mindful of their intimate relationships. This gives a whole new meaning to "safer sex."

CLUSTERS

The concept of clusters was revealed to me directly from the Fair Folk and, to my understanding, is not an element in the old traditional teachings. The nature of consciousness is that it combines itself into new patterns and clusters with other forms that have a magnetic affinity with it. In fact, consciousness is refined through this process. It forms symbiotic relationships with other streams of consciousness and thus families, clans, ecosystems and organisms are born. What appears as one being is actually a cluster. A human being is a cluster of cells, elementals and microbes that have affinity around a central spiritual core (the soul) and act as one. Therefore, the being called by your name is a composite cluster centered around a central point of intelligence. Ecosystems, like woodland areas and water-sheds, work the same way. They are a cluster of cells (in this case living plants and creatures) that have an affinity with each other around a central point of intelligence, the *genii loci*. If you communicate from the central point of intelligence within you (the Child of Promise) to the central point of intelligence of a woodland ecosystem, much powerful work can be achieved. The universal intelligence called the "Ancient One" flows through form into patterns that gather in pools of intelligence and interlock with each other. The concept of the "inscape" is the discovery of a land area's clusters, the function of each cluster, component parts and intelligences of the cluster, and their relationship with the central point of intelligence.

ATTUNING TO THE POWER OF PLACE

Before you can encounter the tribes within Faery, you must tune into the power of place. The best way for the seeker to begin their attunement to the interior world of the land is through changing their approach to, and resonance with, the inner power of nature and her power places in the surface world. Understand that, as far as the Fay and the Dreamer are concerned, all land and sea is sacred and powerful. We humans experience some natural places as more powerful, and thus sacred, because either they have been relatively undisturbed by us, they have been restored to health through human/Fay partnership, the *genii loci* are very powerful, or something of human significance has occurred at the place. However, *all* places have inner power. The Faery well exercise is good technique to begin attuning to the inner power or toradh of a place.

VISION #2: The Faery Well Exercise

This exercise is most effective if performed outside on the land, though it can be performed inside if there are no other options. A large pot of soil can be brought in and used for this as well (please, no potting soil). This exercise parts the physical substance of the surface world (in this case, land) and reveals the pool of inner power within it.

a) Draw your senses inward into yourself. Be aware of your presence here and now. Be also aware of the sounds and sensations around you, allowing them to pass through you unaffected, like water through a sieve. Close your eyes to draw your awareness inward.

b) Be aware of your breathing which mimics the breath of the universe as it passes in and out of the void – creating and de-creating. Allow all cares of the human world to pass away from you and be left behind as you enter into the eternal communion of spirit. Approach stillness.

c) Be aware of the sun above you that shines its radiance on the backdrop of the dark spaces. This is the star that dances on the infinity of night. Feel its presence as it radiates power onto the earth and all who dwell upon her. Be also aware of the sun within the earth that gives light to the mysterious underworld – the home of Faery, ancestral, deep planetary being and your soul. Now be aware of the fire that burns within your heart, for it is the center of your inner universe and its light shines into all of the areas of your body and mind. Envision these three suns coming together in a light line connecting you to all above, below and within. This is the Bilé or sacred tree.

d) Now open your eyes. Be aware that, though you too often perceive the land as something you are walking on, you are indeed floating on it, and an ocean of power and vitality lies just below the sheath of form.

e) Reach out before you and with your index finger (either hand) draw a sun wise (clockwise) circle on the soil before you while feeling that you are demarcating the boundaries of a well that shall open into the land.

f) Holding this feeling, reach out before you and draw a line on the soil in the circle from the top to bottom vertical to you and declare, "let the powers of above …"

g) Still holding this feeling, draw a line on the soil from left to right across the first one horizontally to form an equal-arm cross while stating, "… unite with the powers of below." You should have before you an equal armed cross with a circle around it with the points of the cross extended to the edge of the inside of the circle.

h) Now there are four quadrants in this circle. These are like the glass in a window or the skin of an onion that you peel back revealing the interior. Reach into one quarter and peel it back like you are opening it. Do this with the other three sections while holding the vision and feeling that you are opening a well, one section at a time.

i) Once the well is opened, feel the power that surges within it. This is the power of the sacred land that lies at the root of substance, feeding it. Reach in with your hands as to cup water, scooping some of the toradh into your hands. Pour this down over your body, feeling it cleanse and attune you to the land. Wash yourself with this toradh. This is similar to the smudging techniques used by Native Americans.

j)   Take these feelings of clarity, purification, holiness, and attunement to the land within yourself.

k)   Now gently close the well by taking each section that you opened and folding it back into the center, one by one. Continue to feel the power of the underworld surging within the well.

l)   Once you have closed each section, take your hand and trace the horizontal line (the powers of below) from the right to the left. Then do the same with the vertical line (the powers of above) and draw it from the bottom to the top. Thus you are undoing the equal-arm cross.

m) Now, take your hand and trace the circle counter-clockwise to fully close the well. Sit and feel the well completely recede into the land.

n)   Sit for a few moments and commune with the feeling of attunement that comes to you. Document your thoughts and feelings in a journal.

This exercise should be performed before doing any Faery work on unfamiliar land. In the beginning of your work, it should be performed 2-3 times weekly for a month to attune to the power of the land where you live or do spiritual work.

CHAPTER 7:
THE ANCESTOR SPIRITS
AND THE RIVER OF BLOOD

O they rade on, and farther on,
And they waded thro' rivers aboon the knee,
And they saw neither sun nor moon,
Buth they heard the roaring of the sea.

It was amirk mirk night, and they nae stern light,
And they waded thro' red blude to the knee;
For a' the blude that's shed on earth;
Rins through the springs of that countrie.

— *"The Ballad of Thomas the Rhymer"*

The Ballad of Thomas the Rhymer is an old folkloric account of the taking of a mortal human by the Faery Queen into the underworld for seven years, which is the traditional "tithe to hell," also called a "kain." This tithe is an initiatory period wherein the soul of the human is changed and made Fay over a period of time, during which he or she is neither human nor Faery, but betwixt and between. This ballad also recounts the folk connections between the human dead (through the imagery of blood) and the Faery realm and its inhabitants. For the blood that Thomas the Rhymer waded through is the traditional River of Blood, which is the living stream of all human and other life on the earth's surface, as indicated by the line "for a' the blude [blood] that's shed on earth; rins [runs] through the springs of that countrie." This shows us the connection between the surface world of humanity and the underworld of the Faery races. For as the essence of the Fay fills our world like honey into a honeycomb, thereby giving it life; so too, our blood (life essence) fills the springs of the Faery realms like honey flowing backward into the inner worlds. Once again, we are led back to the question of "who are the fairies?" How are they connected to the human ancestral dead? Leslie Shephard, in her forward to *Fairy Faith in Celtic Countries* provides insight to this question by saying

> What are those fairies — those romantic and sometimes mischievous little people — pixies, nixies, elves, fauns, brownies, dwarfs, leprechauns, and all other forms of the *daoine sidhe* (fairy people)? Are they real? Folklorist say they were fragments of ancient religious beliefs, occultists thought they were nature spirits; the peasant traditions said they were fallen angels who were not good enough to be saved nor bad enough to be lost. There is some truth in all these views.

Traditional Faery lore and magic cannot be approached without addressing the interconnections between the Faery people and the ancestral dead. Again, Faery Seership and necromancy, which is the practice of conjuring and communicating with the dead, are *absolutely inseparable*. If one is to study and understand the Faery races, they must and will work with the shades of the dead. Evans-Wentz notes that:

> ... the striking likenesses constantly appearing in our evidence between the ordinary apparitional fairies and the ghosts of the dead show that there is often no essential and sometimes no distinguishable difference between these two orders of beings, nor between the world of the dead and fairyland.

Evans-Wentz found, as he was collecting Faery lore from throughout many Celtic countries (as all anthropologists and folklorists have found), that there is a constant reoccurring connection between these two orders of beings. This connection is so reoccurring that many researchers have assumed that the Faery people are the ancestral dead and that the whole practice is a cult of the dead. This assertion is close to, but not in keeping with the deeper teachings of Faery tradition.

"The fairy faith is inseparably connected with that same area of human consciousness that has to do with religious experience, with metaphysical insight. It is concerned with a greater reality beyond the everyday world of human frailty and limitations." (*Forward, Fairy Faith*, Shephard)

In short, experience of the Faery realms taps into that same stream of life that brings prophecy, spiritual awareness, connection with the guiding hands of destiny, and at-one-ment with the source of life as we know it. It also offers humanity a reconnection to their place as individuals and a species within a greater tapestry of life and purpose. The most personal stratum on this continuum of life relates to ancestry, which is the life that flows through each one of us. This ancestral life is the "Well of Memories," a reoccurring concept in many legends across cultures and time periods. When we partake of this wellspring of inner life, ancient abiding wisdom, vision and purpose opens up to us. This is the legendary drop of inspiration from the cauldron of Cerridwen, a drink from the Holy Grail or wading through the River of Blood. The student of the Faery mysteries must understand that contact with the river is what opens the deeper streams of inner life to us. Then the "intraterrestrial life" of the Faery races and the Shining Ones can be revealed to the attuned sight of those marked with the old blood.

Oral tradition teaches that the Fair Folk are present and involved in child birthing and death. In truth, these occasions are mirrors of each other. The only difference is the direction of the movement of the human soul into or out of physical form.

In one, the spirit is leaving the Faery realms and entering into the outer strata of human life. In the other, the spirit is leaving human life and re-entering the mystical Faery realm. There are many folk sayings that capture this sentiment such as "your mother has gone with the fairies." This statement or concept is still alive and in use throughout Ireland, Scotland, Britain, Wales and the old families in America, as reported by seers in these areas. This saying suggests that the belief in the connection between ancestral human dead and the Faery realms is very much alive and well. It also suggests that there are folk beliefs in which it is clear that the two beings (ancestral and Faery) are interconnected, but not the same.

"Some European peasants believe that the dead belong to the fairies, and they [the fairies] therefore celebrate the death of a [human] person like a festival, with music and dancing." (*Teutonic Mythology*, Grimm) However, tradition is clear that the Fair Folk are not captors of the human dead. Rather, they are guardians and guides of the death process and the destiny of the soul as it moves out of time and space, and across the aeonic ocean of Annwn to the under and inner world. Likewise, there are many Celtic beliefs that the soul of the dead goes to an inner world, island, happy hunting ground, or Summerland of warmth where it never grows old. For, if the Faery people are ever-young, as tradition suggests, and our dead step into their realm, perhaps we too become ever-young and this is the heaven we await – living in the paradisiacal vision of the Dreamer with the elder races of Fay. That is a question left for you, the reader, to explore as you wade through the River of Blood into the under-country of the Good People. But beware, not all of your ancestors are at peace.

HUMAN GHOSTS AND THE FAERY RADE

It is impossible to discuss the necromantic elements of Faery Seership practices without discussing the Celtic festival of death known today as "Halloween." Interestingly, this type of festival honoring the dead occurs at the same point on the calendar all over the world in many cultures. Alexander Montgomerie wrote a poem in 1585 entitled "Flyting" that illustrates the Faery revelries at this time:

In the hinder end of harvest, on Hallowe'en,
When our Good Neigbors (the Faery) does ride; if I read richt,
Some buckled on a bunewand and some on a bean,
Ay trottand in troups from the twighlight;
Some saidled a she-ape, all grathed in green,
Some hobland on a hemp-stalk, hovand to the hight;
The King of Pharie and his court, with the Elf Queen,
With many elfish Incubus was ridand that night.

As discussed in previous chapters, there are two primary fire festivals in the Celtic variants of the Faery tradition; they are the festival of death and ancestry called Samhain, Hallowmas or Halloween, and the celebration of renewed life called Beltane or May Eve. These festivals mark the points in the yearly cycle where the doors of life open and close, hence the concepts of such times being when the veil between the worlds is thinnest. At Hallowmas, the gates of the underworld open and the cold breath of death is issued forth from the Cave of Voices. The Cave of Voices is a Faery concept that embodies the opening between inner and outer life and the levels or depth that it contains. The opening of the gates brings forth winter and the season of death. It also marks the beginning of the "blooding time" when the weakest of the livestock are butchered. This illustrates how life consumes life through death, which in turn bears forth sustained life. For life and death are the same process in reverse, twin poles of an engine of transformation on a great wheel of life transporting life on our planet to its destiny. The Faery people, seers and witches are the mechanics of this wheel. One teaching suggests that the blood of the sacrificed animal in the autumn stirs the sleeping ones in the dust. Another teaching tells us that the horns of each animal slain and consumed for their life sustenance become the crown of the Horned God, the Lord of the Underworld.

The natural dynamic illustrated in these teachings is akin to the breathing process which draws life inward, regenerates it and uses its constituents to feed the greater life, and then breaths out again issuing forth new life patterns. "On the eve of Hallowe'en, the old Keltic festival of Samhain, the dead ghosts and fairies were thought of as mingling together in unholy revels." (*British Fairy Origins*, Spence) Traditionally, October 31st marks the eve of Hallows, which runs until the end of November. During this time, suspended between life and death, expression and repose, the otherworld powers of Fay and ancestry weave their tapestries into all other orders of life, including humanity. Our ancestors took Hallowmas very seriously. Any crops that were not harvested by October 31 belonged to the "shrouded one," known by many names including the *Bucca* and *Ankou*. This being is a type of Faery connected to the primal powers of death and regeneration. Modern humans would be wise to note the wisdom of our ancestors in this custom. The soil is, in fact, becoming depleted as we strip the land and leave nothing to decompose and regenerate the soil with nutrients. Traditionally, ancestors not honored at this time could plague the living with ill health and bad luck. The Faery people work their magic of regeneration at this time. The circular dances employed in modern witchcraft are remnants of these Faery practices called the "Mill of Magic" which mimics, on this occasion, the turning of life into the soil through decomposition.

Faery beings disturbed in their dance upon the mill of magic could strike the wandering human with paralysis, bad luck or ill health. Only those humans who keep with the old ways knew (and still know) the secret ways of the dead and the elder race. At this auspicious time, the Faery Rade, lead by the Lord of the Faery, rides forth with the hosts of the dead across the land, sweeping up the souls of those who have died within that year and smiting all with his cold breath and touch of winter. In many traditions, the god of death and the Faery king are one and the same.

In Ireland it was thought that the fairies and the dead were very close to each other. Finvara, one of the fairy kings, was also King of the Dead, and it was thought to be very dangerous to be out after nightfall on Hallows Eve (October 31) and for a month after it, till the end of November. (*Vanishing People*, Briggs)

Likewise, Lady Wilde recounts a folk story called "the Dance of the Dead":

It is especially dangerous to be out on the last night of November, for it is the closing scene of the revels – the last night when the dead have leave to dance on the hill with the fairies, and after that they must all go back to their graves and lie in the chill, cold earth without music or wine till the next November comes round, when they all spring up again in their shrouds and rush out into the moonlight with mad laughter. (Wilde)

Though Hallowmas marks a specific time of the year when folklore tells us that both the dead and the Fay walk about, the Faery teachings are clear that there is a constant connection between them.

At Beltane, the gates of the underworld open and the warm breath of life issues forth from the Cave of Voices, bringing the Faery powers of life to the land. This brings forth summer and the season of renewed life. It marks the beginning of an outpouring of life patterns from the inner to the outer worlds and the start of the "seedling time" and the season of the White Goddess. At Hallowmas, the gates open and the Faery powers of death enter onto the surface world bringing death and decay. The traditional colors of the Faery tradition are red for the blooding time and green of the greening or summer time. The Faery powers reflect the regenerative qualities of nature as seen in the winter and summer seasons.

THE RELATIONSHIP BETWEEN THE ANCESTRAL DEAD AND THE FAIR FOLK

The Faery people live in a stratum of life one shift of awareness away from human surface life. They are our closest next of
kin, second only to our ancestors. They live in the sea of life that
connects the earth where humans, plants and other animals live
and the sky which is the realm of planets and beings that dwell
in the stars. This re-illustrates the Celtic cosmology dividing the
three worlds of creation into sky, sea and earth. Tradition teaches
that some ancestors may come back into form, even into our
families, while others live within the River of Blood and surface
through the blood of the living in a symbiosis. Many traditional
mystic teachings, including Celtic, African, Afro-Caribbean and
Egyptian, tell how at death the soul travels across the waters of
life to another realm. These waters are one and the same as the
Faery River of Blood. In this process, the soul forgets who it was
in life. Ancestral worship assists these shades in remembering
who they were in life and their connection to the living.
The novice seer is wise to note that ancestor spirits constantly
influence the destiny of their living loved ones. They can open
or bar the way to the Faery realms. There are elaborate rites to
ensure that the soul does not forget, get trapped, break its ties
with the living family or become angry and wreak havoc on the
living. It is the duty of the seer to address these issues.

When I was being taught as a seer, I was instructed that the
more we travel into the Faery realms, the less we will fear death
when it comes. Through exchange with the Fay, humans understand the greater truth of life – incarnate and discarnate. The
more we travel these hidden paths, the more we understand the
words of the truly inspired song "We Do Not Die" which says:

We are not dead, we are alive.
We are just on the other side.
We are alive.

   – Millard & Doss, Dreamtrybe

Our fear of death departs us because there simply is no death. Life is a state of being far beyond the mere confines of flesh and physical form. Dividing, yet connecting the realms of inner and outer life is the River of Blood, which is a border that carries the consciousness of all that has ever lived within it. Perhaps when we cross it, a part of our soul is carried by it to some deep inner region of planetary being where all knowledge originates and is stored.

There are stories of the human otherworld traveler who wades through the River of Blood, haunted by the voices of the dead crying out for redemption. This is a haunting reminder that when we go inward, we first encounter the voices that dwell within our own blood – the voices of those who preceded us. They can bar the entry to the Faery realms or act as intermediary spirits, guiding and guarding the living through the halls of death into deeper realms of life and truth. Beyond the River of Blood are the voices of those ancestors and the Faery beings that lead humanity, from the inside out, to spiritual revelation and atonement. All humans will be touched closely by the Fay, if not in life, then in death and beyond. We do better to engage the enchanted self or sith, explore those realms and open the paths between them consciously and while we are embodied. It is reassuring to know that the Faery allies we make in life will follow and assist us when we move into their world at death.

WORKING WITH THE DEAD IN FAERY SEERSHIP

Often, the ancestors are the first beings that the human traveler encounters when entering the inner formative worlds. Anyone who has worked with meditative and visionary techniques will attest that, at least in the early training phases when they attempted to look inward and still themselves, a cacophony of voices and meaningless mind chatter surfaced. We are too often told that these voices are simply mind chatter when they are often the voices of ancestors in our blood. When we allow these voices to pass through us, they often fade away leaving a few voices that may surface as ancestors who can and will work with us in the liminal state through dreams, visions and inspirations. There are several areas where the ancestors come into Faery work:

A) *Work with ancestor spirits as guides and go-between beings that assist the human traveler in making connections in the Faery realms*

Of all of the spirits in the Faery realms, the ancestors are the most familiar with the living human seeker. They are the beings most invested in the development and affairs of the humanity, since they have lived in the human experience and have descendents currently in physical form. The growth of the human feeds back into the River of Blood through the blood of the human which brings illumination to the dead. Ancestral spirits can block or open the way for further explorations in the otherworld. It is always good to have friends when you travel in a strange land. Work with the dead is an important component of traditional magical practices including those of Faery Seership. In visionary work, the student seer will encounter ancestors that become a part of the working team of the seer.

B) *Work with friendly ancestor spirits to assess whether other spirits are blocking the road for other inner work and outer harmony*

A fellow southern conjureman once told me, "ma Pappy always lets me know when someone's a workin gainst me." This American folk sorcerer was simply telling me that his deceased father gives him inner perception of other forces at work on his destiny. This is common among Faery seers and root doctors. If the seer works with the spirit of a deceased loved one who they knew and loved in life, they have a powerful inner ally for looking into the inner worlds and acting with magical and divinatory precision.

C) *Work with the River of Blood to redeem the ancestors, thereby moving the familial bloodline and humanity forward in spiritual development*

This is perhaps the most potent aspect of ancestral work in Faery Seership. The teachings tell us that each of us is born to redeem our bloodline and its inner power. The concept of redemption is rarely addressed in modern mystical practices. Redemption involves resolution and movement of the bloodline spiritually forward. It most often entails encountering certain ancestors, hearing the voice of their crying in the River of Blood and assuring that their problems are not carried forward through you into the next generation. This is one major way which we, the living, purify the blood and redeem the dead. The ancestors of the past flow through us and give us context. We redeem them by bringing forth balance in both the inner and outer worlds. Let us not be revisited by the sins of our mothers and fathers. Let us meet them straight on and redeem them.

Some of this work can be quite disturbing and requires intense supervision by an experienced seer. For example, I once worked with a woman who had insanity in her family and was on treatment for severe depression and bipolar disorder. In the Faery work, I led her back through the blood of her mothers (a Faery technique) until we found the last woman with the second sight. In the contact, it became clear that her emotional condition was introduced into the bloodline in the 1700s when a female ancestor closed off her second sight to prevent accusation of practicing witchcraft and the resulting death sentence. Once my student contacted her and bridged a part of her forward in time into her current life where she (the student) had developed her second sight, a burst of joy and completion came into her. Later that year, she informed me that she was no longer on medications and that her psychiatrist and therapist said she was moving forward in her healing at an incredibly accelerated rate. It's been five years now and her healing appears to be permanent. Perhaps it was a coincidence, but this is not the only case I have encountered where there was a radical example of healing associated with this work.

D) *Work with the River of Blood changes incarnate human perception of time, place and death*

In this aspect of Faery work, the student contacts and encounters ancestors of the past and future. Humans are, by nature, very time and space oriented. This is the way we have been trained to interpret reality and the information around and within us. However, work with the Fair Folk and the ancestral beings forces us to realize the ever-present now. When we tap into timeless states of Faery being, we realize that behind us we have ancestors of the past that flow up through us and anchor us, and before us are ancestors of the future drawing us forward through time and into new expression. In another time, we are already the voices of the ancestors. We appear in their visions and dreams in another place and time. Perhaps, we even warn them not to repeat our mistakes. Do not confuse time with reality. Time is only a means of explaining the relationship between matter and change. It is a measure of cycles of form caused by change. The concept of time never touches in on energy and its perpetual life. Forms change but the essence remains the same. The ancestors of the future give us the next goal. We (the chronological present) open the way for them as we approach them to become the ancestors of their past.

E) *Work with the mysteries of the soil*

Traditionally, the ancestors (human and other) govern the powers of the soil. The soil is comprised of the memories of their form – dust to dust. It is a custom in Faery Seership to pray to the ancestral spirits for prosperity and blessings on any seed before planting it into the ground. Another custom is to pour wine, ale or beer over the ploughshare or hang cheese on it to feed the ancestors during the first tilling of the soil in the spring. The soil is their domain and they should be honored and placated before tapping into the power that is theirs alone.

THE ANCESTOR SPIRITS AND THE RIVER OF BLOOD 101

F) *Understanding that ancestors influence luck and fertility*

The ancestors and Faery beings live in a stratum of life that is ever-becoming. When humans stretch their consciousness beyond outer life to encompass the inner workings which are the very foundations of life, they are entering into the world where luck and fertility are determined. Faery and ancestral beings dwell at these intersect points between possibility and performance, and can (and do) influence balance, harmony and well-being. Work with the ancestors is the quickest way to remove obstacles to these states. It is also the most effective and efficient way to reach the Faery races and encounter a co-walker being.

G) *Mysteries of the blood as embodied in the River of Blood*

The River of Blood embodies the ancestral consciousness that flows through the living form of each human being, through their physical blood. When the river is contacted, the incarnate human experiences a flow of consciousness containing patterns of personalities that flow up through them from the springs of the underworld. With this quickening comes deep wisdom, inner knowing and the ability to see forward into the future. This stream of being is alive in the ever-becoming and yet is rooted in the accumulative wisdom of the past. This powerful intelligence is a state of consciousness "alive in another time cycle." (*Underworld Initiation*, Stewart) Faery Seership works with the memory contained in the blood that is awakened through contact with the first race (the Fair Folk) and the River of Blood. Remember, your body and blood is your personal entry point into the inner Faery realms.

Faery Seership work with the ancestors does not involve possession or mediumship. Rather, is involves an inter-plane communication process wherein the seer is mediating between outer human awareness and the inner life of a being (in this case, ancestral) that lives in a non-physical energetic state.

In popular mediumship as practiced by spiritualist groups, the person acting as the medium, an agent of transmission, does not act in full individual awareness. In extreme examples, the personality of the human is supposed to be replaced by an entity from another state of consciousness, ostensibly for communication.

... These beings are close to the human time-stream, and can make themselves known through *displacement*.

In seership, the operation of displacement does not occur. The individual is in control of the ability, and is able to communicate with the entities in the Innerworlds. Such beings are very different in type and quality to those that associate with the psyche of the displacement medium, or of the partial-displacement clairvoyant and sensitive.

(*Underworld Initiation*, Stewart)

Work with the River of Blood can be very useful in transitioning humans who are dying into the other world. This can be done through two primary approaches:

- *Engaging Faery contacts into the transition work*: Faery contacts (or cousins) are very helpful is assisting the human spirit to release its current form. Once contacts have been made and sustained by the Seership student, they can help the dying human move easily to the other side. This relationship must be developed by the human and their Faery contact for this technique to be effective.

- *Bridging the River of Blood*: In vision, the Seership student can meet the spirit of the dying human at the edge of the River of Blood and provide them with the *Prudwyn*, the glass boat that carries them to the other side. It is helpful to send a familiar redeemed ancestor spirit who already dwells beyond the river to assist the transitioning loved one.

MAKING GOOD WITH THE ANCESTORS

There are many techniques to begin work with the ancestor spirits. However, some are more involved than others. There are four basic classes of ancestor spirits which the traveler beyond the hedge will encounter:

- *Ancestors of the Blood*: These are the actual ancestors of the current bloodlines(s) of the seeker and are usually the first encountered. The seeker can call for them or the ancestor will find the seeker. They are often the most familiar.

- *Ancestors of the Order*: These are beings that have been a living part of a spiritual tradition, but are now disincarnate. They may be a part of the seeker's current spiritual or religious tradition or of one that they will be entering. These beings are often a coveted part of the inner workings of an occult order, traditional witchcraft line or other spiritual tradition.

- *Ancestors of the Races*: These beings are connected to the other lives or incarnations embodied by the seeker across cultures and races. They usually approach the seeker and lead them into the knowledge of other lives. They will present themselves and what they have for you.

- *Ancestors of the Anointing*: These are ancestors that have never been connected to the living seeker at any time or in any life, though they were once embodied humans. They live in the underworld as mentors to humanity and are often called to work with the seeker to bring forward (from another time) or outward (from an inner source) some way of being or stream of spiritual power. They choose you to be the transmitter of their ways. You do not choose them.

Below are a few easily employed techniques that will increase the harmonious relationship between the human seeker and the ancestors that influence them.

- *Ancestral Altars:* This is an interface point to work with the ancestors. They are never worshiped. Rather, they are honored and engaged for assistance. Altars can be simple or elaborate. Pictures or other icons of the deceased are placed on the altar. The only pictures (or other objects) used should be those to whom the living human wants a renewed and living connection. Ancestors can be, and often are, removed from the altar. Traditionally, a glass of water is placed on the altar and refreshed each week. This provides toradh to the spirits. They consume it as sustenance. There should be a "+" or "x" carved into the altar or sewn onto a simple cloth of black or white. The marking is the crossroads that marks an opening between the worlds. A simple white candle is kept on the altar and is lit when the ancestors are worked with. Other colors can be used, if the spirits enlisted favor them. The candle and offerings are placed at the center of the marking. The flame and the offering of water give energy to the spirits to allow them to work in this world. Ancestral work is *not a hobby.* It is ill advised to start and stop this practice. The commitment of the student is noticed by all spirits. When working with these spirits, it is nice to reward them for jobs well done or help they have provided. I like to brew coffee for mine since all of them drank copious amounts of it in their incarnate lives. I also offer whiskey or rum when they have been particularly helpful. Do not offer much of the alcoholic beverages, as they do get intoxicated and dependent on it. Only give these rewards at Hallowmas or after they have helped with an endeavor. Honey is also useful.

- *Prayer:* Most, if not all, of our ancestors were involved in some type of prayer when they were incarnate. Prayer is active communion with spiritual forces. It is very powerful when we, the living, pray for the spirits of the deceased. The ancestors hear the prayer and receive the blessings. We should pray for their well being and safe travels through the other world and into incarnation. We should pray that they find truth, joy and all of the good things of life. This simple act empowers our connections with the ancestors and engages them into a mutually supportive relationship. Remember, they may be praying for you!

- *Soil Blessing:* Many of the ancestors that sustain our life were not human. They (along with the human ancestors) still live, in part, within the soil. This soil sustains life as we know it. It is good practice to bring a small vessel of soil from the land we live on, as well as the land where we were raised, and place it on our ancestral altars as an honoring. When gardening or sowing seeds, this soil should be honored at the altar and at the place of the working. While planting, simply take a handful of soil and pray into it. Ask for a blessing. Bless the spirits that dwell within it. Take this soil and scatter it over the garden area. Many types of spirits will take notice of this action and will be enlisted to help. If one is planting in a pot for indoor cultivation, simply take soil from an area near you which you honor. Soil from the graves of loved ones can also be mixed in and this enhances the power of the work.

The core of true spiritual work is about coming into a harmonious relationship with the realms of life. Ancestor and Faery work is at the forefront. However, no deep work will be lasting without engaging the ancient heritage that lives within each of our bloodlines. All honor to the spirits in your blood! All honor to the first mother and father who dwells within you! I leave you with this lovely poem, written by Rudyard Kipling:

A Charm

Take of English earth as much
As either hand may rightly clutch.
In taking of it breathe
Prayer for all who lie beneath-
Not the great or well bespoke,

But the mere uncounted folk
Of whose life and death is none
Report or lamentation.
> Lay that earth upon thy heart,
> And thy sickness shall depart!

It shall sweeten and make whole
Fevered breath and festered soul;
It shall mightily restrain
Over-busy hand and brain;
It shall ease thy mortal strife
'Gainst the immortal woe of life,
Till thyself restored shall prove
By what grace the Heavens do move.

Take of English flowers these-
Spring's full-faced primroses,
Summer's wild wide-hearted rose,
Autumn's wall-flower of the close,
And thy darkness to illume,
Winter's bee-thronged ivy-bloom.
Seek and serve them where they bide
From Candlemas to Christmas-tide,
> For these simples used aright
> Can restore a failing sight.

These shall cleanse and purify
Webbed and inward turning eye;
These shall show thee treasure hid,
Thy familiar fields amid;
And reveal (which is thy need)
Every man a King indeed!

– "Rewards and Fairies," Kipling

CHAPTER 8:
THE SACRED LAND
AND THE POWER OF PLACE

Have not all races had their first unity from
a mythology that marries them to rock and hill?

– William Butler Yeats

All indigenous folk magic traditions originate from a human desire to understand and control death, life, luck, and nature. The rituals and magical practices in these traditions are intended to tap, control or cajole the unseen influences of these states into a harmonious relationship with the humanity. Mystical practices and folk magic in their earliest forms grew out of the generations of human life in a specific geographic area and the relationship that evolved between humanity and the land, waterways and sky. Within these practices, nature reveals a magical process to which humans endeavor to understand and relate. These revelations, beliefs and rituals evolve into mystical teachings, practices and wisdom traditions over generations of time and through the process of birth, life, and death, and the effects on humanity.

THE KEEPERS OF THE FAERY WAYS

The keepers of the wisdom traditions, often referred to a seers, conjurers, witches, and medicine men or women, are wise in the inner ways of a place and of the ancestral power of a race, clan, family, or tribe. These insights come from the realm of the spirits, which is the realm of the Faery beings. They know things that are unknown to others.

Throughout Great Britain and Ireland, but more particularly in the latter country, a very considerable number of persons are known to have functioned during the last three or four centuries as magical intermediaries between fairies and mankind. (*The Fairy Tradition in Britain*, Spence)

These healers and seers are known as Fairy doctors in Ireland and Scotland, *dynion hysbys* (charmers) in Wales, and as wise wives, wood witches, and hedge witches in Britain. "In Cardiganshire, a conjurer is called 'Dyn Hysbys', where hysbys ... means 'informed': it is the man who is *informed* on matters which are dark to others." (*Celtic Folklore: Welsh and Manx*, Rhys) In Welsh and other traditions throughout the isles and continental Europe, this otherwise unknown information comes from an alliance between the conjurer and supernatural beings, specifically the *Tylwyth Teg*, or Fair Family, which is a name applied to the Faeries.

THE OTHER WORLD

In keeping with Yeats, the most ancient of mythologies and folk beliefs bring humanity into a marriage with the land, for it was clear to our ancestors that humanity lives within a greater fabric of life. This fabric has an outer pattern, as seen in weather, seasons, plant and animal life, and the substance of the land, yet the weaver is invisible. The hands that weave these patterns are of the other world which includes Faeries, ghosts, nature spirits, demons, and deities. The interface between these two worlds is the realm of the Faery seer. It was also clear to our ancestors that the inner landscape, its denizens, and their relationship with the surface world determined such things as health, luck, prosperity, and fertility. The seer was, and still is, skilled in their perception of this relationship and its secret ways and knows the necessary rituals to retain or regain the balance or mitigate harmful forces.

The material world is like the reflective surface of a pool of water. It is a reflection of the real source world. It is not the source world in itself. In this pool bubbles constantly surface changing the pattern, form and appearance of the pool. At this time in our evolution, most of humanity is only conscious of the surface of the pool. Some may take note of the bubbles, but they never really delve into the deeper source of its motions. At best, post-industrial humanity examines the source world from the vantage point of human-based scientific approaches. Science tells us much about how the physical world and its processes may appear and act, but little about the forces that brings these patterns forward. Most of the modern sciences strip the intelligence from nature and attempts to turn her (nature) into a clump of chemical and energetic processes. Though technology is good, it must evolve in balance with the natural forces to have sustainable positive results.

The result of hundreds of years of this surface-based, ma-terialist lifestyle and mindset is that human beings have relocated their awareness to the plane of effects (the surface world) leaving much of the plane of causes (the Faery realms) behind, relegating it to the hidden realms of the occult. The human senses have been trained to only perceive the densest of elements through the five senses. Human consciousness has been trained to only accept that which can be proven through the hard sciences. This limited approach has also dulled the inner sense of intuition while sharpening the outer senses. This has been a detriment to the spiritual skills of our species and the cost of this loss is high. The consensus reality that forms the basic norms of modern human society simply leaves minimal room for actual non-physical, spiritual contact. It puts what is acceptable at odds with religion and mysticism. This leaves most humans in a quandary about whether they should respond to the voices of the spirit or whether it is forbidden and wrong to do so. Responding to the pull of the spirit forces puts a modern human at risk of incurring ridicule (and even being ostracized) from their fellow humans for not adhering to the consensus rule that what cannot be directly measured by science and the senses is not real. However, this is a chance that must be taken by the student of Faery Seership who listens to these impulses and dives into the hidden pools of Faery which reveal the deeper nature barely touched by modern science.

The surface-based approach limits our awareness to appearances and apparent relationships. This is a world of glamoury and illusion. It leaves the intelligence, vision and soul of the natural and spiritual worlds hidden in the underworld where the dragons of dogma and the Cerberus of politics guard it. Often, this leads its adherents to a feeling of emptiness and a sense of isolation from the spiritual world. Most humans have bound their sciences and senses to a perception and explanation of the surface world only; the courageous step into the ancient borderland where the comfortable formula of modern life reveals itself to be feeble superstition and a lure away from the truth. The spiritually curious soon discover that their beliefs only limit their perception about what is real; it never has prevented the deep abiding spiritual forces from existing. Rather, it only raises a boundary between the comfortable world of men and the domain of the spirits. This boundary has become a stranglehold suffocating the spirit and soul of humanity and everything it touches.

The Faery people instruct us that "at this time, humans *must* re-acquire an attuned awareness of the tides and motions that occur beneath the surface, at the foundation of the creative process." They send their ancient call outward from our blood, the land and the very breath of creation. Spiritual restlessness is awakened, and the otherworld is calling for humanity to reclaim its place in the mystical fabric of the land. This otherworld is the Faery realm, the world of enchantment. Without reconnection with its power and wisdom, human endeavors will continue to lack balance and eventually lead us all to ecological disaster. Likewise without this understanding humanity will continue to reach upward and outward for spiritual insight and meaning to realms that are beyond its grasp, thus leading it further away from its place upon the sacred land and its place in the spiritual landscape. The Faery realms are the true roots of the material world. Humanity must understand and live by the laws of this realm. All of the biochemical processes measured and analyzed by our sciences are mere pictures of the astral dance of the Faery forces. The first step to reconnection is re-opening the hidden paths through which the soul of nature surfaces into the human and non-human surface world. The most sacred and personal of hidden paths are the ones that open into you, the land where you live, and the land you were conceived on.

This step requires an expansion of what we perceive and an extension of our senses into the inner realms. This awakens the inner senses of vision, spirit, and life forces in motion. This step begins the journey to the sacred land – that heavenly source-world of Avalon that exists just on the other side of the illusive mists of time, space, and matter. This sacred land is the true heritage of all of humanity – including you! The search for the hidden paths is an exercise in free will whereby the human seeker re-establishes his or herself as an active co-creator with the spiritual forces.

THE TWO EARTHS

As previously stated, tradition tells us there are three interpenetrating realms that comprise all of existence. These realms are symbolized by the strata of sky, sea and land. The sea

is the underworld (or within world) and the skies, or stars, are
the over-world (or around world), while the land or stone is the
surface world. The Faery seer works with the surface and
underworlds which exist in parallel states superimposed over
and within each other. Primarily, the seer works with the
underworld, which is the source world for all surface world
affairs. It is of primary concern since it is at the root of
all substance and the patterns of our world. Deep in the
underworld resides the original plan of our world, held close to
the heart of the planet.

The deepest strata of the underworld include a state of
being called the "Sacred Land," also known as the Earth of Light
or the Blessed Isles. This state houses the Dreamer within the
Land, often known as Lucifer, the sun at midnight, and the star
within the stone. The surface world is the Isle of Stone and Bone
where mortality and the seasons of change reign. These worlds
interpenetrate each other and are connected by hidden paths,
which are interface points between them. Faery Seership is
concerned with reaching deep into and through the substance
of the surface world to that state where the Lord of Light holds
the original vision of the earth and her creatures in the sacred
land. The Faery seer seeks to be as one with the Dreamer and
to open this sacred land into the surface world thereby healing
and re-vivifying it. The mystical ways of the Faery seer involve
opening these hidden paths out into human awareness to
re-establish the ancient alliance between humanity, the Faery
races, and all other living creatures, and to bridge the worlds of
source and effect, creation and created, and spiritual essence and
spiritual form.

The sacred land is the original vision of the world in its
balanced and paradisiacal state. This state of being surfaces in all
natural areas but it is stronger in some. All natural places are an
outgrowth of this deep abiding pattern or vision, which is alive
and active in the sacred land. Nature, left undisturbed, reflects
the sacred land into the surface world as surely as the moon
reflects the suns rays onto our planet in the dark of night, but

with softer, silver rays of light. As a fellow seer friend of mine put it, "the sacred land is the land the way God intended it to be – a Garden of Eden." This statement is in keeping with some of the deeper teachings of Faery Seership which say that the Garden of Eden receded into the inner worlds as humanity moved forward into the surface world. This is the mystical legend of the exile of Adam and Eve, the primal parents of humanity, from Paradise.

The goal of Faery work centers on re-surfacing Eden into our surface world, thereby closing the gap between the sacred land and the Isle of Stone and Bone; closing the gap between humanity and our spiritual cousins. When this occurs, great healing and magic returns to the land and us. Hence, the separation between humanity and God (the creation forces) is resolved and the oneness of creation is made manifest. Divine will and human will become unified again. In Faery Seership, humanity was not exiled from Eden for eternity. Rather, the unconditional availability of Eden was traded for the gift of free will. The post-exile shift in the human condition now requires us to seek, find, and claim our place in Eden as an act of choice. To do this humanity must also reclaim its responsibility and accountability as caretakers of the sacred garden of Earth. This is a big leap of consciousness for the modern human who tends to see the earth as absent of consciousness and existing to be an exploitable resource for his or her needs and desires.

WHAT BARS THE GATE?

In most cases, the more human contact a land area has – the more convoluted and dissipated are both its inner and outer resources. There are exceptions to this however, such as: a) land that is protected by humans as a sanctuary or holy place; b) land that has been abused, then reclaimed and rehabilitated by humans; and c) land maintained by humans in a relationship integrating indigenous folk practices (i.e. magic, ceremonies, etc.)

spanning generations of human time and using techniques for working with the physical and spiritual substance. Sadly however, in most cases, humanity introduces destructive forces to the ecosystem and the inscape of nature.

There are two primary destructive forces or patterns that humanity introduces into the otherwise balanced state of nature:

- *Parasitic* – Humans migrate onto a land area and exploit its resources by introducing a pattern of constant and insatiable consumption of resources. This often continues to expand into unbalanced and destructive results. This pattern appears to be born out of greed which has its foundations in a survival instinct based on fear. As a result, the inner beings and living plants and creatures of that area absorb the pattern and reflect it back as a change in the natural balance. This shift in balance is a primary cause for an over-population of parasitic insects, invasive plants and other pests that challenge the health of a local ecosystem and humanity's ability to sustain itself through hunting and agriculture. Land surface area, nutrients, metals, gems (and other stones), water and other elements in and beneath the soil, as well as plant and animal life, are the aspects of nature most exploited by humans. This parasitic pattern, once introduced and nurtured over time supports life forms that literally devour an area and leave it devoid of contact with the innate balance of the sacred land. It is a rare (and sacred) situation when humanity takes into account the natural balance of an area and plans its utilization of resources around this.

- *War* – This type of pattern is not limited to man's relationship with man. It can be seen throughout many facets of relationships between humanity and nature itself. When humans migrate onto a land area, they tend to engage in battle with many of the creatures that are indigenous and a part of the natural balance. The words we humans choose to describe many of the indigenous beings that dwell in nature and that do not possess exploitable aspects, or somehow hinder the production of otherwise human-useful resources, tell us much about the human perception of itself and nature. For example, plants that are not useful in ornamental or food gardening are named "weeds." Insects are often termed "bugs." Any creature that poses a threat to human comfort is termed a "pest." There are whole industries for the manufacture and distribution of pesticides and herbicides. Perhaps these products have some long-term use that can be balanced, but the terms and overall intention is war. In response, these beings shift their balance and produce new resilient life forms that can be dangerous to humanity. It becomes survival of the fittest and toughest. No one kingdom of creatures has endured this assault more than insects. This war pattern, once introduced and nurtured over time, closes the hidden ways and introduces destruction to a living natural area.

These two destructive patterns offer the student of Faery Seership much meditation material. For they are not only energy forms that humans introduce to the natural world, we also cultivate them within us. Likely, they are the origins of most of the mental, emotional, physical, and spiritual diseases that plague our species. The Faery beings can show us how to re-engage a healthy, balanced and true relationship with the patterns, processes and practices of nature, an immense living being of which we are a part. However, one simple truth is thus: how we approach life and its many patterns and beings defines much of what we receive from it. If we approach it only to defend ourselves against it or to consume all it has to offer, then we will harvest the fruits of this engagement. These fruits may very well be more virulent strains of life that can wage war and consume humanity, challenging us to create more powerful assaults on the natural forces. This is a no-win approach for us since nature is a being of ancient profound knowledge and power. This is a war *we are destined to lose* if we continue to engage in it. If we shift our patterns to partnership with nature and her custodians, then we may re-enter the doors of Edenic paradise. This legendary paradise is the original vision for this planet. It lies latent, yet alive and it dwells within the Earth of Light, which is that sacred land in the heart of the planet.

THE GARDEN OF EDEN

Nature holds a memory and resonance of paradise, even though most of humanity has forgotten it. Humanity does, however, remember at a deep, almost cellular level. This memory has to be re-awakened through contact with the spiritual world and, more specifically, with our cousins, the Faery races and the ancestors. Until this occurs, humanity is driven to search for that elusive missing something. This ancestral memory lives within our blood and drives us to seek, find and share spiritual insight and meaning. Luckily for us nature remembers and holds its essence within its processes. We can approach this deep abiding memory in nature, the earth, and our blood and attune to the voices that rise from the underworld and lead us into the realms of enchantment. This is why we humans often feel a sense of balance and return to self when we escape into the natural world of the ocean, woods, mountains, and lakes to re-connect with ourselves and nature, or true nature. It is as if the harbingers of truth rise up to us from the land, the waters and out of the air itself to say "come home ... remember and heal thyself."

It is advised that the Faery Seership student spend time in natural areas that have been minimally impacted by human life. These areas can be wooded, watery, desert-like, or basically any area that has retained its natural power. This technique of self-finding is effective for four basic reasons: 1) these areas are free from the human created larvae of the city; 2) contact with the un-altered sacred landscape re-establishes the human connection with both the individual soul and the collective soul of humanity through contact with the natural balance inherent in nature before human influence; 3) the inner beings of the natural place live in balance if unaltered by humanity, and will

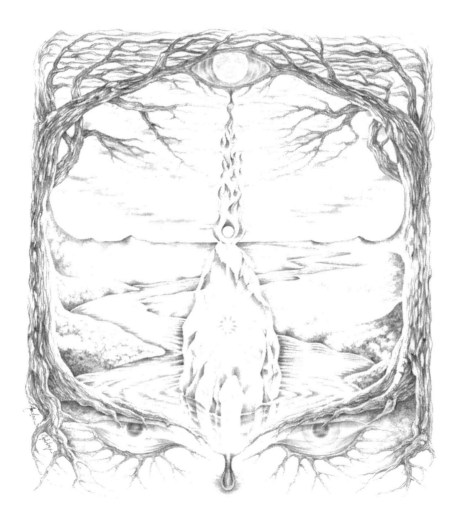

work to integrate the human into the sacred landscape; and 4) the inner beings of the land de-energize the larvae carried in the human's energy field and re-generate them into pure creative life force that is more useful and less vampiric to its human hosts.

The vision of Eden is held by the Dreamer in the Land and it is the very life source of the surface world and ourselves. It is the living flame that vivifies all of life on this planet. The Faery people are ever-young because they live close to, and care for it.

They live in constant communion with the sun within the earth. This Faery paradise awaits the bridge-builders (human and other species) to open it out again through their bodies and the body of the land – for they are in fact, the same. We long for this. Our fellow humans search for this illusive "it" (the sense of vision, balance and connection) in the physical world through many means including psychoactive drug abuse, flagellation, bondage, past life regression, and other mind-altering behaviors. The alarming concern with these behaviors is not in their basic practice. Rather, the need for re-connecting with the vision can be so overwhelming that these behaviors are taken to excess and produce harm and the opposite of the desired results. However, the impulse that drives this is a part of our ancestral memory and of the longing for our place upon the sacred land. It is important to remember that beings, especially humans, do not quest for something that is totally unknown to them. Rather, they quest for something they have tasted, loved, coveted, and then crave. In this instance we are questing for something that we remember at a basic ancestral level.

Our body and senses dwell in the surface world while our spirit dwells in this sacred land where it too is one of the "Shining Ones of the Sacred Flame." A part of our quest is to retrieve this fire from heaven from within the body of planetary being, only the path to this heaven is within us and the planet, not in the distant stars. Within each of us is a part of this sacred flame. Our spirits are like sparks from the bonfire of the gods. Our foremothers and fathers spent time listening to the deep voice of the land. This connected them to a sense of their place upon the sacred land. They listened to the voices of the ancestors and the ancestral memory in their blood. They spent time watching the patterns of life, death and rebirth, and seeing and honoring the power of place. In doing this, they attuned themselves to the sacred land and consequently to their true selves and their purpose. They developed sacred rites and customs to bring the sacred land closer to their world and their destiny. They also developed rites to attune to the balance inherent in the power of place – the place where they were born, lived and died.

Sadly, our current world culture is more interested in the symbolic power of monetary resources. Thus, it is rapidly losing touch with the real prosperity that comes with living in partnership with the guiding hands of our destiny, which are the powers resident within the planet of which we are a part. Let us not forget that the planet earth is the being that holds residence in this part of the universal space and we live on her ... not she on us. Our destiny is intertwined with the earth's, so it stands to reason that we should understand her visions and work to achieve them. Otherwise, we become a replaceable species. This planet holds our dreams within; we only have to reach for them. This light, and those Faery beings that guard it, can part the darkness of our sorrows and loneliness and show us the Child of Promise, which lies within us and which is the messenger of the Dreamer in the Land. In short, at the heart of the great earth mother is the Lord of Light, the crowned jeweled son of the holy mother, which lives to illuminate all living things with truth. This is the true star within the stone. The path to this star begins within and leads deeper into the planet where our spirit finds its place in the planetary visionary pattern. This pattern is the sacred land.

A foundational step to doing this is to reach into the depths of the land we live on and take the hand of our Faery cousins as they reach upward offering guidance. We must explore the internal environment of our place on the Isle of Stone and Bone and map out its ecology and inner mechanisms; by doing so, we re-enter the sacred land and claim our place there. I call this process mapping the inscape. This involves looking into the internal environment of a place to assess and access the beings that live there, and their roles in preserving the harmony and balance of that place. This understanding reveals the power of place. There is a dynamic balance between the Faery realms and our world. The old teachings say that "when we prosper in our orchards and fields, the Faery lack" and thus, we should care for our enchanted cousins to keep fortune balanced and cycles turning. Working with the power of place is a fundamental step toward this aim.

THE POWER OF PLACE AND THE GENII LOCI

The "power of place" is a term used to describe the inherent virtue and living being of a physical location. Literally, it is the power resident in a specific location. In the context of the three worlds, which are really three "conditions," the power of place is the underworld virtues reflected into a land space by the intelligences and patterns deep within it at its creative foundation. It is the point where the sacred land surfaces in a specific land area. In other words, it is the aspect of the Dreamer's vision as it moves outward at a specific location on the planet in relationship to the stars above. You might say that it is the relationship between the Lord of Light (the Dreamer) in the land and the stars, moon and sun above the land, and the patterns and beings that result. This pattern is the *axis mundi* or Bilé – the sacred unifying pillar that holds open the inner temple of a place for beings to move inward and outward across the worlds. It holds the universal pattern in place. This power is pre-human and is always present, though it may recede deeper into the land from human contact and pollution.

Indigenous spiritual traditions tap into this power to work with it and to ensure that humanity is woven into its fabric. The Faery practices involve mapping this out and developing rites and customs based on an actual living relationship with this power and the beings that attend it. Doing this opens the hidden paths of place and revivifies it.

To understand and tap the power of place you must open up to its power without preconceived judgments about what it is or is not. Do not name anything, rather allow it to express its inherent power of being without the false name constructions we humans allocate. This power is mediated to our world by the Faery and other beings that dwell within a place. As we humans attune to it and to the Fay, we too become a mediator for the land. This brings forth the second sight and other magical talents. There are simple exercises that help one approach the power of place.

VISION #3: Contacting The Power

Much of the initial stages of development involve approaching and engaging the formless power of a place, then the beings that dwell within and work with it. This requires a skill that humans rarely use. It is the ability to simply be with something (or someone) without defining it. It requires the human seeker to let the presence of a thing or place present itself without the vessels (or prisons) of human nomenclature. One practical approach to contacting the power is the following:

a) Pick an area to do this exercise. It should be a natural place with woods, gardens, a pond, or stream. The place should be of some importance to you, such as the land where your home is located, where you grew up, or somewhere else of meaning.

b) Seat yourself or stand comfortably. Draw your awareness to the present while casually dismissing all other influences from you while breathing in the present deeply and comfortably.

c) Close your eyes and open your awareness to the feelings, smell, and sounds of the place.

d) Allow this to lead you away from human affairs and inward to a more still, silent, content, and pure place. This place is at the edge of the sacred land, which exists just under the surface of your senses. It is alive, pulsing, and inviting.

e) Envision, in your mind, that all of your senses are drawing in the essence of this place through your ears, nose, and across your skin.

f) Allow the feeling of the place to surface within you. When you feel full, open your eyes and allow the feelings to flow out into the images you perceive around you. Note how vivid the images around you become. They are filled with the light of the land.

g) Experience this feeling until it draws back into you and your awareness drifts back into the affairs of human life.

It is beneficial to practice this exercise as often as possible so that it becomes more vivid and informing. Eventually beings will present themselves in the form of feelings, communications that rise out of you, or in patterns of light perceived with your eyes open or closed. A version of this technique can be used to approach the "power of person" which is the inherent power of an individual being and its feeling or resonance in the sacred land. True love taps into the power of person. It evolves out of an ability to be at one with the true nature of another person. Try this exercise with a tree. Except, dismiss the name and concept of "tree" and approach it as a being to be understood in its own right, without labels.

VISION #4: Attuning Through The Substance Of The Land

The living presence and power of the sacred land is not a distant concept. This power is imprinted into the very fabric of the land. Remember that the surface and under-worlds interpenetrate each other. Therefore, the human seeker can approach this power through the physical substance of a place.

a) Still the mind chatter and approach silence.

b) Close your eyes and move through the essence of the place and let its feeling be revealed as you did in the previous exercise.

c) Now, with your eyes closed, reach your fingers into the soil. How does it physically feel (texture of the ground, temperature, etc.)?

d) Bring your soiled fingers to your nose. How does it smell?

e) Do any emotional feelings rise within you? What other sensory feeling comes to you?

f) What comes into your mind (free floating images, contacts from intelligences in the location, etc.)?

g) Envision that all of these feelings and sensory perceptions come together in a single stream of golden light that draws a circle around you. This is the travel tunnel of the seer and the golden cord that connects all things.

h) Feel yourself sink into this tube just below the surface of the soil into the inner realms of this place.

i) Let the feeling and presence of this place rise up and flow into and around you as a massive living contact flowing into you. It completely enfolds and cradles you in its immense presence. Let yourself be as one being within it as it fills you with the light of the land.

j) Once full, let the presence of the tube completely fade as you rise to the surface world filled with the light of the land and a sense of being interwoven with the intelligence of the land.

k) Open your eyes and feel the contact with the land's power, presence and consciousness flow out of you and into your surroundings.

This exercise will bring about a feeling of connectedness and exchange between you and the place.

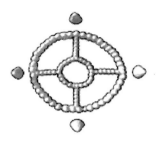

CHAPTER 9:
OF SLEEPERS AND SEEKERS

If my humanity I'd loose,
Which seduction would I choose?
The angels' voice eternal in the stars,
Or faery folk, immortal mid the flowers?

The angels sing of boundless light and joy
And spirit's flight to high rebirth,
The faery folk are in the land
And love the sacred earth.

– "Seduction," R.J. Stewart 1992

There is a pulse that beats in each of us, driving us to seek meaning in our lives. For all who have experienced and responded to it, this pulse feels like it is something that grips us and leads us to some unknown but fascinating territory of life. It drives us to seek answers to the sacred questions. It often feels like a guiding hand reaching out of us, waking us in the middle of the night, or steering us in our waking hours onto some path yet to be revealed. Anyone who has walked a path of spirit will understand this concept. Anyone who has not knows of the deep longing for the illusive "something" that seems to be missing from their lives, no matter how much money, sex, power, social position, or fame they acquire. That longing in the seeker is the pulse moving outward from the depths of their being and rattling the familiar foundation of their worldly affairs.

The Faery mysteries teach us that there is a great stellar being known as the Utterer who breathes forth all of life from the void, and there is a being called the Dreamer who lives deep in the planet and pulses forth its vision to our surface world. Perhaps our human hearts beat in sync with the Dreamer and our breath draws essence in and out of the void in harmony with the Utterer. To take this thought one step further, perhaps we are an embodiment of these vast beings and thus, we are driven to carry out their (and our) destinies. To accomplish this, we must first awaken. It seems that most religions speak of initiation or being born again. The old craft speaks of "once-borns," referring to those people who have been born into flesh but have not awakened to their spiritual being. This is not unlike the mystical Christian concept of being re-born. In the Christian version, when we awaken and surrender to Christ, we become a part of the body of Christ.

Though this teaching has too often been misused as a political stance, it is profound in its deeper mystical implications because it implies that a part of us must die so that a deeper, more profound part of us that is dormant may be awakened. This deeper aspect is the Christ spirit in the Christian mythos and the Child of Promise in Faery Seership. When we surrender into it, we are regenerated, reborn and made whole. The Faery teachings of Robert Kirk imply that we are incomplete. To become complete, we must form the three-fold alliance of human, Faery, and other living creature (plant or animal). This awakens the enchanted spiritual self. In many occult practices, and even in mainstream religions, there is a spiritual re-birth that opens us to becoming totally or truly alive. It is as if we are dead matter until a more profound co-existing spiritual intelligence opens into or out of us and brings us to life – true life.

Elements of a death and rebirth saga are an integral part of all mystical initiation ceremonies. They are often coupled with an introduction to otherworldly beings (be they Christ, the Goddess, Loa, Fay, or a host of beings) that will "speak" for the reborn human. As the old hymn speaks "I once was lost but now am found; was blind and now I see." Many people describe their lives before this spiritual unfolding as a time when they felt lost, forlorn, hopeless, and without vision. It is as if there is a greater purpose unfolding in the universe, without which, each of us is nothing, or incomplete at best. The path to this unfoldment is littered with discovery. We humans tend to cling to the familiar shadows of our past and embrace them as companions. Far too often we are more comfortable with a familiar pain than an unfamiliar joy. We like predictability and familiarity; however, the touch of the spirit world shatters this and brings us an exhilarating spontaneity. There are many ways we are introduced into this new life. Sometimes it is through formal processes that involve instruction and ceremony. Sometimes it is through the chthonic processes of a near death or out-of-body experience, or during times of immense stress or grief when the fabric of life becomes tenuous and some deeper impulse rises and takes the driver's seat of our lives. Whatever the entry point is into the greater life, we all will pass through it at some point. When it occurs for us, may we become one of the blessed.

THE SLEEPING GIANT

It is unfortunate that much of humanity has lulled itself into a type of ignorant, spiritual sleep by our modern culture. It continuously sings the lullaby of political, social, and even religious rhetoric to seduce the inborn divine discontent into an opiate-type sleep to prevent straying from the consensus boundaries of conformance. We have great world religions, yet the bulk of the people alive today seem to be starving for meaning, purpose, and connection. In our attempts to master the elemental world and make it serve our materialist ends, we have left behind our ancient kindredship with nature and each other. In the end, these approaches leave us with full hands and empty souls. This has created a divorce between human consciousness and the rest of the natural world. When human-kind thinks of the natural world, the tendency is not to immediately think of the human species as being a part of it. Instead, when told to envision nature, most see woods, streams, birds, flowers, and animals. It is unlikely that the average person would see this scene with a condominium community in the center or even humans living in cooperation with the land. Rather, we think of nature "out there" or "over there" in the woods, oceans, mountains, deserts, and plains.

Yet there is a vast potential, a wellspring of spiritual power if we can humble ourselves and embrace the fact that *we are a part of nature*. We are kindred with all of the forces and beings of the natural world. Our electric lights, automobiles and cement buildings are not insulating us from this fact. However, we are not the *only* intelligent beings in the natural world. In fact, we are not the *most* intelligent beings in the natural world. We humans see like a laser that considers nothing around its beam. If this were not so, we would have never created a lifestyle dependent on machines and chemicals that are destroying the very environment that sustains us.

If we can expand ourselves beyond the horizon of our belief systems, we may spy the dawn of a new, yet ancient knowing. Inside us is the core essence of nature, a spark of divinity which is the same essence shared with all of creation. When we awaken our consciousness to this essence, we will then know the universal language. We will then know that our purpose is not only an individualized one. It is to fulfill the destiny of our species and ourselves in balance with the other visible and invisible beings of the natural world. Our roles as humans can only be understood in relationship to the rest of the surface world and the inner creative intelligences of which we are a part. To find our place upon the sacred land, we must see the underlying pattern of life and the part of the design that we humans fulfill. To accomplish this task, we must embrace certain core facts:

1) humanity is neither the only, nor the most intelligent being in nature; 2) humanity has intelligence and a soul, but then so does everything else (regardless of what our human-created religions tell us); 3) humanity has a distinct role within the greater vision of the planet, but then so does everything else with which we co-exist; 4) humanity must discard its arrogant assumption of dominion over nature; 5) the human experience is directly influenced by other beings in the natural and spiritual world of whom we have little or nor real control or comprehension; and 6) the access point to unity with nature and spirit is within us.

Humanity was born with "free will" and it is both a blessing and a curse. This faculty defines our species as an individuated soul type, which is driven to seek reconnection to the collective species soul and to the soul of nature. The tendency for most of humanity is to mis-translate this drive from one of reconnection to one of dominion, control and exploitation. The latter is aimed at creating a feeling of completion, satisfaction, safety, and worth by a surface-based mastery over the elemental forces. For some these shadows move apart and love (the quest for harmony) is made manifest. I share with you an insight given to me by my Faery Queen:

> There are two types of humans: sleepers and seekers. Sleepers are those persons who are moved through life by selfish motivations, chance, or the tides around them and they never take responsibility for their actions. Seekers are those persons who consciously seek meaning, vision and unification with the unfolding mystery of life.

This concept reveals how we are perceived by the inner-world contacts. In a further explanation of this statement, she also noted:

> Until your senses and your presence are awakened in the inner realms, your sleep [lack of consciousness in and of the inner worlds] makes you nearly invisible to us. Most of your lives are awake in your world and asleep in ours. Until you awaken here, you will not be complete. A piece of you is

here [in the Faery realms], but it is not fully alive until it is re-united with the surface walker. At times you slip into our world in your dreaming time, in times of great stress, or when you momentarily fade from form [what we humans would call death or near-death experiences] and you become fully visible to us. We are, however, always aware that you exist, for you have an entire stream of ancestry which rises from our world, into you. We know you by that stream.

These statements reveal a great deal about spirituality as the active process of a life in the spirit world. Therefore, to become spiritual, we must become active and conscious participants in this process. It leads us back to the Faery myths of Eden wherein the paradise receded into the inner world where, to be found, it must be consciously sought through an act of free will. The "sleepers" are those humans who have not been awakened to the inner world.

The first steps to this awakening come with the following realizations: 1) there must be a greater purpose for us (i.e. we live within a context relative to the whole of life); 2) there are other intelligences than humans that know the greater plan (e.g. deity, angels, Faery beings, etc.); 3) there will be no sustainable happiness until the spiritual world and our place in it is sought out (i.e. a conscious commitment to the quest is made); and 4) fully awakening this faculty require works and deliberate transformation of ourselves, our lifestyles and our paradigms (i.e. initiation). The surface world is a busy place and humans have made it even busier with the cacophony of sounds, movements, expectations, social roles, and other distractions we have created. The Faery beings call humanity "the distracted ones" because of this fact. Approaching inner stillness and attuning our senses to the voices of the subtle forces working through and around us will truly require a conscious commitment and considerable inner work. I ask you, the seeker, are you ready to live for a purpose that includes you, but is not singly focused on you? Are you prepared to nurture the seeds of your soul by planting them in the garden of nature?

Approaching the Universal Language

There are a few concepts that the Faery Seership student must grasp to begin opening to core spirituality: soul, intelligence, individuated and collective existence, the three-fold life, actualized and latent awareness types, and the universal language (also known as the spirit tongue). The "soul" is a hard concept to explain and grasp. Following is the working definition developed through partnership between myself and my inner contacts:

A soul is an individualized unit of creative life force (toradh), which expresses and evolves through physical form. It is not eternal, though it moves through multiple expressions over vast amounts of time (time defined as a metaphor to describe the interaction between matter and change). It moves through multiple levels of life concurrently even while fused to a physical pattern.

The use of a soul is a primary part of the Ancient One's means of moving toradh through experience (cycles of change) and form (patterns of experience) as a means of:

- *extension* – expansion from the universal source into a myriad of experiential patterns

- *incarnation* – fusion of universal creative intelligence to a pattern of form

- *movement* – the active principle of the Ancient One that uses a soul and its form as a point of focus for traveling and carrying the specific units through experience and form

- *assimilation* – building the inter-form relationships necessary for attaining the balance that liberates form from the cycles of change.

All beings have a soul, though some are collective while others are individuated in their experience. At the core of the Ancient One's existence is intelligence, for it is intelligent on all levels of its being: creative and regenerative, soul and form, elemental and existential, planetary, lunar and stellar, seen and unseen, human and other. There are no exceptions to this rule. *This is the very basis on which the Seership student builds his or her paradigm.*

A being uses its principle intelligence to structure its experiences. Any state of existence that has pattern and that includes movement, heat, structures, etc., has intelligence moving through or into it. It cannot exist without this intelligence. The Faery teachings suggest that the toradh is intelligent in itself and thus causes the coalescence of patterns and forms as a part of its curious quest. The universe is driven into creativity by its own brooding and divine discontent. All beings have intelligence because they exist. To exist, they must have a subtle or overt pattern (addressed in the sacred sciences of numerology, geometry, etc.). To have a pattern, organization and structure is inherent and thus intelligence is inherent. However, all of life and form is intelligent and no being is more intelligent than another. Rather, each being in the creative world has its own distinct properties of intelligence.

THE SEEKER, SUMMONER AND THE THREE-FOLD LIFE

All beings operate from a soul type, meaning that there is a point of coalescence within each being that receives, packages, and designs its experiences. The soul type finds its origins in the eternal spiritual essence, but may be collective or individuated in its operation and experience. Collective soul types (summoners) are connected to beings that have a high degree of collective intelligence. The individuated soul types (seekers) are connected to beings that have a high degree of individualized intelligence and free will.

When discussing free will, it is important to understand that it is this specific characteristic or dynamic that allows (or even promotes) the individuated soul to create and refine new patterns of life and being. This element, imparted into a being by universal (Utterer) and planetary (Dreamer) beings, allows them to explore and discover new ways of experience and feed this back to the core creative intelligence (the Dreamer, and consequently, the Utterer). In this way, individualized beings are the great explorers of the natural world.

Free will is a mechanism whereby the creator explores itself through its creations. Although this form of will (defined as the drive and ability to create and implement change) allows these beings a certain amount of freedom, there is no such thing as free will meaning without cost. All seeker beings have an awareness of their mortality and in-born feeling of isolation from the collective. Humanity falls on the extreme range of individuated beings. This is why humans search for spiritual meaning for a sense of who they are within the collective. The price of becoming a defined wave that is aware of itself uniquely is that it often loses touch with the ocean of its origins.

Collective soul types are called summoners because they draw their experiences to them, unlike the individuated soul types that search or "seek" them out. Stationary beings (such as trees and plants) have no need for an individualized soul, for they do not seek and search for information, they simply receive it. Beings that share collective intelligences have an in-born sense of purpose and direction. Beings that are individualized do not have this sense. They have to purposefully open out connection with the deeper collective states of being through forming spiritual clusters.

There are three aspects to the soul of an individuated being collectively referred to as "the three-fold life:"

- *The Surface Walker* – the aspect of the soul in the surface world. This is your consciousness (often called ego), including the personality and is the soul of your physical form.

- *The Dream Walker* – the classical soul aspect which lives in the underworld as the co-walker

- The *Star Walker* – the quintessential spirit that lives at the edge of the stellar world. This is the guiding hand behind it all. The Star Walker is the core essence of ourselves that is stellar in nature and partakes of the Dreamer in the Land, for it is also the indwelling Child of Promise. It is the point where soul merges with infinite spirit.

Individuated beings experience their soul as a part of their specific incarnate selves. To this type of being, mortality is very real because it experiences its individual incarnations. Its experiences are solitary and, to a degree, measured. And, indeed this is true if this being only lives in the outer world through its Surface Walker. Seekers would have more of a sense of soul purpose and direction, but the free will characteristic brings through high intellectual functioning, which in turn causes these beings to rationalize and dissect their lives and perceptions until the quiet soul-voice of intuition is barely distinguishable. This is the payment for free will.

The quiet soul voice is inherent in the summoner and in the Dream Walker. An outgrowth of this characteristic is that the more individuated a being is, the less inherent balance it has. After all, if a being has inherent balance, then it cannot operate outside of the parameters of this balance and thus cannot apply free will. Humans have the most distinct level of individualized intelligence and thus the highest concentration of free will. The cost of these dynamics is that they tend to feel a sense of disconnection. However, this is not an irreversible state. An actualized human being, conscious of its Dreaming Soul and in partnership with a summoner can use its free will to see the interconnections between all levels of beings and care for the integrity of them. The role of the human species is in keeping with Gene Roddenberry's statement in the popular sci-fi series Star Trek "to boldly go where no man [or other being] has gone before." Therefore, free will and the individuated intellectual capacity are crucial attributes that define what the human species contributes to nature.

The seeker is, by nature, lonely and overwhelmingly curious. Thus, humanity (which is the very embodiment of the seeker) must ally its Surface Walker with soul types that are collective (summoners) to re-align itself with its underworld Dreaming Soul. There is a reciprocal exchange between these two soul types when they form into teams, councils, or clusters. The Dream Walker holds the vision of each individuated soul and its relationship to the whole. The summoner experiences the great quest through the seeker. The seeker experiences oneness through the summoner. This is the delightful experiential balance of the universe. Blessedness is attained through a partnership that is the assimilation of soul and the remembrance of the oneness. Through these partnerships, the universe is re-assembled into wholeness. There are beings that bridge between collective and individuated souls for they either have aspects of both or they function in this way in the natural world. They include Faery, animal and some trees.

The two primary modes of intelligence (individualized and collective) share in a vast universal, planetary intelligence that connects all things through the essential toradh. This is the universal language for it is the shared organizing force of universal intelligence (i.e. energy and resonance). Seekers connect to the Ancient One primarily through the three-fold life. Summoners connect primarily through the *nar*. The more collective the intelligence, the more attuned it is to its over-arching species intelligence. This type of intelligence is often described as the over-soul or deva, but is called a nar in Faery Seership. The nar holds the pattern and very being of a summoner. When working with collective beings, we tend to work with an apparent individuated form that leads us quickly to its nar (if plant, tree, mineral), or king or queen (if Faery or elemental).

When working with individuated beings (primarily human) we will tend to work with one or more of the aspects of their three-fold life. There are nars associated with humanity too, but humans tend to operate less within them. These nars evolved through shared races and cultures. Sadly, our current movement away from shared tradition is damaging these nars. They do not die, however, for they live outside of time and space. They simply recede into the primal waters of human spiritual life. Nars also evolved through other shared commonalities such as nation or state collectives and religions, and are sometimes referred to in modern tradition as archetypes or over-souls. The difference in the operations of the nar is that collective beings inherently operate from the nar level while individuated ones inherently operate from the soul aspects, primarily from the Surface Walker which implements free will. If we were to identify a nar for all of humanity, it would be the Divine Ancestor. The Divine Ancestor is a deep underworld being that is the ancestral parentage of humanity.

Humanity as an operative individuated intelligence is, by its nature, less attuned to the Divine Ancestor or the nars of races and cultures. Consequently, racism and other forms of intra-species discrimination occur. On a broader level, humans tend toward speciesism, meaning that humans tend to see themselves as greater or more intelligent than animals, plants, and minerals. *However, the difference between ourselves and other beings sharing this planet is not in the level of intelligence, it is in the type of intelligence possessed.* Each major class of beings in nature has its own operative mode of intelligence. Below, is a list of some of the overarching classes of beings and their mode of intelligence:

- *Mineral* – These beings share collective intelligence, are incarnate and have no need for a soul since they do not re-incarnate. They are powerful summoner intelligences that live in the surface world for vast periods of time. All mineral beings are evolving to become crystalline, which is their last mode of incarnate life. They differ from plants and trees in the length of time they are incarnate in physical form, and thus in the depth of their experiences. These beings are the great scribes or bookkeepers of the creative world. Like other collective types, they receive information which they both hold and transmit through resonance to the natural world around them. These beings remember the beginnings of surface world creation and record all events since that time.

There are Faery beings associated with the mineral kingdom such as the Scottish *Frideans*. It is unclear whether these beings are extensions of the stones themselves or beings that live in a symbiotic relationship with them. Either, way, the Frids are powerful allies that are contacted through the stones.

- *Trees and Plants* – These incarnate beings do not have individuated intelligence types. They implement a collective nar. They have no need for individualized intelligence or soul typing as their existence and experience is of *we* not *me*. It would be foolish for a human to perceive them as less intelligent, for they have a greater intelligence than human as it relates to collective awareness and natural balance. Each plant or tree species has the awareness of its entire variety. This means it thinks, feels, and expresses through all of the trees or plants in the world which share its type. For example, one oak tree knows the experience of all oak trees. These stationary beings require elemental care for their survival. Thus, elementals and nature spirits are often linked to trees and plants in historical Faery lore. The powerful sacred plants and trees in the Faery practices are able to bridge collective awareness to the individualized beings. In doing so, they become powerful forces in the unfolding spiritual awareness.

- *Animals* – All of these incarnate beings have individuated intelligence and free will in varying degrees. This is why these types of beings (and humans) tend to be passionate and curious. Animals, especially those that are mobile, are seekers and thus they move about to collect their experiences. This is unlike plants, trees and minerals, which are stationary. Some non-human animals actually bridge between individualized and collective beings. These are beings to which humans ascribe some amount of intelligence such as cats, dogs, wolves, chimps, lions, dolphins, and whales. These beings have a strong resonance with humanity because there is a similarity in their mode of intelligence and soul type. Humans arrogantly see these beings as more intelligent and sentient than other animals because they act like humans more than other animals do. When we form relationships with these beings, they often assimilate some of our characteristics, which stimulates their individuated intelligence or seeker characteristics.

- *Faery* – Where plant, tree and mineral beings live in an outer surface world of form (i.e. incarnate), Faery beings do not and never have. These beings may appear as independent individuated (solitary) or collective (hive) intelligences. At their core they are summoners. The Fay bridge between the two types of intelligences. This is why they are seen as companions to humanity. They tend to live in one region or continental area, which restricts their ability to travel to other surface world areas. Again, this is another summoner aspect.

  They do not have or need a soul *per-se* because they never embody physical form. This does not make them a lower life form. In fact, it would be unwise for any human to attempt to denigrate these pre-human, ancient and powerful beings. They live close to the eternal spiritual fire that burns at the heart of our planet and ofttimes are more spiritually evolved than humans. They experience soul transitions through a symbiosis with humanity. Humanity experiences the vision of the Dreamer through Faery companionship. They live in a non-carnate condition of form though they are inexorably intertwined with incarnate life. They are the caretakers of the rhythms of surface and natural life. Interestingly though, they do not merely receive their experiences, they seek experiences and feed them into the hive. In a hosting, they can coalesce into one being sharing a central core of intelligence, which in tradition is seen as a king or queen. They are highly evolved collective beings that can share a symbiotic relationship with humanity.

Some Faery beings, especially those who are the guardians of a place, share intelligence with all of the natural world in the area where they live. In a human/Faery alliance, the human partner re-connects with inherent balance and collective intelligence, while the Faery partner experiences individualized soul-based experiences. This allows the human to evolve patterns of life that are in balance and the Faery being to explore new ranges of life.

THE SPIRIT TONGUE

The seer works to fuse his or her outer interpretive individuated intelligence with a being possessing collective awareness. In doing so, the human partner remembers the universal language of resonance that is spoken through the one thing we share in common with all beings, the core intelligence. This state of being is not communicated through human-based language and movement. Rather, it is communicated through resonance at the most profoundly rich level of our being. If we work from the vantage point of this "spirit tongue" we are able to transcend the illusionary divisions of species and intelligence to speak the universal language of resonance. Initially we work through visionary constructs that we humans have developed to shift our perception and to give a shared interface to communicate with otherworld beings. Eventually, these fade away as the human expands beyond its self-set rules and is able to speak from the indwelling Child of Promise to all of its family, both seen and unseen. In the end, the human then finds its place in the sacred circle and rejoins the family of life.

Earlier chapters presented the concept of clusters. This phenomenon occurs in both the surface and underworlds and involves a teaming of symbiotic relationships between apparently distinct beings or groups of beings around a central point on intelligence. In an ecosystem, some traditions would call this the deva or oversoul. This clustering effect appears to be the natural state of the universe. We can see this all around us embodied in ecosystems, human social groupings, multi-cell biological organisms, solar systems, and galaxies. It would appear that natural balance involves team-building or implementation of partnerships that result in the birth of new, more evolved collective beings. In short, the universe operates on parts in resonance forming colonies with collective purpose and intent. This seems to occur on every level of life from the extreme microscopic to the massive intergalactic. Clearly, life is filled with micro-systems building macro-systems unfolding one purpose, which the parts are discovering through the active process.

So, why is it important to understand the different aspects of your human soul? Why is it important to understand the types of intelligences operating throughout the natural world? Why is it important to build partnerships or teams with other beings? What role does this really play in human, planetary, and universal life? The answer is simply that the universe is one massive being that has both individuated and collective parts that are carrying forth its expansion and exploration. Each part has a distinct mission or role as surely as every cell and organ in your body has a purpose for the whole body's life and functions. In our everyday human life, we understand that all parts of the body must function with health and vitality for the well being of the total person. This forms a basic part of the concept of holism.

Therefore, it stands to reason that humanity must both embody its individuated nature while teaming up with other beings. In doing this it assists in the assimilation work of the planet, and thereby the universe. The one statement that is at the core of human experience is that:

We are in pieces, striving to be made whole;
We are alone, seeking to be at home;
We are curious, yet we are afraid; and
We want to reach out but are afraid we may be consumed.

Each being (human and other) is incarnated through a symbiosis with elemental beings and inner world beings that include ancestral and Faery streams of life. In a way, there is a team or council assigned to every human. Each human must initiate contact with this team, though if they do not, the team will awaken them in often disturbing but effective ways.

Though a big part of our human experience is declaring independence from all of nature, we soon find that we must balance that with relationships. This search for independence echoes the adolescent human quest for balancing dependence and independence, the characteristics of child and adult. Sadly, we often confuse our longing for connection with a longing for sex and intimate human relationships only. Such relationships can be fulfilling spiritually, physically and emotionally, but they cannot meet the full demands of the soul. Humanity must re-connect with its enchanted self (Dreaming Walker) and spiritual self (Star Walker). This is done through alliances with other humans, plants and animals in the surface world, and with ancestral and Faery contacts in the underworld. Again, core to the Faery path is understanding that we humans do not live only for ourselves. Our spiritual quest is not merely a quest for our own fulfillment. It must involve other beings. The spiritual world is not filled with little islands of consciousness. It is alive with an ocean of being, complete and fulfilled in itself. The ocean is whole, only the fleeting waves are distinct.

THE PATH OF INITIATORY TRANSFORMATION

There is a path to the awakening or "quickening" of core intelligence that requires inner work and commitment if it is to be opened. The Seership student will need to clean their inner house and change many bad habits (physical, emotional, and mental), attune to the voice within them that is theirs, then humbly and sincerely reach in to the inner worlds for a hand to reach back. This is not a quick process, nor is it one without difficulty. For the road to Faery is strewn with thorn thickets and glamoury. This ancient inner path has been long neglected by an arrogant humanity and the Fay beings will test the seeker. But then, all true spiritual traditions require a transformation of self. However, the Faery way does not support abdicating personal responsibility to family, employment and other responsibilities. If anything, the more attuned the human becomes, the more sacred their responsibilities become.

So, the true seeker of the Faery way is advised to search for balance in all areas of their life, so that, when contacted, the regenerative powers of the underworld do not bear forth the haunts that have been relegated to our mental closets. The Faery beings understand oaths, family, clanship, and responsibility more than nearly any other type of spirit beings, for they care for the balance of our planet and they have lived as our cousins since before we were aspiring apes.

All beings are composed of spiritual essence, but not all beings have good intent. We know this to be true in our dealings with fellow humans. Many humans do bad things, though at their core they may not be bad people at all. Otherworld beings are no different. If a being requests you to do anything outside of your moral structure or they suggest that you harm yourself or another in any way, then rebuke them. In most cases the type of spirit being that a seeker encounters will be proportionate to their own inner wiring. If a hateful person seeks, they will find a hateful being. If a fearful person seeks, they will find a fearful being. This is not always the case, but is applicable most of the time. The deeper levels of beings will never ask baneful things of you. The Faery have no interest in our destruction. However, there are unbalanced and sick discarnate humans, larvae, and even Faery beings who do not like us. After all, there are humans who hate humans. We humans have given the natural world a lot of reasons to be wary of us. Therefore, spiritual discernment is a virtue. Faery work is a process of engagement and reciprocity. Spiritual development will involve the engagement of other world beings into reciprocal sharing.

Ultimately, all of us seek for happiness. We may become misguided or deluded in that quest. We may even become depressed or disheartened and give up our search. It is truly sad when this occurs. In fact, I suspect that all of us have been, or will become, distracted from our true quest at some point in our incarnate lives. This is a normal part of our experience. But through it all, we all have a pulsing drive to seek. We have an inborn Dream Walker that envisions a vaster life. We have an inborn Star Walker that knows the plan and calls us to loftier heights of life. Often we are not even conscious of what it is we are seeking, but we know we want to feel complete, satisfied and fulfilled. This pulse that drives us is the ancestral memory that remembers when we walked as one with God. Sometimes our greed, vanity, fear, anger, and other less than favorable attributes lead us astray. But with luck, we awaken to some level before we pass out of form, unresolved, incomplete, and destined to repeat our quest.

The curiosity that drives us to seek is a form of divine discontent or restlessness. Without it, we would surely die of boredom. Without it we would lack the drive to implement our free will. We have broken pieces and, like a shattered urn, we must put ourselves together with glue made of love, devotion, service, and respect.

Before we reach to the other worlds, we must know as many of the voices that live in our head as possible. We must inventory our inner demons and give them license to depart. This is by no means an instant process. However, if the seeker is unwilling to do this work, then why should the Faery beings, or any other profound spiritual intelligence, trust us? Why should they believe that we seek harmony and balance when we are all too ready to bring harm to ourselves and to others?

It is a golden staircase that leads down into the underworld of ancestry and Faery being. Each turn in the stair holds a mirror reflecting your true self. If you would walk the Faery way, be ready to look into the mirror, embrace, and transform what you see. In the underworld, there is no submissive power waiting to place itself in the hands of humanity. There is only deep and profound wisdom, regenerative power, spiritual healing, and connectedness. If the human seeker is seeking the Faery realms to exploit it, they will find themselves quickly on the receiving end of such a destructive quest. Initiation implies "to begin again" and this is truly what occurs. There are nexus points in our development where it seems we are starting over. But then, was childhood the end of infancy? Was adolescence the end of childhood? Or, do they all become a part of a greater self?

We know at our core, that there is a co-existing, enchanted life just under the surface of our everyday, waking consciousness. We have all touched or been touched by it at times when we have stood at the crossroads where the Surface and Dream Walkers unite and the gate of enchantment is opened. We have experienced this when we met the flooding tide of dreams that rushed up from the underworld when we have been taken to ecstasy by the rhythm of a drum, the electricity of dance, or the secret waterways of dream.

What will you, the seeker find in your Faery quest? That depends on your intention. What do you seek? It also depends on your willingness to alter your life and live in harmony with the natural world as much as is possible and feasible. The Faery path is not one of slow evolution, it is one of total transformation. These changes can be disturbing but they are always revealing. You see, a part of the Dreamer in the Land already dwells within you. It is the Child of Promise. To connect with it, you must reach to the enchanted realms of the underworld where your Faery treasure is buried under the soil of your mind-clutter, the dust of your ancestral line, and the limits of your intellect. Only you can change, for you are the gate to Faery. I share with you a brief poem:

Ancestral Memory

There is a world out there; though really, it is less out than in.

It is in you and in me and it is the most profound silence and beautiful perfection.

I am not referring to the mere memorized, ritualized, consensus reality of the visible world, which is contaminated by human greed; but rather the infinite worlds within worlds within you and me.

They are within and around you and me; and interpenetrating the greater "us."

This vast world is a living being in itself; and it is not waiting to be discovered like we humans too often think.

It is already there waiting for us to arrive.

When we knock, the door shall be opened to us.

It is waiting to be remembered ... by you and me.

It is comforting to know that all things, all beings (human and non-human) are in the process of exploring this ancestral memory of Eden, a garden of oneness.

It is the shared inheritance of all things, all beings.

Moment by moment we re-link, remember and return. We are all doing it ... right now ... no exceptions, yes, you too!

When we remember ... we re-member and become one with the infinite spirit.

When we fully remember, we can be content for we are home.

– Orion Foxwood, Lammas 1998

VISION #5: Approaching Silence

In a world that is so task and results oriented, the ability to think (or un-think) in process is often turned off. Inner stillness is a state wherein the seeker is both centered in the moment and flowing with internal and universal rhythm. Approaching inner stillness requires a turning inward of the mind through three distinct levels of inner life: 1) the Surface Walker, which bears forth a cacophony of mind chatter; 2) the Dream Walker, which bears forth less sound and distraction but does include ancestral and subconscious voices as well as Faery voices; and 3) the Star Walker, the deepest level which bears forth the voice of the Child of Promise, who is the same as the Dreamer. Faery Seership terms this process as "approaching the voice" or "approaching silence" through the Cave of Voices. The cave image embodies the entry point to the underworld and, just as there are breezes that rise from within the land to the mouth of a deep cave, there are levels of voices that rise from within us to the opening of our minds. This is normal, for the nature of spirit is that it pulses outward into expression, while the nature of the soul is to draw experiences into itself. Here is one practical technique to approach the silence:

You will need a chair to sit in, a single white candle (the glass enclosed kind is safest and most useful) and matches.

a)　Sit yourself upright, yet comfortably in a chair that has arms (this is important for the chair embodies the throne of dominion). Begin by breathing deeply, slowly, and evenly to signify to your mind that you are changing modes of awareness.

b)　Be aware that your breath synchronizes with first breath of the Utterer that breaths forth the stars from the void. Light one single white candle before you. It embodies your communion with the holy and formless fire and the light of your quest for truth.

c)　Close your eyes and, as you feel the curtain of your eyelids soften the outer light into inner embracing darkness, envision an opening in the darkness before you. This is the Cave of Voices. Project your mind into the cave and, as you do, be aware of the sounds and feelings that flow up to you. You may feel your physical self lean slightly forward in your chair. If so, hold onto the arms.

d) Be aware that the flame that burns before you becomes a beacon light leading you deeper into the cave.

e) Soft hands reach out of the fabric of the cave walls and they brush you gently, pulling from you the spectral ghosts of all that clings to you. You are aware of all the distractions of the outside world being lovingly removed from you as you pass deeper into the cave. As you move deeper into the cave, you are aware that your breath and the voice of the cave are as one.

f) The sounds and feelings become less cacophonous and more distinct as you move deeper into the cave. You hear the voices of your redeemed ancestors and inner guides as they welcome you in whispers of power and guidance. The holy fire leads you deeper into the cave.

g) Move deeper into the cave until you feel a sense of peace and quiet come over you. Before you, at the back of the cave, is a stone chair. This is the throne of inner dominion. The holy flame sits itself on a stone pillar that rests to the right of the throne. Hidden behind the throne is an opening to the deepest realms of the underworld. It opens to the Dreamer. Be aware of this, for the voice of the planetary being rises through the throne.

h) Sit yourself upon this throne and let the power of the voice that speaks in the cave move silently into you. Feel the presence of the still voice that flows through you, embodied in the breath of your physical form as it moves in and out of you, synchronized with the voice of creation itself.

i) Maintain this feeling for a few moments then rise from the vision throne (and the physical chair). Lift your arms as if embracing someone and feel the throne recede into you and stillness take root deep within your being. Then close your arms in a soft embrace over the mid-section of your body. Now the throne of dominion is within you.

j) Open your eyes, continuing to breathe evenly, deeply, softly for a few moments. Extinguish the candle while feeling the light recede into your inner chamber. This is the living flame that is your eternal guide.

This vision should be repeated daily for at least three weeks or until it is so ingrained that you can simply sit in a chair, close your eyes, and adjust your breathing to approach silence.

Eventually, you should be able to be call forth this experience anywhere simply by adjusting your breathing and feeling the presence of the throne within you. It is not the specific content of the visionary exercise that is most important; it is the state of inner stillness. Understand that this state cannot be maintained continually. It is the working state of the seer who moves into it at will and when in need. It is also a very useful state for drawing forth creative inspiration, and for stilling the mind and steering it away from stressful functioning.

CHAPTER 10:
BEYOND THE HEDGE:
LIVING IN TWO WORLDS

The Queen of Fairies keppit me
*   In yon green hill to dwell;*
And I'm a fairy, lyth and limb;
*   Fair ladye, view me well.*

'But we, that live in Fairy-land,
*   No sickness know, nor pain,*
I quit my body when I will,
*   And take to it again.*

'I quit my body when I please,
*   Or unto it repair;*
We can inhabit, at our ease,
*   In either, earth or air.*

'Our shapes and size we can covert
*   To either large or small;*
An old nut-shells's the same to us
*   As is the lofty hall.*

*   – "The Young Tamlane," Sir Walter Scott's version*
*   of the Scottish Tamlin Ballad*

The old lore is filled with accounts of humans who somehow enter the Faery realms or are abducted and taken there to dwell. The Faery realms are seen as being in the planet or "under the hill." This ballad points out that the Faery realms are a world separate from the human world. It also informs us that a human can be taken there fully, not just in spirit. All who escape these realms back into human life are permanently changed. Often there are ordeals for the human seeker that take them through multiple encounters and transformations as they move through the inner orders of life. At the end of this quest, they attain freedom, a beautiful princess, or some great treasure and, again, they are permanently changed.

This is a reoccurring theme throughout historical Faery tradition. For the underworld is a place of primal and chthonic power. Its secrets cannot be stolen or taken without great peril. Rather, they are received through a series of exchanges with other world beings. They are received only after the seeker has fulfilled certain tasks and inner changes to accommodate them. Ballads such as *Tamlin*, preserve some of these core elements of the Faery tradition. This ballad ends with a human lover freeing the young Tamlin, but she encounters many strange forces in her quest to do so.

Other core themes that reoccur in the ballads and tales include transport (bodily or in spirit forms) to the other realm, movement to and from multiple levels and orders of life as the human moves into and out of the Faery realms, a sacrifice or tithe to these realms offered (often every seven years), acquisition of allies and inner contacts in the quest, and the gift of prophesy and other magical powers to the human seeker at the end of the journey. Only after the adventure is the seeker able to live "happily ever after." In this quest is found true love, purpose, and morality.

Those who seek the hawthorn road to Faery will find that they may initially face the frightening shadows that dwell in the personal underworld. These shadows embody the primary guardians of our great inner treasure. They are most often the guardians that we put here to cage certain aspects of our soul. Simply, we created them. But alas, our shadows are but feeble fears that must be faced so the seeker may encounter the powers of the underworld that pre-existed him or her and which are the great initiators into the house of wisdom. After the seeker faces the shadows and the ancient guardians who stand at the threshold of that borderland between humanity and the unseen company, they pass through the great powers of the elemental worlds to wade through the River of Blood and encounter the Faery races.

Once these powers have modified the human seeker's consciousness, then they may be greeted by the Lordly Ones and, lastly, by the Dreamer in the Land. But, the seeker must realize that they will change their shape as they tap the deeper powers of humanity, the planet, and the Faery realms. This aspect of the work is not optional, it is inherent. Once we are touched by the hands of the Fay, we too become enchanted, for we now see into two worlds, one of illusion and appearances (the surface world) and one of beauty, vision and truth (the underworld). Once this sight is spied, the human seeker no longer walks the hidden roads of spiritual life for only themselves.

THE SEER AS SHAPE-SHIFTER

In the process of traveling to the underworld, the human seeker changes shape to bring magic into and across the worlds. Faery and magical lore throughout Europe tells of witches and other world beings changing their shape to travel in a new form or simulacrum. But what is "our shape?" It is not simply our physical form, for that is a vessel modified and created by what dwells within it (the soul). The image we use to design our shape is often inherited from our families, communities and cultures. It is often falsely composed of hopes and fears rather than the substance and vision of the soul. To be able to change shape, we must confront the boundaries of form, perception and consensus reality; we must challenge and cross them. This can be beautifully inspiring or a difficult process, depending on the seeker's desire and ability to be honest, motivated, ready and willing to transform. The power of our soul will not compromise.

THE ORDEAL AND THE FAERY PROHIBITIONS

The shape changes are a part of the *ordeal*, a concept that cannot be over-stressed in this inner work. There will always be ordeals to test, tempt and temper us. Some ordeals are harder than others depending on the seekers inner life. The shape changes may require major modifications in how you look at yourself and the world around and within you. Your shape may be changed by the fusion of inner power (which has been latent in your soul) with earthly life. It may require you to change such things as what you eat or drink, whether you smoke or not, or your attitudes. A part of the ordeal brings forth the deepest resonance of your soul and the Fairy contacts will set forth *prohibitions* or *requirements* as a part of the process.

Prohibitions will include things you are no longer able or allowed to do, and requirements (promises) are things you must always do. Invariably, those things that you are instructed never to do are, in the end, for your best emotional, mental, physical, or spiritual health. If they exact promises of things you are to always do, these things will likely be simple to you, but deeply meaningful to the Fay. Do not test these prohibitions. They are given to the seeker in exchange for the powers of enchantment gifted by the Fay (i.e. the second sight, healing powers, spirit knowledge, magical ability, etc.). The price can be high and difficult if the agreement is broken. I assure you this is true, for I have experienced it first-hand. Your word is your oath in the other world, period – no exceptions. You must keep it unless the Fay have lifted it from you and instructed you of such.

Young Tamlin tells us that the Faery Queen took him away from the human world and now he too has become Fay. He is no longer confined to his physical shape for he has traveled through the worlds and been changed. His gifts now are to see the world in its infancy. That is to see life in its process and therefore the direction it moves. Hence he, and others like him who have made this journey, are gifted with prophetic skills or the "tongue that cannot lie." He has moved beyond the mere laws of human life and physicality. He is able to travel into the world of humanity through his physical form as he pleases and leaves it to travel the other world in multiple forms.

The Separable Soul

This theme of traveling between the worlds is central in all branches of Faery Seership. The mechanism for this spirit travel is the *separable soul*, which combines three major teachings; 1) the soul can be separated from the body and they both can continue to function; 2) the soul can be hidden somewhere to prevent it from incurring any of the risks that come to the physical body, and 3) a person cannot be truly destroyed unless their soul is found and destroyed. These teachings tell us much about the core practices of Faery Seership. Macleod Yearsley, in his work entitled *The Folklore of Fairy Tale*, notes that

> What is known as the 'Separable Soul' or 'External Soul,' (is a) 'primitive conception of the dwelling apart from the body of the soul, or heart, as the seat of life, in some secret place. It is a belief which follows naturally upon Animism (meaning that everything is alive), and is referable to the interpretation of dreams as real events.

In *Fairy Tales: Allegories of Inner Life*, J. C. Cooper states "with the idea of the separable soul goes the belief that the soul can leave the body in sleep, or in ecstatic experience, and maintain separate existence in life, though it finally leaves the body at death." In Faery Seership, an aspect of the soul can be willed by its Walking Soul partner to travel and work in the other worlds.

In many of the old Faery tales, an enchanted being holds sway over a human and cannot be defeated until their soul (which is external and hidden) is found and destroyed. More importantly, this illustrates the Faery belief that the soul can move externally to the body and thus, we can travel to and through it. This is a very important Faery teaching, as it infers that there is a timeless aspect to us (the soul) that moves in many shapes and places without the confines of physicality. Robert Kirk reinforces this notion with the co-walker as follows:

> They [the Seers] call this Reflex-man a *coimimeadh* or Co-walker, every way like the man [or woman], as a Twin-brother and Companion, haunting him as his shadow and is oft seen and known among men, resembling the Original both before and after the Original is dead. And [this Co-walker] was often seen, of old, to enter a house; by which the people knew that the person of that likeness was to visit them within a few days. (Stewart)

SOUL CAGES

Some tales speak of the soul being captured and hidden some-where by a sorcerer or other magical being. Other tales speak of a human being poisoned or enchanted into a sleeping, almost soul-less state until the power of true love awakens or rescues them. This is the case in Sleeping Beauty and many other tales. It may be that all of us have a part of our soul trapped in a castle in the underworld where it is caged, and perhaps a major part of our quest is to find our soul and where it is hidden. Perhaps our ordeal is to re-unify with this Dream Walker who lies sleeping in a hidden cave awaiting the kiss of the seeker as the prince. Our spiritual power is in finding this soul, unifying with it, then keeping it safe and secret from prying harmful eyes. Always, it must be awakened through contact with the other world. This contact, when unplanned, can be very frightening. A more effective way of opening the inner sight is to attune to the underworld and develop the capacity to slip into it through our soul, specifically the Dream Walker.

Once this occurs, a piece of us will continue to reside in the other world as it always has, except the unity of Surface Walker and Dream Walker brings through the power of enchantment. Once this change occurs and we have become enchanted, we can then travel to and fro as desired, but again, there are payments for this in terms of continued commitment and the prohibitions that may be required by the Faery contacts.

Know this: all of us have incurred some soul damage in our journeys through form. In our underworld journeys, we may find that a piece of us is locked in a soul cage which we must find and open to liberate the powers of the soul. This is a deeper part of our Seership work. Shape (in this world and the other) becomes a fluid concept as the human seeker becomes more enchanted. Just as the Faery folk can take many shapes in our world, we can take many shapes in theirs. First, we must know our self-imposed image in this world and then break free of it into the other one. There are many tales about the separable soul, usually with a Faery being having a soul hidden somewhere, which allows it to move in the surface world without harm. This leaves us to wonder if our soul is hidden in the other world to keep it away from the destructive powers of the surface world. To reclaim the Faery treasure, which may be one's soul, the second sight, magical prowess, or marriage to the spirits of the land, there will always be the ordeal that modifies and transforms us. I offer you a Gaelic tale that contains many of the core elements of ordeal. Read and ponder.

The Young King of Easaidh Ruadh

In *Popular Tales of the West Highlands*, J.F. Campbell provides us with the tale of the Young King of Easaidh Ruadh, which contains many of the core concepts of the Faery tradition:

The young king of Easaidh Ruadh, after he had come to his kingdom, resolved to go and play a bout of chess games against a Gruagach called Gruagach carsalach donn - that is, the brown curly-haired Gruagach - who lived in the neighbourhood. He went to his soothsayer about it, who advised him to have nothing to do with the Gruagach, but when he insisted on going told him to take nothing as his stakes but the cropped rough-skinned maid behind the door. He went and had a good reception, and that day he won the game, and named as his stakes the cropped rough-skinned maid behind the door. The Gruagach tried to make him change his mind and brought out twenty pretty maids, one after the other, but the young king refused them all till the cropped rough-skinned maid came out, when he said, "That is mine." So they went away, and they had not gone far when the maid's appearance changed, and she became the most beautiful woman in the world.

They went home in great joy and contentment and spent a happy night together; but the next morning the young king got up early to spend another day with Gruagach. His wife advised against it. She said that Gruagach was her father and meant him no good, but he said he must go. She advised him, if he won, to take nothing for his prize but the dun shaggy filly with the stick saddle. That day he won again, and when he put his leg over the filly he found she was the best mount he had ever ridden. That night they spent together in great enjoyment, but the young queen said that she would rather that he did not go to the Gruagach that day. "For," she said, "if he wins he will put trouble on thy head." He answered that he must go, so they kissed each other and parted.

It seemed to him that the Gruagach was glad to see him that day, and they settled to gaming again, but this time the Gruagach won. "Lift the stake of thy game," the young king said, "and be heavy on me, for I cannot stand to it." "The stake of my play is," said the Gruagach, "that I lay it as crosses and spells on thee that the cropped rough-skinned creature, more uncouth and unworthy than thou thyself, should take thy head, and thy neck if thou dust not get for me the Glaive of Light of the King of the Oak Windows."

The young king went home heavily and gloomily that night, and, though he got some pleasure from the young queen's greeting and her beauty, his heart was so heavy when he drew her to him that it cracked the chair beneath them. "What is it ails you that you cannot tell it to me?" said the young queen; so he told her all that happened and of the crosses laid on them. "You have no cause to mind that," she said. "You have the best wife in all Erin and the next to the best horse, and if you take heed to me you will come well out of this yet." In the morning the young queen got up early to prepare everything for the king's journey and brought out the dun shaggy filly to him. He mounted her, and the queen kissed him and wished him victory of battlefields. "I need not tell you anything," she said, "for the filly will be your friend and your companion, and she will tell you all that you must do."

So the young king set off and the filly galloped so fast that she left the March wind behind her and outstripped the wind in front of her. It was far they went, but it did not seem far until they got to the court and castle of the King of the Oak Windows. They stopped then, and the dun filly said, "We are come to the end of our journey, and if you listen to my advice you can carry the Sword of Light away. The King of the Oak Windows is at dinner now, and the Sword of Light is in his chamber. I will take you to it; there is a knob on its end; lean in at the window and draw out the sword very gently."

They went to the window. The young king leaned in and drew out the sword. It came softly, but when the point passed the window-frame it gave a kind of "sgread." "It is no stopping time for us here," said the dun filly. "I know the king has felt us taking out the sword." And they sped away. After a time the filly paused and said to him, "Look and see what is behind us." "I see a crowd of brown horses coming madly," said the young king. "We are swifter than those ones," said the dun filly, and sped on. When they had gone some long way she paused, and said, "Look, and see what is behind us." "I see a crowd of brown horses coming madly," said the young king, "and in front of them is a black horse with a white face, and I think there is a rider on him." "That horse is my brother and he is the swiftest horse in Erin. He will come past us like a flash of light. As they pass his rider will look round, and try then if you can cut his head off. He is the King of the Oaken Windows, and the sword in your hand is the only sword that could take the head off him."

The young king did just that and the dun filly caught the head in her teeth. "Leave the carcass," she said. "Mount the black horse and ride home with the Sword of Light, and I will follow as best I can."

He leapt on the black horse and it carried him as if he were flying, and he got home before the night was over, with the dun filly behind him. The queen had had no rest while he was away, and be sure they got a hero's welcome, and they raised music in the music place and feasting in the feasting place; but in the morning the young king said, "I must go now to the Gruagach, and see if I can lift the spells he has laid on me."

"He will not meet you as before," said the young queen. "The King of the Oaken Windows is his brother, and he will know that he would never part with the Glaive of Light unless he was dead. He will ask you how you got it, but only answer that if it were not for the knob at its end you would not have got it, and if he asks again give the same answer. Then he will lift himself to look at the knob and you will see a wart on his neck. Stab it quickly with the Glaive of Light, for that is the only way in which he can be killed, and if it is not done we are both destroyed." She kissed him and called on victory of battlefields to be with him and he went on his way. The Gruagach met him in the same place as before. "Did you get the sword?" "I got the sword." "How did you get the sword?" "If it had not been for the knob on its end I had not got it." "Let me see the sword." "It was not laid on me to let you see it." "How did you get the sword?" "If it were not for the knob that was at its end I got it not." The Gruagach lifted his head to look at the sword; the young king saw the mole; he was sharp and quick, he plunged the sword into it and the Gruagach fell down dead.

The young king went back rejoicing, but he found small cause of rejoicing at home. His guards and servants were tied end to back, and his queen and the two horses were nowhere to be seen. When the king loosed his servants, they told him that a huge giant had come and carried away the queen and the two horses. The young king set off at once to find them. He followed the giant's track all day long, and in the evening he found the ashes of a fire. He was blowing it up to spend the night there when the slim dog of the green forest came up to him. "Alas," he said, "thy wife and the two horses were in a bad plight here last night." "Alas indeed," said the young king. "It is for them I am seeking, and I fear that I shall never find them."

The dog spoke cheerily to him and caught him food. He watched over him through the night, and in the morning he promised that the young king had only to think of him if he was in need, and he would be there. They wished blessings on each other, and parted. The young king traveled on all day, and at night found the ashes of another fire, and was cheered, fed and guarded by the hoary hawk of the gray rock. They parted with the same promise of help. The third night he spent with the brown otter of the river, who fed and guarded him as the others had done and was able to tell him that he would see his queen that night. Sure enough he came that night to a deep chasm in which was the giant's cave, where he saw his wife and the two horses.

His wife began to weep when she saw him, for she was afraid for his safety, but the two horses said he could hide in the front of their stable and they would make sure that the giant would not find them.

They were as good as their word, for when the giant came to feed them they plunged and kicked, till the giant was almost destroyed. "Take care," said the queen. "They will kill you!" "Oh, they'd have killed me long ago," said the giant, "if I'd had my soul in my body, but it is in a place of safety." "Where do you keep it, my love?" said the queen. "I'll guard it for you." "It's in that great stone," said the giant.

So next day when the giant had gone out, the queen decked the stone with flowers and cleaned all around it. When the giant came back at night he asked why she had dressed up the stone. "Because your soul is in it, my dear love," she replied. "Oh, I see you really respect it," said the giant. "But it's not there." "Where is it then?" "It is in the threshold." So next day she cleaned and dressed up the threshold.

This time the giant was really convinced that she cared for him, and he told her where it was hidden - beneath a great stone under the threshold there was a living wether, and in the wether's belly was a duck, and in the duck's belly was an egg, and in the egg was the giant's soul. When the giant was fairly away next morning they set to work. They lifted the great stone, and the wether leapt out and escaped, but she was fetched back by the slim dog of the green forest and the duck was caught by the hoary falcon and the egg found and brought back from the sea by the brown otter.

By this time the giant was returning; the queen crumbled the egg in her fingers and he fell dead to the ground. They parted lovingly from their helpers and returned to the young king's castle where they had a hero's banquet, and lived lucky and happy after that.

THE CYCLIC NATURE OF EXISTENCES

Shape shifting and traveling is inherent to the natural world, which means that all of nature, including humanity, moves through cycles of change in form, purpose, expression, and relationships as it constructs, destructs and reconstructs its destiny and vehicle of travel. This is seen in the seasonal cycles, as a human moves through the infancy, adolescence, adulthood and old age, and as day follows night. All of these express the rising and falling, generative and re-generative qualities of life. Life feeds upon life to fulfill and sustain life, but life never ends. This is an ever-turning wheel moved by the action of energy through form, spirit through matter, and change against inertia.

The sentient toradh moves through cycles of life expression pulsing outwardly into physical form and drawing inward into the invisible life. In the physical cycle, the spirit embodies (takes a form) and travels (lives) through the seasons of change to move the spirit towards its vision. Once completed, the soul will cast the robe of flesh away as surely as we trade in one broken car for a new, more equipped one.

There is no death, only change and transformation as the soul rides the horse of form (incarnation) through the cycles of change, into the haunted woods of adventure (life), to the castle of sovereignty (fulfillment of destiny and return to the source). This is a pilgrimage that all living things, seen and unseen make – to return again to the primordial source of life at the heart of creation.

The toradh, once uttered from the void, moves through many cycles of change and life expression as it explores, grows, and functions. It moves through incarnate, discarnate and non-carnate beings. It moves through the three-fold life. In the surface world, it moves through a circular cycle of change wherein it embodies form, then disembodies it and may continue its life in this condition in many places at many times, even at the same time. It then re-enters the wheel of fortune that spins the seasons of surface life. All points in this circle of life are alive with intelligence and vision. This means that regardless of whether a being is fused to a physical form, it is alive with intelligence and sentience. The great River of Blood marks the borderland between incarnate, discarnate and non-incarnate life where forms emerge and descend. This border is also seen as the hedgeway between the well-lit township of human and other surface world life and the wild dark forest of the Faery realms.

As we move across the River of Blood, the only change is in the shapes and functions through which the creative intelligence expresses. Some shapes don't make complete transformations, such as the Star Walker and the Dream Walker, for they have mutable shapes that are beyond time and space. However, others do, such as the physical form and the Surface Walker. So often, humans fear that when the physical form and ego (Surface Walker) die, the actual being is dead. This is not so, for the shapes of the body and the outer consciousness (Surface Walker) provide a vessel for the deeper soul aspects (the Dream Walker and Star Walker) to express and explore, they are not separate realities in themselves. The death of form is merely expanded life beyond the hedge. Physical form is the product of multiple shapes converging through and into a fixed pattern. These shapes are the siths expressed in the three-fold life. All physical form beings, especially seekers, can and must travel through the siths to find their place upon the sacred land.

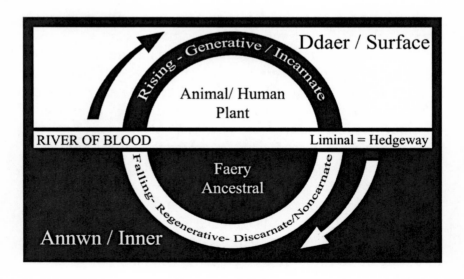

THE SITHS AND THE THREE-FOLD LIFE

The siths are our co-existing bodies within the three-fold life. They are alive and live in a symbiotic relationship with each other. The actualized seer is fully attuned to these siths and can shift their awareness from the Surface Walker (where it tends to spend most of its activities) to the other bodies, or to locate their awareness in all of the siths at the same time. Shifting surface world awareness into these siths helps to unify them and bring harmony and a wellspring of wisdom and inner knowing to the Surface Walker. Without this, the seeker will continue to seek, but never find what will bring comfort to their discontent.

To live consciously through the three-fold life is to be fully alive. It is to reclaim your right to live with the support of your ancestral and spiritual heritage. It is the destiny of all of humanity, without which we are mere robots without souls, trapped in the soul cage of human social life. But, we are so much more than mere family members, lovers, employees, bill payers, car drivers, and taxpayers. We are multilevel beings who are human and spirit, surface, dream, and star walkers all at the same time. To reach this heritage we must be willing to reach into the dark hidden crevices of our being and shine the light of enquiry and devotion. Awakening into the siths awakens us into enchantment and magic. As surely as we have the five senses of touch, sight, smell, hearing, and taste, we have a hidden sixth sense. Really though, this sixth sense is an extension or more rarified level of the five senses. We all have this sense though some are born with a higher capacity, like some people being born as natural dancers or musicians.

The five senses work in the other worlds as well. The more you work with the siths, the more you are able to, first, attune to them, second, to transfer your awareness to them, and third, to operate through your senses in the siths. You could call this a form of astral projection in that this concept deals with the star body and movement through and into it. The difference is, in working with the siths, you are not projecting out of your form. You are transferring awareness into your co-existing bodies, never leaving one but expanding to work with them all. The seer seeks to be able to do this expansion whenever and wherever they are physically located.

They work to maintain awareness of two primary siths (Surface and Dream Walkers) at the same time. This technique, called bi-location, is where the seeker is in two places at one time and yet is fully aware of both. As the seeker travels and works through the siths, they will note that the worlds or strata of life where these soul aspects dwell have recognizable traits. There is a type of inner landscape (the inscape) with characteristics that indicate the location where awareness is activated. These general indicators are relative to the appearance, feeling, sounds, and inner ecology of the place, as well as its inhabitants.

The following table is a general overview of the world where our siths abide. There are beings that pass back and forth across the worlds. These worlds and the siths also have interface points in nature or created by humanity including, but not limited to: 1) wells, springs, caves, temples, and graveyards as interface points between the surface and underworlds; 2) mountains, temples, and meteor craters as interface points between the surface and over-worlds; and 3) the indwelling flame (Child of Promise) and core of the planet (Dreamer) as interface points between the under and over-worlds. This list gives basic examples, but there are many others. Some interfaces have been discovered by seers and magic workers, some have not. Perhaps you will discover many more. The siths, the worlds, and the living beings live in a visible and invisible symbiosis that interpenetrates the worlds and influences each other's very existence.

Sith	Topology	Location	Resident Being	Characteristics
Surface Walker	Surface world, concrete substance and locations, human social life, Elemental climates, oceans of water and bodies of land, the red/orange flame	Land, the "stone" world, embodied, Incarnate, the plane of effects	Plants, trees, animals, humans, minerals, bacteria, insects and other embodied beings, the Ancestor, the Guardian	Time and space orientated, four elements and seven directional, concrete, five sense perception, measurable, generative
Dream Walker	Underworld, cave of voices, river of blood, beyond the hedge, inner world, the blue flame	Sea, the "sea world", discarnate, non-carnate, the plane of causes	Ancestral/ ghosts and faery beings, giants and elementals, the Dreamer, the Weaver Goddess, the Stone of Destiny, inner guardians	No time, fluid space and forms, felt and intuitive, stars within the land, ever-becoming
Star Walker	Upperworld/overworld, the white place of the stars, edge of the void of nothingness, the white flame	Stars and sky, the "star world", non-carnate the plane of origins	The Utterer, Star Father, the Holy Formless Fire	Timeless, formless, imperishable, pure, felt, energetic, no images

THE WEAVER'S CORD AND PREPARING THE VESSEL

The siths or "walkers" are the primary mechanism for traveling the other worlds. Traveling is the mode in which awareness is projected by a being into different components of itself or other modes of life. The walkers are like a horse that is ridden by our awareness into and from the hidden lands. Awareness is a specific mode of intelligence that receives into itself as well as directs the sacred flame of toradh.

However, the walkers are physical and non-physical body functions that must be maintained and healthy to be particularly useful. These bodies are specific modes of operations that work together to bring intelligence into form or coalescence.

The connection between the walkers manifests from the underworld through the golden cord of the Weaver Goddess. It passes up from the earth and into us, connecting us to the life of the planet and giving us ongoing sustenance. In practical terms this cord is awareness, for this is the force that connects all things. In this way the cord is the life cord to all of our bodies, and awareness is the life force. The more aware a being is of itself, the more it exists. This cord passes into each one of us, connecting us to everything. It operates as the connector between each sith. Therefore, the way in which we use our consciousness and the elemental forces it employs will strengthen, or weaken, the cord and its connections. This in turn strengthens or weakens the siths themselves especially the connection between the Surface Walker and Dream Walker and the Star Walker. Breaking this connection opens a being to all forms of disease and vulnerabilities.

The threefold nature of the walkers corresponds to general areas of life and modes of expression. There are influences affecting them and modifications (the prohibitions) that can support and sustain them. The prohibitions are things that must be stopped while the requirements represent things that must be instituted as consistent practice.

As you work with ancestral and Faery beings, prohibitions will be set forth. You, the seeker in the inter-world relationship, cannot (and will not) engage in life experiences that are harmful to you as a participant, and the Faery beings will make this abundantly clear. The reason for this is simple: the destructive use of awareness, intelligence and action weakens the cord that connects the siths and their ability to function. This results in poor health on all levels. Poor sith function means poor traveling ability and poor inter-plane communication skills which consequentially makes the human participant useless in the relationship. Additionally, inner power is opened outward through the siths in Faery work and, if the inner and outer wiring is poor regeneration and destruction can occur. Inner world beings will find those areas and require commitments of change from you in the form of the prohibitions and promises. I could never provide you with an exhaustive list of these for they are specific to the seeker. But they will be set and they may not be the choice of the seeker though they will be in their best interest. Be ready to examine your poor habits and change them as well as to integrate new improvements to the health and well being of the Siths.

Sith	Area of Human Experience	Influences	Key Words	Potential Prohibitions (P) and Requirements (R)
Surface Walker	Physical states including health and sensory experience, outer surface world awareness, interpersonal and social experiences, behavior, touch, cognitive knowing that flows from the outside in.	Nutrition, exercise, all forms of physical health maintenance, mental and sensory perceptions, sleep, sexual and social relationships	I think, I express and I relate	P – Substance abuse and addictions, P/R – specific foods or beverages, modification of sexual proclivities, colors used in clothing R – use of physical exercises
Dream Walker	Emotional, intra-psychic, inner, sensual, self-perception, intuitive, knowing that flows from the inside outward	Attitudes, beliefs, feelings, emotional perceptions, repetitive thought patterns, self-esteem, unseen energetic influences	I feel, I believe and I attract or receive	P/R – Certain types of emotional relationships, use of self perceptions including self talk, change in thought patterns and perceptions, R – use of mantras or affirmations
Star Walker	Spiritual, inspiration, vision, faith, passions and drives	Paradigms (world views), commitments, religions and spiritual doctrines and practices	I am, I manifest and I create or project	R – Prayers, meditations, specific areas of study, daily spiritual practices aimed at inner stillness and connection to a "higher power," use of altars and shrines

VISION #6: Traveling Beyond the Hedge

Traveling beyond the hedgeway of everyday consciousness to the realms of enchantment requires the seeker to attune to the inner worlds and clear the influences that compromise the siths. Attunement is the first part of the process. Health and maintenance are the subsequent ones. This exercise will tune you, the seeker, into moving awareness into the siths and communing with the inner worlds.

By the time you work with this exercise, you should have worked with inner stillness and cultivated a feeling for it. Therefore, when you sit in a chair and assume the throne of dominion, you should be able to enter into stillness easily. This state is the entrance into and exit from all visionary work. It precedes and succeeds it. Traveling beyond the hedge involves a transfer of awareness attuned through stillness into a place that is timeless, where all the creative intelligences of the inner world partake of the central flame of life. According to oral Faery lore, it is central to the traditional witch's flight to the sabbat, for it employs the traditional visionary process for the witch (or seer, in this case) to enter into communion with the inner spiritual worlds. I advise that the seeker do this at least two times per month to keep the pathway open and attuned to the subtle forces. Eventually, you can do work while you are beyond the hedge, then leave that work there to be sustained by the holy flame and grow outward into embodied expression.

You will need a chair to sit in, a single white candle (the glass enclosed kind is safest and most useful) and matches.

a) Sit in your chair, draw your awareness inward with your eyes open and enter into stillness.

b) Light the central candle, which embodies the holy formless fire and the light of your quest for truth.

c) Close your eyes, breathe deeply and evenly.

d) Allow the outer world to fade away and envision the central candle flame becoming the fire in a fireplace in an old cottage.

e) Envision an old wise woman sitting in a chair at the fireplace stirring a cauldron. She is a powerful inner contact in this work who has held open the path beyond the hedge for hundreds of years and through the fires of persecution.

f)   She tells you of the journey to the witch's sabbat, which is at the center of creation where the holy light of the Child of Promise guides, guards, inspires, and inspirits all of creation on earth. The beings that attend it are the sacred Fair Folk who work with humans that come in search of magic and fulfillment of the triple will.

g)   She offers you a ladle full of the bitter fluid that is brewed in her cauldron. This fluid makes the changes within your awareness that allow you to fly beyond the hedge. You receive her gift and drink the contents of the ladle.

h)   You feel yourself become light headed as you begin to float like a wisp of smoke.

i)   Suddenly, you are drawn by the Faery blast, a vortex of energy that sweeps you up the chimney and out over the roof of the cottage and village where you see other seekers flying through the air.

j)   You can see the lights of this village below you and, off in the distance, you see where the lights end. You cross a river to the place where the dark forest begins.

k)   At this borderland, you can see that there is a hedge thicket filled with brambles, thorns and rose blossoms.

l)   You are set down by the Faery blast at the hedge.

m) The wise woman greets you again and tells you her secret name, one that is for you only. She tells you that you must not reveal it, for this is the secret name that opens the gate in the hedge to the hidden path into a sacred grove.

n)   As you approach the hedge, you speak the secret name and it opens for you to enter.

p) There is a bonfire in the center where elementals, Faery, ghosts, witches, and all forms of beings move in a circular dance around the luminous flames while singing the joy of creation.

p) One being beckons for you to enter and join in the dance.

q) The assembly dances in a circle about the fire, faster and faster until you are drawn up into the smoke of the fire.

r) You feel whispers of truth move through you as the smoke carries you away.

s) Suddenly you are aware that you are above the old cottage again. As you descend the chimney, you are aware that you are in fact settling into your physical body.

t) Allow the experience to settle in you, then open your eyes, remembering the feeling of this experience.

In future travels beyond the hedge, you can spend time there spinning the living light around specific inner workings. Sometimes a being will beckon you to the side of the flames where they will instruct you. In this way, seekers often find new inner contacts.

CHAPTER 11:
SPIRIT COMMUNICATION
AND THE SECOND SIGHT

I saw the Weaver of Dream, an immortal shape of the star-eyed Silence; and the Weaver of Death, a lovely Dusk with a heart of hidden flame: and each wove with the shuttles of Beauty and Wonder and Mystery. I knew not which was the more fair: for Death seemed to me as love, and in the eyes of Dream I saw joy. Oh come, come to me, Weaver of Dream! Come, oh come unto me, O Lovely Dusk, thou that hast the heart of hidden flame!

– "Where the Forest Murmurs," Fiona Macleod

This haunting poem speaks of a vision that emerges from the silence of dreams. Could this be speaking of the inner visionary world of the seer? A seer is simply one who sees, a prophet, soothsayer, diviner, and sometimes a magic-worker. In the world of the seer, death and life are living beings that dwell in the twilight of the second sight. The second sight appears throughout all Celtic cultures as a primary trait in the mystical, magical and spiritual practices of these indigenous peoples. There are many terms to describe this faculty, those persons possessing it, and the rites, spells, initiations, and other practices related to it.

There are several Gaelic terms for this phenomena including: *an-da-shealladh* (meaning "the two sights"), *Da-radharc* (meaning "the power of vision"), and *Taibhsearachd* (meaning "the gift of supernatural sight"). It appears in countless other cultures around the world and is called by many colloquial names which translate to "the gift," "the sight," "the knowing," "the spirit sight," and even as extra-sensory perception in the modern research world. All of these terms describe a type of seeing that is a "pre-vision," or the ability to perceive occurrences before they manifest. All of the lore connects it to a relationship between the seer and deities, devils, Faeries, ghosts, and other spirit beings. Perhaps, this connection is nowhere more graphic than in those cultures with the Faery tradition.

Connections with other world beings such as the Fay always seem to be related to visions, poetic inspiration, spirit vision, and other gifts that cause the "see-er" to tap an otherwise unknown strata of inward sight or "insight." In fact, it is impossible to discuss traditional Faery practices, especially Seership, without addressing the mystical virtues of sight. However, I am not referring to the ordinary seeing capacity that perceives the solid world around us. Rather, it is the sight that sees the finer, invisible world and its inhabitants illuminated by a subtle light that flows from within, exposing the object of its gaze. The Gaelic people, specifically those of Scottish heritage, call this "the second sight" implying an additional faculty beyond our normal mundane sight perception.

In the course of this chapter, I will simply refer to "the sight" to describe all of the senses plus the inner ones based on intuition and emotion. Although these senses may be experienced through outward faculties (nose, mouth, eyes, touch, ears), they are also applied in the dream world, and a less iden-tifiable sense of inner knowing. Sometimes it comes in the form of visions, other times in voices, olfactory influences, touch senses, "dreaming true," or simply knowing things that are not within the capacity of most people. It may even involve a certain feeling that my Queen in the old craft calls "the delicious shivers." You know that feeling we get when we walk alone into a graveyard, civil war battlefield, haunted house, or ancient ruins in the darkest of night. It is that feeling that both scares and exhilarates us at the same time. It is that feeling that says "something is going on here and I cannot see it" or "something (or someone) else is here with me and I cannot see it, but I can feel it in my spirit and in my goose-bumps." This can be both stimulating and daunting in its effect.

The sight is the primary means by which the seer sees. It is the mechanism for communication with beings that live in a stratum of life that is not composed of the base elements that give form, depth, structure, solidity, and substance as we know it. In its more evolved stages this sight involves both the capacities of communication and interpretation. Some people are born with it through genetic inheritance, others acquire it through strange life experiences that usually involve trauma or contact with the spirit world and others develop it through training and discipline. Robert Kirk speaks to this thusly:

> And again [the seer teaches] that men of the Second Sight, being designed to give warnings against the secret engines [that is, devices and occurrences] surpass the vision of ordinary men, which is a native habit in some, descended from their ancestors, but acquired as an artificial improvement of their natural sight in [the case of] others. (*Kirk*, Stewart)

Most Faery lore asserts that the sight is either given by the spirits or, in most instances, the seer is born with the faculty and it is awakened through contact with the spirit world. In Gaelic lore it is passed on from parent to child through the blood. Again Kirk states:

> Some have this Second Sight transmitted from father to son through the whole family, without their own consent or the teachings of others, proceeding only from a bounty of providence, it seems, or by a compact, or a complexional quality of the first acquirer [of the sight]. (*Kirk*, Stewart)

This aspect of Gaelic lore suggests that it is passed from parent to child and, when transmitted, it is not the choice of the child as to whether the sight will awaken. In this case, the only choice a gifted person may have is how, or when, it will awaken. Ms. F. Marian McNeill in her book, *The Silver Bough* asserts:

> The faculty of the second sight he (a friend of the author) attributed to the high development of the sympathetic nervous system as compared to the cerebro-spinal system in a simple people living in close and harmonious relationship with nature-one might call it 'in tune with the elements'- but the faculty, he held, tends to decline where this contact is slackened or lost or where the cerebro-spinal system is more fully developed. It seems to be almost a matter of blood versus brain.

If this is correct, the close contact with nature opens the subtle capacities of the sight. Since the Fair Ones are beings inherent within nature, this would begin to explain how they influence the potentials of the sight.

Those who are born with it tend to have a greater degree of skill, although they often possess a lesser degree of control over the sight. An experienced seer, however, can train their control. Those born with it in a culture (ethnic, racial, family or geographic) where it is integrated into everyday life and socially sanctioned practices tend to be even more proficient. These individuals may not actually receive it until a particular time in their life. For them, the sight may sleep in dormancy until the onset of puberty, mid-life, or some other developmental point in their life. Then, it is suddenly activated and starts working. Those who develop it through disciplines may have considerable skill, but never have quite the intensity or clarity of those who receive it through genetics. Many people may disagree with me, but that is the position of most folk practitioners and it has been my experience over many years of living with the sight.

FAERY TRADITION AND THE SIGHT

Faery tradition and the sight are inexorably intertwined. It is this mystical faculty, together with the practice of the magical, musical (and other artistic forms), and healing arts that form the foundation of the Faery/human exchange and the seer's skills. The sight has been a consistent factor in the long history of folkloric practices that address human, Faery and ancestral encounters. It has always been those persons with the sight who could perceive and interpret the delicate balance between humans, ancestral spirits and nature via the course of spiritual tides and the subtle forces attending them.

The sight is often given by Faery beings to those humans who have relationships with them. Sometimes this is a sudden bestowing, other times it gradually awakens through consistent contact with the inner realms. The traditional Scottish ballad of *"Thomas the Rhymer"* is a graphic example of a person who received the sight from a Fay encounter. This ballad is based on the actual life of Thomas of Ercledoune, a prophet and seer who lived during the thirteenth century. He is also known as "True Thomas" because of his prophetic ability to see the future, which he attributed as a gift from the Faery Queen. In this ballad, the Faery Queen, clad in green (the primary color of the Fay), takes Thomas to the underworld through the River of Blood where "for forty days and forty nights he wad thro blood to the knee, and he saw neither sun nor moon, but heard the roaring of the sea."

The Queen shows True Thomas a vision of three roads (one of the outer and human world, one of sacrifice, and the middle one that leads to Elfland) and the forbidden fruits of the underworld. She instructs him to travel the "road to fair Elfland" and "hold your tongue, whatever you may hear or see, for if one word you should chance to speak, you will never get back to your ain countrie." After his seven-year period in the underworld, True Thomas returned to the world of humanity clad in the green garb that is the magic of Faeryland and gifted with "the tongue that cannot lie." Lewis Spence in his book *The Fairy Tradition in Britain* comments:

> Thorough examination of the sources of the belief in the second sight leads to the conclusion that it had spiritualistic origin and that it was associated with a highly developed technique for getting *en rapport* with the spirits of the dead, who could endow the living with vision into futurity.... From passages in *The Secret Commonwealth* of Robert Kirk of Aberfoyle, it is manifest that second sight was commonly regarded in the Highlands and Lowlands (of Scotland) as a means of beholding the fairies, whatever its later associations may have developed into.

It must be noted that the land of the dead and the Faery realms are not the same. In *"The Ballad of Thomas the Rhymer,"* the River of Blood is encountered before the road to fair Elfland. However, tradition tells us that those who wander through the Faery world and gain the Faery sight also have the ability to speak with the spirits of the dead.

Some people receive the sight during a time of severe illness wherein they traverse the inner roads of Faery and return changed. W.Y. Evans-Wentz in *The Fairy Faith in Celtic Countries* provides us with a telling interview with Mr. John Glynn, a town clerk in Tuam, Ireland who provides insight into the local lore on the second sight:

> Fairies are said to be immortal, and the fairy world is always described as an immaterial place, though I do not think it is the same as the world of the dead. Sick persons, however, are often said to be with the fairies, and when cured, to have come back. A woman who died here about thirty years ago was commonly believed to have been with the fairies during her seven years' sickness when she was a maiden. She married after coming back, and had children; and she was always able so see the *good people* and to talk to them, for she had the second sight.

The seven-year sacrifice is a re-occurring element in the Faery ballads and stories. This teaching has many interpretations but, it implies that would-be seers will find themselves stretched between the realms, bi-locating to bridge humanity and the Faery realms for up to seven years once they have been accepted and admitted into the Faery realms. This is the primary training period wherein the human seeker is enchanted and made Fay. Some accounts, however, suggest that every seven years, a *kain* or *teind* (tithe) must be paid to the underworld to ensure the favor of the Fair Folk. The oldest forms of this are bread, wheat, barley, milk, whiskey, and any food that has no salt in it. The traditional amount that should be given to the Good People is one tenth (a tithe) of what you (the human) need to survive. Other interpretations of the *kain* suggest that, once every seven years, a human must be introduced into the second sight and Faery arts.

Some of the clearest and most concise accounts of the sight and its connection to Faery practices come from the Gaelic traditions, specifically Irish and Scottish. The material provided by Robert Kirk gives some of the most detailed information on Faery Seership and the sight. R.J. Stewart in his edition of Kirk's *The Secret Commonwealth of Elves, Fauns and Fairies*, gives us many insights into traditional Scottish approaches on this subject. Kirk speaks about the trance state used by the seer to gain inner information: "The men of that Second Sight do not [simply] discover strange things when asked, but at [that is, in] fits and Raptures, as if inspired with some Genius at that instant, which before did lurk in or about them."

Our ancestors on both sides of the Atlantic Ocean were clear that those persons who understand the seen and unseen ways of the natural world may also peer into the spiritual realms. Again Kirk states:

As the Birds and Beasts whose bodies are much used to the change of the free and open air [thus] foresee storms, so those invisible people are more sagacious to understand by [using] the Book of Nature, things [yet] to come, than we [are], who are pestered with the grosser dregs of all Elementary mixtures, and have our purer spirits choked by them.

The seer gains a type of clarity from their contact with the Faery realms that allows them to read the "Book of Nature." The "grosser dregs" addressed by Kirk are not merely the aspects of physical life, but the distractions of human social life; this statement points back to the need for approaching inner stillness to move beyond the grosser dregs. Perhaps we can learn much from the creatures of nature about the workings of inner sight.

All Seership traditions hold that the gift is enhanced by the seer's inner spiritual alliances which usually include beings such as gods, angels, Faeries, ancestral dead, and nature sprits. If the seer can develop the faculty to not only communicate with these beings, but to understand their hidden ways, they will be able to predict (the art of prophecy) and even influence (the art as magic) the future as well as to interrupt or correct harm (the art of healing). Kirk states, "Thus a Man of the Second Sight perceiving the operations of these forecasting invisible [fairy] people among us, indulged through stupendous providence to give warnings of certain events, either in the Air, Earth, or Waters..." Clearly, by tradition, if a man (or woman) can perceive the inner working and see creation from the inside out, they will know the direction of outcomes.

THE SITH AND THE SECOND SIGHT

W. Grant Stewart, in his *The Popular Superstitions of the Highlanders of Scotland* comments on the connection between the sith and the second sight:

From the birth of the mortal to the eve of his death, the ghost, in point of similitude, is a perfect counterpoint or representative of his early yoke-fellow. As the child grows toward manhood, his ghost keeps pace with him, and so exactly do they resemble each other in the features, complexions and aspects, when seen by a third party that, without the use of prescribed spells, no human observer can distinguish the mortal from the immortal, Nor is this resemblance confined to the personal appearance alone - it is likewise extended to the habiliments ... The ghost is supposed either to accompany or precede, at some distance, his human partner (of course invisible to those not possessing the second sight) in all those multifarious journeys and duties which the mortal performs throughout the course of his eventful life, and the mortal utility of the ghost is supposed to consist in propitiating the mortal's undertakings by guarding him from the influence of evil spirits.

This ghost is the co-walker, also referred to in the Irish Faery tradition as "the fetch" (not to be confused with the fetch common in the western mystery traditions), and, in my practices, as the Dream Walker. Kirk suggests that this sith guards its living host from evil. However, in Seership practices, it is actually the mechanism for the sight itself. The seer attunes to this body and opens their awareness into it. Thus, they can see into the world where the sith abides. As a point of clarification, the term "sith" is a Gaelic term representing the Faery beings themselves. But, the lore in Faery Seership identifies the co-walker/sith as enchanted aspects of who we are. Therefore, work with the sith is work with our "Faery selves." It is through this apparition, that the seer moves about, perceives, and lives in the Faery realms while his or her Surface Walker travels the surface world of physical substance.

Every person has a door into the other realms through one of their senses that is sensitive to the finer subtle forces. The sensitivity may be mild, but likely you have perceived the other world through one or more of these senses at some time in your life. As the seeker travels the inner realms using the visionary techniques provided in this book, one of these senses will become the obvious area of inherent talent. This means that the seeker will note that they always use one of their senses more so than any other. It is advisable to allow oneself to be comfortable with that sense and allow other senses to follow it into unfoldment over time. If this does not happen, just use your psychic sense and do not try to force the others.

Each seeker's soul will not only have a propensity for specific senses to be clearer in their operations in the other world, they will note that communications extended from the inner world outwardly will often emerge through specific elements. The seeker receives information from the Faery through some sense in relationship to an elemental force. I call this the tap on the shoulder. The inner contacts tend to use a device that works well with the seer to get their attention and then deliver a direct message through one or more of the human's senses. Examples of these may include:

The Element of Air

- Hearing voices on the wind
- Seeing a vision in the wind or the patterns the wind makes on grass or trees
- A haunted wind that blows over the seer bring with it a vision
- Asking a question of the wind and waiting for the answer to come at that time or in dreams
- Smelling influences (ex. smelling danger)
- A breeze blowing over leaving a taste in their mouth that always means something

The Element of Fire

- Seeing visions in any flame
- Hearing a voice coming from the flame that gives messages
- Seeing "spirit lights" like little balls of flame that bring a vision or messages
- Having a specific way of working with a fire to bring forth visions

- Circling around a bonfire (known as hallowing) to connect with the underworld and receive visions or messages
- Reading ashes or coals in (or after) a fire to get visual messages from the patterns.

The Element of Water

- Receiving visual messages through patterns on moving or still water, whether it be a pond, lake, river, creek, ocean, glass of fluid, crystal ball, or other fluid-like tool
- Hearing voices from water-ways
- Sending a request across still water or down the stream of a moving waterway and waiting for visual, auditory, or other messages to come
- Seeing images surface in a still pool of water (or other fluid)

The Element of Earth

- Hearing voices from stones
- Receiving messages from the patterns on or in stones
- Carrying certain stones that give messages in dreams, through voices, or a sudden knowing
- Listening to the ground for voices in the soil, particularly in graveyards
- Sitting on a large stone or boulder to receive messages
- Reading the signs in nature

This list is by no means exhaustive. Rather, it gives you (the seeker) some insights on the many ways that the senses and the elements come together to transmit inner contact from the Dream Walker to the Surface Walker. Other interfaces can be used such as pendulums, tarot or playing cards, kinesiology (such as those used in the Perelandra techniques), and countless others.

There are also certain times which are more propitious for communicating with the denizens of the other world. From the human standpoint, you are more receptive at liminal times such as at the point of wakening in the morning, just as you are falling asleep, quest times at natural places, or when you have entered into silence and moved the waking mind into its subtle modes. There are times when both the human and the inner beings can contact each other more easily such as the twilight hour before sunset, midnight, the dawning hour before sunrise, noon, Summer Solstice (hence Shakespeare's *A Mid-Summer Nights Dream*), and Beltane and Hallowmas.

FOLK TRADITION AND SEERSHIP IN THE AMERICAN SOUTH

It is important for you to understand that these traditions are not a part of the distant past or of distant lands. Likely, no matter where you are, there are Seership practices and (I assure you) there are Faery beings.

I grew up in a small area outside of Winchester, Virginia located in the Shenandoah Valley in the United States of America. This wonderful area is rich in folkloric farming, hunting, magical, and music lore and practices including those associated with the intuitive arts. Being born and growing up in this area exposed me to the sight, faith healers, and conjurers. As anyone who grew up anywhere in the southern states can tell you, there are fascinating practices in the folk life of the South. These traditions blend European, African, and Native American practices into a delicious gumbo.

Sadly, slavery was a major factor in the history of Virginia and the African slaves brought with them many spiritual and magical practices. Over long periods of exposure and cultural synergy, many of these practices were incorporated into those of the British, Irish and Scottish settlers, and merged with the practices of the local Native American tribes. After hundreds of years of cross-fertilization, these influences have become potent magical traditions in their own rights. The magical practices are simply referred to as "conjure" and occasionally as witchcraft. Sometimes the locals will say that people who do these kinds of things are root workers or doctors. In the deeper south, the names for these practices change, as do some of the practices themselves. In the Carolinas and further south, such practices may be called root working, conjure magic, or even hoodoo. The changes in the traditions and their names were influenced by the specific African tribes imported into that area, the local Native American tribes and their practices, and the magical practices of the European settlers, which included British, Scottish, Irish, Spanish, French (including Creole/Acadian as you move deeper south) and others.

My life experiences in the South echo similar patterns to those in the Celtic countries. My mother was born with the veil, or caul, which is a certain way the placental sheath falls across the baby's eyes. I was also born with it. The folks back home believe that this signifies a person who has the gift to see into the future, speak to spirits, or both. It has been my experience that this folk belief is very accurate. Everyone I know who was born with the veil has the gift. Sadly, for some it is more like a curse because they only get messages of bad things to come. In my experience, this trend can be changed, but it takes inner work and training.

A person who is born with the veil may receive messages in one or more of many forms. My mother called it "the knowing" when she simply knew things, or "the knowing told her." She also received "tokens." A token is a specific way the spirits give a message to you. Sadly, my mother only received tokens of death. Her token worked through an old wooden door that was on the home of her birth. In fact, she took that door with her when she left home and it traveled wherever we lived. It is still at our old home in Virginia. When her token came, she would hear a knock on the old door. She would open it and then get a vision of who was next on death's list. She had other tokens, but that is the one that came to her most often. She also received messages from something she called "quaking." Always, wherever she lived, there would be a shrub or small bush that would signify a message by shaking or quaking. Then she would hear the voices of a funeral procession discussing the life of the person who just died. In this way, the token would inform her of who was about to die. She rarely received visions. Her messages came indirectly through these tokens.

My gift started to open up when I was very young. Initially, I would simply get visions. My earliest vision alerted me to my grandfather's death. This one was a clear, powerful and frightening vision of how and when he would die his very gruesome death. Imagine how traumatic that was for an eight year old boy. Then, after my puberty, it kicked into high gear. I would hear a knock on a wall (any wall), put my ear to it and receive my token. The token would be in the form of a voice that would tell me things that were to happen in the future. Now, at forty, I get direct visions and messages from the spirits. The visions come in the form of visual pictures, dreams, spirit visitations, and voices. They are a balance of good, bad and even relatively insignificant events.

There were also magical practices, which my mother taught me, including the lore of the crossroads, the Gray Lady of Death, "cleaning your shoes" (ways that someone may pick up bad influences then cleanse them away), and special ways to pray for healing that involved water and soil. However, she would have rarely identified these practices as magic. Instead, she would have simply identified them as things you need to do to get things done, and things you need to know about to get through life.

All of the exercises given in this book help the seeker refine their perceptions and stretch them beyond the usual mode of activity. Through consistent work with subtle forces, the mind is cued to move into a different function, one that operates from the inner senses. The mind works like a muscle, if you work it and stretch it, it becomes stronger and more flexible. Work with the envisioning process teaches you awareness to work in an inner way and to use the imaging process as an interface for expressing and interpreting other world communications. No exercise can guarantee the sight, but with repeated practice, they do enhance your sight capacity and attract the attention of inner world beings. These beings are fully capable of granting the sight if they think it is in their (and your) best interest.

VISION #7: Traveling Eyes

Any exercise that strengthens the golden cord that connects the siths will expand awareness and inner sensitivity. This results in clearer and more meaningful interactions with the Faery beings and subsequently, meaningful and accurate visions. Working toward developing the sight will only open and strengthen the seeker's awareness of the siths and their inner life. This, in turn, becomes the interface to the inner worlds and its inhabitants. The traveling eyes exercise opens a connection between the eyes of the Service Walker and those of the Dream Walker. Initially, it can be somewhat unsettling because it shifts the seeker's mode of perception so drastically. With practice, it unifies the siths, increases the comfort level of the seeker as he or she bi-locates, and improves the quality of the vision. It also helps the seeker establish their conscious presence in the underworld.

a) You can begin this exercise standing or sitting. However, you will eventually be standing and moving.

b) Draw your awareness inward by approaching silence. Breathe deeply and evenly.

c) Be aware that at the bottom of your feet begins the bottoms of another set of your feet that extends downward (upside down) and is connected to another you, your Dreaming Soul in the Faery realms. This is the part of you that always lives in the other world regardless of your conscious awareness of it.

d) Now poise your attention on your physical eyes. Close them and imagine that they (or at least your capacity to see) are rolling down your form until they rest in the eye sockets of your co-walker.

e) Open your inner eyes in that world with your outer eyes closed.

f) Note what you see.

g) Now, holding on to that feeling, open your physical eyes and be aware of "seeing" in both places (the surface and underworlds) at the same time.

h) Walk around the room and experience the feeling of being in two places at once. After a few moments, close your physical eyes again.

i) Feel your eyes roll up your underworld sith until they come to your physical body and let them rest in your outer eyes.

j) When you are ready, open your eyes into this world and let the uneasiness fade.

k) Resume your normal breathing pattern.

This exercise should be repeated weekly until you are comfortable and can move into your inner sight at will and with minimal discomfort.

VISION #8: Fire Circling

This exercise strengthens the golden cord between the siths. It can be done using a candle flame or a bonfire. Be sure to give adequate fire-hazard clearance as you circumambulate (also known as hallowing) so that you do not knock over your candle or get to close to the flames. Position the source of the flame at the center of the working area for it embodies the flame at the center of all-being. This exercise is a very ancient form of working with the Faery people. I suggest that someone else be with you during this exercise, especially if using a bonfire. The trance state achieved can be very deep.

a) Enter into stillness with your eyes open.

b) If you are using a candle, light it. It embodies the holy formless fire and your eternal quest for truth.

c) Roll your eyes into the eyes of your Dream Walker as you did in the previous exercise.

d) Begin hallowing the sacred flame (circling it) while seeing into both worlds.

e) Feel the attention of all of the beings around both bodies as their spirits approach in this dance of life.

f) Continue circling as you feel your underworld and surface bodies merge and the borderland between the worlds fades away.

g) Continue this for a while and allow yourself to receive messages from the Faery contacts. If one in particular approaches you, work with it. It may become a consistent ally.

h) Slowly roll your inner eyes upward to merge with your Surface Walker and, when ready, open your outer eyes and feel the presence of the rapture.

i) Extinguish the candle or other flame as appropriate, while feeling a part of this sacred flame merge with you.

CHAPTER 12:
FAERY MAGIC

The desire of the Fairy women, dew:
The desire of the Fairy host, wind:
The desire of the raven: blood:
The desire of the snipe: the wilderness:
The desire of the seamew: the lawns of the sea:
The desire of the poet: the soft low music
*   of the Tribe of the Green Mantles:*
The desire of man, the love of woman:
The desire of women, the little clan:
The desire of the soul, wisdom.

— *"Nine Desires," Fiona Macleod*

All beings have an object of yearning and desire. So, if the desire of the soul is wisdom, which is knowledge applied, what then is the role of magic? In fact, what is magic from the viewpoint of Faery Seership?

Magic is a principle, a living dynamic of creation and regeneration that brings about constant change and transformation throughout all worlds, on all levels and in all planes. It is the creativity of the life force, the expressed imagination of the Ancient One. All beings that exist are a part of magic or they would not exist. In fact, all of existence is magic in action. It was magic that inspired the utterance from the void and the visions of the Dreamer. It is magic that gives creation its wings to fly through experience where it becomes wise, transformed and whole.

The myriad of life forms (seen and unseen) in our surface world alone is a testimony to the creativity and magical prowess of the Ancient One. Magic is perhaps the deepest source and expression of wisdom for it is creativity and knowledge applied. The ancients call it "the most sublime and profound of sciences." To understand the ways of magic as a principle and an art is to understand the secret ways of nature. These are the secrets of creation, destruction, regeneration, attraction, repulsion and the mysteries of life, love and death. All of these are perfect and profound spells in the hidden grimoires of nature and her elder race, the Faery people. These are the mysteries well understood by the Faery races and offered to a humanity that *truly* seeks. To understand them is to become truly wise. To sail their inner tides and apply their mystical ways is the practice of magic. Once touched by the hand of Fay, magic is with us to stay.

SOME CORE ELEMENTS OF FAERY MAGIC

There are some basic principles in the magical practices of Faery Seership including:

- *That Faery magic causes visible change through invisible means*: This form of magic involves: 1) engaging inner world beings and dynamics that are pre-substance (or pre-manifestation), 2) working with the inherent virtues and patterns within a thing (such as an herb, stone, metal, etc.) or with patterns occurring in nature (such as seasonal changes, the circular movement of the heavenly bodies, the stream of toradh pouring from the stars into the earth, etc.), and 3) mediating these forces through objects, places, rituals and even through the seer to the outside world where they become visible changes.

- *The seer works with the invisible connections between all things*: Often things or occurrences that seem unconnected in the surface world are intertwined at their source. The hidden paths are the points of connection. If a seer understands or attunes to these connections, they will have a deeper understanding of how future events will evolve and how to mitigate or support them.

- *Faery magic works with creation from the inside out*: This form of magic works directly with the creative process and its attending intelligences in the active mode of creation. In this way, the human participant works as a co-creator instead of manipulator. This aspect of magic either works without tools by using the visionary techniques, or with tools in simple rites or practices.

- *The visions are the primary tools used in Faery magic*: They are used to enter and exit the Faery realms as well as to facilitate work in these inner planes. The topological descriptions encoded into the visions are also primary tools. Any physical implements are simple and usually natural objects or items found in the household. These practices are remnants of an ancient folk tradition, not a temple tradition. The tools are objects that a simple, financially poor and often illiterate person could access. All of the forces that are worked with are natural. There are no Faery beings created by humans. In fact, this approach is impossible as these beings pre-exist humanity as an independent species.

- *Historical Celtic magical techniques will recognize some of the Faery magic practices*: These practices are at the very core of the Celtic mystical mindset. Therefore, the Faery magical practices have a strong resonance with any form of Celtic spirituality and magic. This is not to say that they cannot be incorporated with other practices. On the contrary, they can and have been successfully meshed with other practices. Remember, Faery Seership is a practice and an art, not a religion.

- *This form of magic taps into the inherent power of a place:* This is distinctive among magical traditions. Most traditions engage inner contacts by language and cultural names that are not localized to the area in which the practitioner actually works and lives. Faery magic works with what is there in the location where the seer is conjuring.

- *The seer partners with Faery and ancestral allies:* This is an aspect of Faery magic that is relatively unique. There is no worship, invocation, binding (though this does appear in later Victorian ritual magic practices) or summoning. Rather, the relationship between the seer and the Fay is one of partnership, engagement and mutual exchange. Faery Seership acknowledges and respects deity forms, but they are not a part of these practices, although they can be used concurrently.

- *There is a wild force resident in the powers of nature:* It cannot be tamed and commanded. It can only be tapped and worked with. This force becomes a part of the seer's personality as they work closer with it and incorporate it into all aspects of their life. This is different from many magical approaches that infer that the practitioner can command and force a being to do his or her bidding. I strongly advise against this in Faery work. These beings are very potent and can turn the seer's will against them. Power plays with an ancient being are not wise.

- *The seer uses the twilight or enters a rapture:* This is a tipsy state in which the seer accesses alternate paths of perception and reality to engage the realms and beings of enchantment. Sometimes people enter raptures spontaneously for a short time. This is often referred to as *dejá vu*, which is that feeling of familiarity that comes upon you unexpectedly, making you feel as if you have been at that place or in that moment before. This experience is a rapture and at that moment, you have entered the other world of Faery. In that world, you are in a timeless place where the result and the process are happening at the same time. In the Faery realms, life is ever-young, and process is always happening.

- *The use of unguents, oils, scents, and plant allies*: Though the use of these practices is not unique to Faery magic, the ways in which they are used is. Unguents are used to gain the sight or prevent the Fay from becoming invisible to the seer. There are traditional recipes, some of which are provided in this book. Plants and trees are central in Faery magic. We do not charge or consecrate them. Rather, they are lending their magic to us. They are already powerful and blessed, that is why we work with them. For instance, a rowan tree does not need human energy added to it for it to become powerful. It simply is powerful and we humans tap into that power.

General Magical Practices

There are many general types of magical practices in Faery Seership. Some of them have descriptive terms specific to the tradition. I have listed a few of them here. Seekers will find that they are more proficient in some than others. I provide techniques for some of these practices in later sections of this chapter. Malefices (magic to bring harm) and benefices (magic to bring help) are listed so that it is clear that Faery magic is a two-edged sword, like all magical traditions. However, I do not recommend that the Seership student practice maleficent magic, for as the old craft saying warns "the toucher is touched." This means that the focus of your magic becomes the focus of your destiny. Choose your workings wisely, for the ways of magic will not be mocked.

- *Hallowing*: a circumambulating motion around a thing or place. The seer walks (beginning facing the east) around an item, a place or a person three times to bless it. This follows clockwise (*deosil*) which is the path of the sun and growing things. Hallowing is performed to bless something or gather magical power for a working. A spell in Faery Seership is called a "turning."

- *To Bane*: the same motion as in hallowing except that the seer walks counter clockwise (*tuathal*), also known as "star wise" for it moves on the path of the stars. The seer walks opposing the sun for the purposes of cursing and destruction. However, it can also be used to unwind the coil of magic that has been placed on someone or somewhere. Maleficent magic is called "bad washing" and the practitioner is called a "bad-washer."

- *Saining*: blessings made on an item, a place or a person. It is usually done with salt, fire and water. When this is done with people, they may be alive or dead. For the dead, it is traditional to place salt on the left breast and soil on the right breast of the deceased to sain them for safe passage through the Faery realms. For the saining of a child, they may be blessed with the three elements and passed over a sacred oak fire to ward them against the overlook (evil eye) or Fairy shot (the anger of an ill tempered spirit). Sometimes a torch (or candle) was waved over the child or hallowed around them three times to bless the toradh. This can also be done for cattle, especially when they are moved from one pasture to another.

- *Setting of Lights*: a practice for blessing the dead. This term means something completely different in Southern folk magic where it refers to candle magic for any purpose. In this practice, candles are placed at the foot and head of the deceased until they burn out. This is used to drive the darkness out of the corpse as well as bless it against re-animation.

- *Libation*: the practice of feeding the ancestral dead and Faery people for the purposes of strengthening them and the link between the seer and the Fay or ancestors. Offerings such as whiskey, wine, ale, milk, water, honey, grain or apples are poured onto graves, sacred stones and sacred trees, or can be poured directly on the ground or left in vessels for these spiritual beings. They, in turn, consume the toradh of the substance. These offerings are left until they feel cold, clammy and empty. Humans must never eat or drink these libations once they have been offered. It is customary to share a libation with the enchanted ones and the ancestors, but never consume their portion, for this will cause illness or bad luck. *Never offer your blood to them.* Many other world beings would be offended by this and, once the vampiric ones taste blood, they will want more and will not work for you (though they may work against you) unless they have it.

- *Healing*: the practice of repairing or restoring harmony to a person, place or thing by working with siths, Faery companions, blessings, herbal remedies, or the laying on of hands.

- *Flying*: movement or transportation across or between the planes and worlds. An example of this is traveling beyond the hedge.

- *Blessing the Dead*: blessing the dead is an important part of the tradition. Work with the dead cannot be omitted from authentic Seership work in the Faery tradition.

- *Blessing or Blasting*: beneficent (blessing) or maleficent (blasting) magic performed by the seer.

- *Weather Witching*: the use of Faery magic to alter weather patterns.

- *Rogations*: magical techniques to remove or cleanse unwanted influences from the siths of a person.

- *Overlooking, winking or glancing*: a practice of the bad-washer. It is a technique for disrupting the golden cord that connects the sith by projecting toradh through the eyes. In other traditions, it is called "the evil eye" or "the eye that eats."

MAGICAL TIMES

On the eve of the quarter days (Hallowmas, Lammas, Roodmas and Candlemas), the Fay move their houses and the witches gather to greet them. The first Monday after the quarter day is considered most propitious. There are other holidays that they are said to move about, such as Summer Solstice. Lore is clear on one thing about this teaching, the Fay are connected to the movements of the seasons and the life energies through the hidden roads of the land. W.B. Yeats in *Irish Fairy and Folk Tales* shares this lore with us regarding the Faery holidays:

> They [the Faery] have three great festivals in the year – May Eve, Midsummer Eve, November Eve. On May Eve, every seventh year, they fight all round, but mostly on the "Plain-a-Bawn," for the harvest, for the best ears of grain belong to them. An old man told me he saw them fight once; they tore the thatch off a house in the midst of it all. Had anyone else been near they would merely had seen a great wind whirling everything into the air as it passed. When the wind makes the straws and leaves whirl as it passes, that is the fairies, and the peasantry take off their hats and say, "God bless them."
>
> On Midsummer Eve, when the bonfires are lighted on every hill in honor of St. John, the fairies are at their gayest, and sometimes steal away beautiful mortals to be their brides.
>
> On November Eve they are at their gloomiest, for according to the old Gaelic reckoning, this is the first night of winter. This night they dance with the ghosts, and the *pooka* is abroad, and witches make their spells, and girls set a table with food in the name of the devil, that the fetch of their future lover may come through the window and eat of the food. After November Eve the blackberries are no longer wholesome, for the *pooka* has spoiled them.

This quote gives us some important Faery lore: 1) the Fay are connected to the seasons, 2) they act in different ways at different changing points in the seasons (likely, these changes influence the seasonal weather), 3) sacrifices of grain are made to them, 4) The "plain-a-bawn" is probably the plain of plenty in the underworld, since this is a harvest activity occurring it the beginning of summer when the Fay mark the fate of the grain before it grows, 5) they have times of intense activity which brings about whirlwinds that can be destructive (this also shows them tied to the elemental forces), 6) only those humans with the sight can see them, 7) the peasants would bless them for personal protection, and 8) after November Eve (i.e. Hallowmas), all un-harvested vegetative food belongs to the Faery and should not be gathered by humans.

Magical Tools and Their Uses in the Faery Tradition

There are a number of physical implements that are used to conjure or direct the toradh in Faery magic including:

- *The Blasting Rod*: A blackthorn berry or sloe cudgel wand that measures the length of your forearm, or a walking stick or staff. It can be purchased or harvested. This tool is used to summon the dead, for cursing or for removing an influence. If it is harvested, it can be fallen or cut from the tree after you have asked the spirits of the tree and made libations. Traditionally, all cudgels (wooden staves, wands or rods) are harvested on the path of the moon, the direction of the moon's power. This tool is harvested on the dark or waning moon. At least three days prior to the harvest, a thread of cord or twine should be tied around the area marking the place where the limb will be cut. The spirit of the tree should be humbly approached and asked for assistance, and then the thread is tied on so that the spirit will know to draw back its essence from that area. If requested politely, tree spirits will always leave a part of themselves in the rod to give it power. It is preferred that no steel or iron implement be used, though this is not always possible. You will note that metals are rarely used in Faery magic. The lore teaches that metal affects the way the toradh moves. It somehow disrupts its flow. If metals must be used, then gold, silver or copper is used. Stone implements are best. Traditionally, the limb is harvested with one cutting stroke.

- *The Blessing Rod*: A hawthorn (also known as whitethorn) cudgel harvested when the sap is rising during spring or during the growing (waxing) or full moon. Dead or fallen wood is never used, for it bears no fruit. Only live wood is used. Wood that has been struck by lightening or wind-broken can be used if gathered within hours of the strike while the inner bark is still green. Cudgels gathered in this way are very powerful. The blessing rod is used for blessing, healing, enchanting and calling (not commanding) the Fay.

- *The Iron Blade*: A blade of iron with a wooden or bone handle used to severe relationships with a Faery contact or prevent them from entering a space. It can also be used when flying. When it is used while flying, it is traditionally wedged into the door frame of the entryway into the Faery realms. I never use it that way because I am not in an adversarial relationship with these beings. I have used it in rare cases to sever the connection with a contact.

- *The Travelers Rod (the spiral staff)*: A staff that has a natural spiral on it caused by vines such as honeysuckle and wisteria. Because it has been molded into its shape by the fingers of nature, it has great power. It can be of any wood and is harvested live or dead. Its primary use is in visionary traveling, where the seer holds the staff before them and, while slowly turning it, envisions a spiral staircase traveling into the under world. It is also used for opening hidden ways for inter-plane traveling and contact.

- *Silvered Water*: Water that has been blessed with silver. It is used to sain or purify an object, place or person.

- *Hallowed (or) Elf Flame*: A fire that is used for blessing, traveling or calling. It is usually lit without the use of metal (i.e. with flint or the sun's rays). The Beltane fire is an example of an elf flame. It may be a torch used to sain or a bonfire hallowed for traveling or conjuring. It may or may not use specific sacred woods. Even the ashes of the fire and supporting stones can be used in magic and healing.

- *Oak, Ash and Thorn Rods*: This is often called the holy trinity of trees in Faery work. They are very sacred and powerful, and are used for specific purposes. The oak is the guardian tree and is for healing, strength, power and protection. The ash is the traveler's tree and is used for traveling between the worlds. The thorn (hawthorn) is the enchanter's tree and is used for visions and magic.

- *The Ashen Wand*: This wand is made of ash (which is rowan or mountain ash) and is a small cudgel the length of your hand. It is harvested when the rowan berries are ripe and is then stripped, waxed, anointed (with an oil made from the berries) and polished. It is carried to improve communication with Fay.

- *The Hag Stone*: This stone is also called a "Faery stone," "an enchanter's stone" or a "holy stone." It is a stone with a natural hole in it. They are most often found on beaches or near waterways, which is a part of their magic. They can be tied on a red cord and worn or hung in the house (or on an altar) as an amulet to attract the Fay. They can simply be carried as well. Lore says that you can see the Faery by looking through the hole at dusk or dawn. Libations to the Fair Folk are also made through the larger ones. They cannot be purchased. They only have their power if they are found or gifted.

- *The Cup Stone*: This is a naturally occurring cup or vessel shaped stone. Libations are placed in it for the Fair Folk, especially *genii loci* and household spirits such as brownies.

For example, in the Scottish highlands, the *glaistig* is a spirit which steals things, especially cow's milk. Sometimes they are called *Clach na Glaistig*. Theft can be avoided by leaving milk as an offering in a cup stone, also called a glaistig stone.

- *The Talking Stone*: A stone or crystal that speaks to the seer. Literally, it tells the seer magical or prophetic information. It is always either gifted or found and travels with the seer for the duration of their life. It is not any particular type of stone. It can also be a stone from your original homeland. There are other sacred stones used in Faery magic that include the Stone of Destiny and the Ancestral Stone. Often, these stones are from old foundations or from deep within the land.

- *The Silver Branch*: This wand is a single branch of apple wood harvested in the spring before the blossom buds have opened. Apple branches tend to be silver or gray in color. This wand is a key to the other world.

- *The Faery Wind/The Faery Blast*: An enchanted wind that carries either the Fay on the winds or the power of enchantment. This wind is either conjured by the seer or sent by the Fair Folk and is used to curse, bless or cure. It is also called the eddy of wights. Sometimes it is used for flying or traveling. The lore of the wind tells us that it blows from the mystical north and there are charms used to call this wind, such as the following:

"Wind of Wights, eddy of lights ... carry me tonight."

– or –
"Horse and hattock, horse and go in the old ones name."

FAERY HEALING

There are many ways that healing is applied in Faery Seership. Sometimes the seer works with their inner contacts to transmit healing energy to someone or something. In Faery work, healing is not limited to plants, animals and people. It also is used for spirits, places and patterns.

One simple working involves marking the palms of both hands with rose oil in the form of an equal arm cross. Then the seer places their palms on or facing the area to be healed, calls forth the toradh and sends it forth. Usually a partnership with Faery companions is used to mediate this power and knit it into the fabric of the being to be healed. Often Faery beings will stream from the palms (as if the palms were the Faery well) into the patient.

CHARMS AND SPELLS

There are hundred of Faery spells and charms. I have listed only a few of them. These are some of the protective charms used by the conjurer.

- Dig under a mugwort plant on Midsummer's Eve (the night before Summer Solstice). If you find a piece of coal, it will protect you from plague, carbuncles, lightening, burning and many other forms of harm for as long as you live.

- The herb called St. John's wort is a very potent charm against all kinds of illness and bad luck. A sprig of it should be harvested with one single cutting blow using a non-metal edge on the morning of St. John's Eve, also known as Summer Solstice. Carry it that day for good luck and protection and then keep it in your charms bag, in the house or on an altar throughout the year. It should be given back to nature at Yuletide, when the sacred holly is harvested and kept in the house until Candlemas.

- Small stalks of the ragweed plant are carried for flying and traveling between the worlds. In Gaelic tradition they are called *bucolauns* and are seen as one of the steeds of the Fay.

- A piece of antler from the red deer, also known as the Faery steed, ensures strength and health.

- Often coins or silver pins are cast into a river or stream of water before one crosses the bridge to silver or sain it. This is so that the spirits of the water will not vex the crosser.

- Salt is carried (in a packet or pouch) for protection against all forms of maleficent forces.

Oils, Unguents and Teas for Gaining the Sight

All of these oils are provided for your discretionary use and historical insight. They are not to be used for medicinal purposes. Responsibility for the effects of these oils rests solely with the user.

- The following is a Faery Sight unguent recipe from Katherine Briggs' *Encyclopedia of Fairies*. It originates from a 17th century manuscript in the Bodleian Library, University of Oxford (U.K.):

An Ungt. To annoynt under the Eyelids and upon the evninge and morninge, but especially when you call, or finde your sight not perfect. [That is, an ointment to give sight of the fairies] Pt.[precipitate?] sallet oyle and put it into a Viall glasse but first wash it with rose water, and marygold flower water, the flowers be gathered towards the east, wash it til the oyle come white, then put it into the glasse, ut supra. and thou put thereto the budds of holyhocke, the flowers of mary gold; the flowers or toppes of wild time the budds of young hazle, and the time must be gatherred neare the side of a hill where fayries used to go oft, and the grass of a fayrie throne, there, all these putt into the oyle, into the glasse, and sett it to dissolve 3 dayes in the sonne, and thou keep it for thy use; ut supra.

- There is a Faery ointment made of compounded four-leafed clovers. This ointment opens the inner sight to see the Fay. Once the human eye is anointed with it, it is reputed one can see the Faery and into the realms of enchantment.

- The juice from the inner bark of the elder tree applied to the eyelids of a sained child will give them the sight. This will enable them see the Fay especially at Hallowmas, Beltane and the quarter days which mark the changes in the seasons (equinoxes and solstices) when the Fair Ones are moving their homes and trooping.

- A diet that includes eating hazelnuts or acorns also helps to develop the sight.

- An old conjure woman gave me this recipe called Faery Sight Oil. It is reputed to be over 300 years old. I can attest to its effectiveness. When concocted, it should be applied to the forehead (the third eye area). It is ill advised to drive while working with this oil.

  Mix one part of each of the following herbs: 1) dittany of Crete, 2) bucchu leaves, 3) mugwort, 4) Indian hemp (wild collected preferably), 5) mistletoe, and 6) 1/3 part dried (or fresh, which is preferred) broom flowers. Then cook them in oil in a double boiler. I use light mineral oil because it holds the scent well and does not go rancid. Strain the herbs from the oil. It will have a greenish color.

  Add high John (or as we call it "Johnny root") and lavender. The amounts of these two oils depend on the size of the mixture. I add enough to give the scent, but not enough to overpower it. Then, shake well and store in a cool, dark place until the first full moon. Let it set in the light of the moon all night and bring it in before *any* sunrays touch it. It is preferable that sunlight never touches it. Rather, it should only be seen by the light of the moon and stars. The very scent of this oil brings insights and altered consciousness.

- May Day dew is a potent inducer of the sight. On the morning of Beltane, gather a handful of dew from the grass. It is all the better if the dew is from within a ring of dis-colored grass called a Faery ring. This is grass that is greener and thicker than the normal grass around it. Rings of mushrooms or toadstools are also used this way. Simply anoint the eyelids with this dew. I recommend that this rite be performed every year.

SILVER WATER

This is a very old practice for blessing or saining something or someone. Silver is a sacred metal to the Fay and it is magically charged with potency and purity. Silvering involves placing a silver coin or ring into water, praying over it, then drinking it or sprinkling it on a person or thing to protect or heal the subject from malevolent forces. This is the origin of tossing a silver coin into water before you cross it and throwing a coin or pin into a well and making a wish. There are several forms for this working, but the one I received works as follows:

Heat a silver ring or coin over a flame, and then drop it into a bowl or cup of water while saying:

I lift this water in the name of God the Father to do good for the health of the one for whom it is lifted.

White is the Lady.
White is the snow.
By the Lady and by the snow, I do bless this water.
Be thou pure and blessed as the first waters.
All darkness shall flee by your wave.

This water is then sprinkled or drunk.

CHAPTER 13:
GROVES AND SHRINES

Nature stretcheth out her arms to embrace man, only let
his thoughts be of equal greatness. Willingly does she follow
his steps with the rose and the violet, and bend her lines of
grandeur and grace to the decoration of her darling child.
Only let his thoughts be of equal scope, and the frame will
suit the picture. A virtuous man is in unison with her works,
makes the central figure of the visible sphere.

— *"Nature and Other Writings," Ralph Waldo Emerson*

The inherent spirituality of Faery Seership is in the reconnection of humanity with the natural world (its visible and invisible inhabitants) and its life processes, as well as the role of humanity within nature's vast mysteries. However, to tap this wellspring of vision the human seeker must cultivate humility, compassion, courage, grace, and dedication. The mysterious inhabitants of nature's inner world are not as likely as they once were to reach out to a humanity that has turned its back on the mysteries of nature by becoming arrogant, self-righteous, exploitive, self-centered, and greedy. Each human has to part the shades of our self-imposed disbelief and spiritual isolation to reveal a deeper more profound mode of life. This may require long periods of reaching out to the spirit world, only to draw back an empty hand. Eventually, when we give up our need and willfulness, they (the denizens of the unseen company) reach out to acknowledge us.

There are many ways to approach the early steps of building a relationship with the Faery beings and the ancestral spirits. Remember, the majority of humankind has neglected the inner pathways to these worlds for a long period of time. Therefore, there will be brambles and thickets that must be cleared. Most of these thickets exist in our own mental and emotional processes, few are actually in the gateways to Faery. The gateways have never completely closed. There have always been wisdom keepers on both sides of the hedge that have kept the ways open. However, humanity did exert aggressive attempts to close them. Our species has used our own belief systems and sciences (which are often one and the same) to build an iron fence between ourselves and the realms of the spirits and creative forces. The foundations of this fence were reinforced with inquisitions, racism, sexism, ageism, and strategically manipulated social norms that insured that the bulk of the human population would never attempt to tear down the fence. Indeed, most of our kind does not even realize that the fence exists, though so many of the humans we know feel trapped somehow in a life absent of depth, meaning, worth and inner substance. The aims of Faery Seership are not to dispose of the fence. Rather, it is to find and open the gates.

Groves and shrines are intentional gateways to Faery. They are access points into the inner world and places of communion between the species. They are also an intended statement to the inhabitants of the other worlds that we (humanity) are opening our minds, hearts and spirits to rejoin the family of life.

As presented in earlier chapters of this book, there are places all over the surface world where the hidden paths surface naturally. These places are ideal locations for groves and shrines (or what I call interface points). However, these interface points can be opened anywhere, for the hidden paths can always be opened at any place. We do not have to live on a natural place of power for it to become a place of power. When we create the interface points, we have to work diligently and with devotion to keep them open and energized until they are set and integrated into the inscape of the place. The opening of an interface point is sacred. It is a declaration of return and respect to the inner world and should not be taken lightly. The upkeep of a sacred interface point is not a hobby. It is a path and a ministry.

The two general classes of interface points are called shrines and groves. For the sake of clarity and in the context of this book, shrines are interface points that are within a home such as altars and niches. Groves are interface points located outdoors and include cairns (monuments built of small stones in mound, chambered, or ring formations), stones and stone circles, gardens, and outdoor altars. The outdoor groves are the most potent as they are broader in scope and integrated into both the outer and inner landscape of a place. However, indoor shrines are also quite powerful and tap into deep forces if properly and consistently attended. There are many traditional libations, sacred plants, and trees that should be integrated into these practices. They tap into deep and longstanding practices that draw the attention of ancestral contacts, who were wisdom keepers in the human world and are now inner contacts in the Faery realms.

I opened such an interface point on a piece of sacred land in Maryland called the Moonridge Center. Later in this chapter, I will present some of the approaches and general philosophies of the Moonridge work and how they can be applicable to any seeker who works upon the sacred land. Though I know longer dwell at Moonridge, the work shared between the spirits of that sacred land, myself and my students was profound and life changing.

THE INDOOR SHRINE

Indoor shrines are used for two purposes: 1) honoring the spirits of the dead using an ancestral altar, or 2) an area in the house set aside for the house spirit (a Fay) or brownie. It is good practice to have both of these shrines in your house. The brownie is a central figure in the home of a Faery seer. They are a cross between a Faery being and an ancestral spirit. Lewis Spence comments on this connection in *The Fairy Faith in Britain*:

> The "ancestral" character of the brownie appears to me to associate him and his British congeners with the well-established European type connected with the hearth and home, and which may have found a more ancient exemplar in the lar or spirit of the Romans, the dead man, although it is widely distributed throughout the Continent from Russia to Spain and from Scandinavia to the Mediterranean in many forms.

Brownie, is a name derived from the Gaelic word *brunaidh* for house Fays that are usually, but not always, in the form of an old man. Brownies, also called Hobthrusts or Hobthrush, are household spirits which guard and bless the home. They attend the house in the midnight hours and live in the recesses of the house through the day.

They usually reside in a dark area (behind the stairs or in a cubby hole) or behind the door. Traditionally, you should feed them warm milk poured into a brownie stone (a cup stone) every Sunday if possible. However, at a minimum, they should be fed regularly from a dedicated earthen bowl filled with milk and bread or sweet cream and honey. They have great physical strength and prophetic powers which they use to support their adopted human family. It is customary to invite them to warm themselves at the hearth and join in holiday celebrations.

They are very solitary beings and it is rare to have more than one per home. Occasionally there will be one male and one female brownie that attend the home. They tend to stay with a family throughout many generations and be passed on within the human bloodline. To pass them on, the elder of the house must introduce the brownie and their hidden name to their new family head and pass on the customs for feeding and care. They will rarely leave one house to enter another one. However, they are more likely to move if they have a vessel to indwell.

It is relatively simple to attract a brownie into your home. Set aside a place for them as described above and send out a call. When you work with your ancestral shrine, ask an ancestral family member to find one for you or re-introduce one that may already be connected to your bloodline. A warning though: do not treat these beings as pets. They can be loving or grumpy, mischievous or well mannered, but they are never subservient, unintelligent, or dependent. They are powerful Faery contacts that can provide years of protection, prophesy, and good fortune to adults, animals, and children as well as being a guardian against fire, lightening, robbery, and other household concerns. If treated badly, they can leave and take good luck with them. If consistently treated with love, respect and familiarity, they will carry blessings through the family for hundreds of years.

As another brief advice, any time I leave my home for a period of travel, I always let my brownies (and outdoor *genii loci*) know where I am going and when I shall return. I also give them the following request:

Let there be no implosions, explosions, imbalances, or dis-harmonies in our home while I am gone. Welcome all who come here in trust and love. And scare away, but do not harm, any who come here with malice in their hearts.

I always state that I will return a day later than I actually plan to. That way the spirit does not feel deceived or upset by my late return. If something comes up and I cannot return on that date, then I have someone speak to the brownie for me.

This may sound quaint, but I assure you it is not. These

beings are like any other concerned and attached member of the family. Only, the brownie is far more powerful than dear Aunt Dora.

THE OUTDOOR GROVE

The purpose of the outdoor grove is to invite a partnership with the *genii loci*. The location can be identified through the use of dowsing, pendulums, inner work, and observation of the visual landscape. Sometimes it is quite obvious in cases such as an area that already has local superstitions associated with it, an area where all the trees lean inward almost pointing to the power spot, an area where two streams cross, a single hillside, ruins, an opening in the center of the woods, an old graveyard, or any other in-between place. The grove can be as simple as one tree dedicated to the Fair Folk, a small garden, or a small stone circle. If only one tree can be planted, then hawthorn is the most appropriate choice. You may have many or only one stone to mark this area. The most important thing to understand is that, once this area is opened, it is permanently dedicated and consecrated as an interface point between the worlds. It becomes a living classroom where humanity comes to learn about the Fay, and the Fay come to learn about humanity. It is indeed a sacred shrine.

Choose the plants or trees that are sacred to the Faery beings as a good-faith effort toward attracting their attention. Once the area has been identified as a grove, you should perform the Faery well exercise described in Chapter 5, only this time leave the well open. This should be repeated every month until the feeling of enchantment is almost palpable. This exercise opens the inner crossroads or hidden paths to the surface world and affirms that the other-kin are welcomed here. Once a grove has been started, it is permanently holy and open. So, choose wisely and resolve yourself to a long-term commitment. Any wild plants that are removed (erroneously called weeding) should be used as compost. These indigenous plants are composed of the nutrients needed by the soil to be healthy. Avoid using chemicals in the grove. If you must, use them sparingly. Organic fertilizers are always welcomed. Pesticides and herbicides are forbidden. If you must remove destructive insects and other beings, you should first request them to leave. If they do not leave, then you may remove them. If they are persistent, they can be killed, but only using organic approaches and their bodies should be used in the compost. In this manner, these beings are honored as an integral part of the sacred land. There are a number of sacred plants and trees to select from and I have listed some of them below.

SACRED PLANTS

Be mindful of the poisonous plants, especially if you have children or pets. Do not plant them if they may bring potential harm. There are several plants listed that are not poisonous and are safer. I have noted the harmful or baneful ones.

- *Ground Ivy (English Ivy)* – A sacred plant of the under-world. There are initiatory rites wherein the aspirant is wrapped in these vines as a part of the inter-weaving into the underworld.

- *Roses (especially wild varieties with emphasis on red and white colors)* – Both the plant and its scent attract the Fair Folk. Traditionally, a white and red rose bush flanks the entry to the grove. In this, they embody the River of Blood and the River of Tears (semen) also known as the red and white dragon.

- *Flowering broom* – The plant and the blossoms attract the Fair Folk. Often, the dried flowers are used as offerings. *(These are poisonous; do not consume any part of this plant.)*

- *Lavender* – A plant of dark magic. It attracts the ancestral spirits and the knowing ones of the underworld. This herb is used in incense, offerings and tincture preparations.

- *Elecampane (also known as Elfswort)* – This plant attracts the spirits of the woods. The roots, flowers and leaves can also be dried and used as offerings or in spells, charms, and incenses used to work with the Faery people.

- *Foxglove (also known as Fairy Bells or Fairy Caps)* – This plant is very poisonous, but highly attractive to the Faery people.

- *Mugwort (a form of Artemisia)* – This plant can be quite invasive if it seeds, but is very useful in dream and psychic development teas, tinctures, and incenses. It opens the inner sight and is sacred to the hidden company.

- *Datura (also known as Thornapple; very beautiful and very poisonous)* – This plant is a very powerful ally for attracting the ancestral and Faery beings. The seeds can be carried in a leather pouch to open inner sight. The dried whole root is a powerful fetish, but must be handled with gloves when harvested.

- *Thyme* – Used in incenses and tinctures for health and developing the sight, this is one of the lesser known, but more powerful of the Faery herbs. Carrying or consuming this plant enhances the inner sight.

- *Faery Circles* – This phenomenon cannot be cultivated. It has to grow naturally for it to have power. It is a natural circle formed by fungus or molds on grass and believed to be the dancing area of the Fay. They are used as places to leave offerings.

- *Ragwort* – Sadly, in America this plant is often classified as a noxious weed in many regions, but lore has it that the stalks of this plant are used as steeds by the Fay.

- *Clover (especially Oxalis, which is a four leaf clover variety)* – This little plant is always featured in its connection to the Irish solitary Fay called a leprechaun, but in fact it attracts all types of Fay.

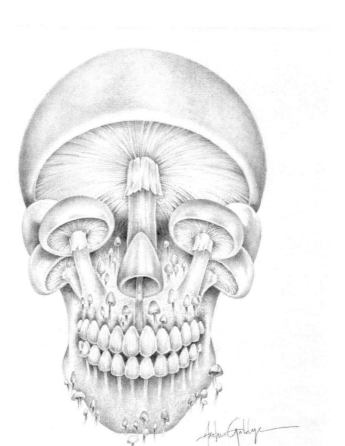

- *St. John's Wort* – This little plant is used in healing and magical work and has been presented earlier in this book as a potent charm. It is also used for developing the second sight.

- *Mushrooms, Toadstools and any Fungus* – They are the Roses of Annwn, the flowers that grow out of death and decay.

- *Marigolds* – The only real folkloric practices associated with this herb is that it is used in 17th century recipes for Faery sight oil. Marigolds, along with Hollyhocks are often mentioned in 17th and 18th century Faery poetry.

- *Any flowers that attract swarming insects (specifically bees), butterflies and birds* – These are all sacred in the Faery ways.

- *Other intoxicating and often-poisonous plants* – Plants such as poppies, belladonna/nightshade, henbane, hellebore, or any of those that have intoxicating scents are also sacred to the Fay.

- *Mandragora* – This is a poisonous sacred herb used to make a special fetish called an *alraun* used as a fetch or guardian spirit. White bryony (sometimes spelled briony) can also be used in this manner.

SACRED TREES

Trees play special roles in Celtic spirituality and magic, including the Faery tradition. There exists a widespread belief that both the souls of the dead and Faery beings inhabit trees. According to tradition, the ancestral dead abide in them while they await reincarnation. Likely, this belief originates from an ancient time when druids and other mystical leaders were interred in trees at death. This has similarity to the lore of burial mounds as abodes of the Fay. Again, we see the connections between the ancestral and Faery traditions. It is still a custom to plant a tree as a memorial to someone deceased in both Celtic and American folk cultures.

An Ulster ballad written by Sir Samuel Ferguson around 1922 and recorded by W.B. Yeats in *Irish Fairy and Folk Tales* speaks beautifully about the lore of some of the Faery trees and their place within magic. There is a great deal of lore in this poem. I have also noted my analysis of the traditional practices addressed in different sections of the poem.

The Fairy Thorn

Get up, our Anna dear, from the weary spinning-wheel:
For your father's on the hill, and your mother is asleep;

Come up above the crags, and we'll dance a highland-reel
Around the fairy thorn on the steep.

Three practices of note are addressed in this stanza: 1) the enchanted hill or mound, 2) the hallowing or dance around a sacred area to open out its power, and 3) the central focus is the thorn (the hawthorn) tree.

At Anna Grace's door 'twas thus the maiden's cried,
Three merry maidens fair in kirtles of the green;
And Anna laid the rock and the weary wheel aside,
The fairest of the four, I ween.

The three maidens are dressed in the primary color of Faery magic (green) suggesting that they were intentionally invoking the powers of the old ways.

They're glancing through the glimmer of the quiet eve,
Away in milky wavings of neck and ankle bare;
The heavy-sliding stream in its sleepy song they leave,
And the crags in the ghostly air:
And linking hand in hand, and singing as they go,
The maids along the hill-side have ta'en their fearless way,
Till they come to where the rowan trees in lonely beauty
*   grow*
Beside the Fairy Hawthorne gray.

The rowan (or mountain ash) also figures strongly in the Faery tradition.

The Hawthorne stands between the ashes tall and slim,
Like matron with her twin grand-daughters at her knee;
The rowan berries cluster o'er her low head gray and dim
In ruddy kisses sweet to see.

This illustrates a triad of trees, which is a common practice in Faery magic. Often, oak, ash and thorn are planted in a triangulated pattern or there may simply be three haunted thorns.

The merry maidens four have ranged them in a row,
Between each lovely couple a stately rowan stem,
And away in mazes wavy, like skimming birds they go,
Oh, never caroll'd bird like them!

But solemn is the silence of the silvery haze
That drinks away their voices in echoless repose,
And dreamily the evening has still'd the haunted braes,
And dreamier the gloaming grows.

As Anna Grace joins the maidens, the magic of their song and dance, coupled with the Faery trees, is shifting the feeling and atmosphere of the place toward an enchanted realm. This is a type of synergistic magic common in Faery workings.

And sinking one by one, like lark-notes from the sky
When the falcon's shadow saileth across the open shaw,
Are hush'd the maiden's voices, as cowering down they lie
In the flutter of their sudden awe.

The "cowering down" and "sudden awe" is indicative of the rapture of the Faery Seer.

For, from the air above, and the grassy ground beneath,
And from the mountain-ashes and old White-thorn
    between,
A Power of faint enchantment doth through their beings
    breathe,
And they sink down together on the green.

The trees themselves are breathing or mediating forth "a power of faint enchantment" as the maidens and the trees (and likely the hill too) sink through substance into the underworld Faery realms.

They sink together silent, and stealing side by side,
They fling their lovely arms o'er their drooping necks
    so fair,
Then vainly strive again their naked arms to hide,
For their shrinking necks are bare.

Thus clasp'd and prostate all, with their heads together
  bow'd,
Soft o'er their bosom's beating- the only human sound-
They hear the silky footsteps of the silent fairy crowd,
Like a river in the air, gliding round.

Now the whole grove has become enchanted. The Faery people enter in as a stream of life in the very air of the place, moving in a circle.

No scream can any raise, no prayer can any say,
But wild, wild, the terror of the speechless three-
For they feel fair Anna Grace drawn silently away,
By whom they dare not look to see.

The three maidens are stricken silent. This is a motif that reoccurs through many old ballads and Faery tales. Also Anna has been taken, because of her fair beauty to the Faery realms. This is another relatively common theme.

They feel their tresses twine with her parting locks of
  gold,
And the curls elastic falling as her head withdraws;
They feel her sliding arms from their tranced arms unfold,
But they may not look to see the cause:
For heavy on their senses the faint enchantment lies
Through all that night of anguish and perilous amaze;
And neither fear nor wonder can open their quivering
  eyes,
Or their limbs from the cold ground raise,

They are caught betwixt and between where they cannot move or speak.

Till out of night the earth has roll'd her dewy side,
With every haunted mountain and streamy vale below;
When, as the mist dissolves in the yellow morning tide,
The maiden's trance dissolveth so.

The haunted mist of the Fay dissolves as dawn arrives and the enchantment retreats. Thus, the maiden's trance is broken and the earth resumes her stance.

Then fly the ghastly three as swiftly as they may,
And tell their tale of sorrow to anxious friends in vain-
They pined away and died within the year and day,
And ne'er was Anna Grace seen again.

Unlike most traditional ballads, Anna Grace did not return to humanity after seven years. The sad ending of the story reveals that the powers of enchantment are not for mere curiosity and delight. Rather, they must be respected. If we open the door to magic with no true intent or purpose, we may be drawn entirely into the Faery realms. It is unclear whether the girls physically die or are initiated into the mysteries of the Faery ways. A year and a day is the traditional period of initial study in the old craft.

There are a number of trees that are sacred to the Fair Folk including: oak, ash, hawthorn, blackthorn, birch, apple, willow, alder, and hazel. Each has their specific magical uses. I rather think of the trees as priests and priestesses in their own right. There are some specific practices related to these trees, some of which were presented in Chapter 12. For example, at Midsummer, it is traditional to *bawm* (adorn) a thorn tree to honor the fertile powers of the Fair Folk. On this same holiday, the alder, also known as elder tree, has the power to grant the Faery sight. The lore also suggests that if one stands under an elder tree at midnight on Midsummer's Eve, they will see the hosts of the Faery ascend from the underworld. An oak should be in or near any grove as it guards against evil spirits.

SACRED STONES

The magical use of stones figures strongly in Faery work. By stones, I do not mean the use of crystals and such in the manner of the New Age movement. Rather, I mean the placement and use of stones as powerful beings and interface points that anchor or mediate certain powers between humanity and the inner powers of the land. I also do not mean a circle of little stones on a dish or drawer. I mean stones that are placed in and on land.

North America, Europe and other countries all over the world are covered with ancient stone monuments. Folk tales abound linking them to Faery beings and ancestral spirits. However, few of us have direct access to ancient stone monuments, so we can,

and should, build ones of our own, for our use and for the generations to come. After all, ancient stone monuments were not always ancient. Someone built them for later use. Stones have multiple functions in Faery and ancestral work including:

- marking a place of power
- holding open an inner gateway
- guarding a place of power
- housing spiritual forces
- bridging between two realms
- mediating certain spiritual potencies
- stabilizing destructive forces

Some lore likens standing (upright and elongated) stones to "soul houses" for their shape resembles a coffin. Tales are prevalent of the Fair Folk dancing around sacred stones, which suggest that stones have always been figured as primary interface points between the worlds of humanity and enchantment. Some lore presents the placement of upright stones as a type of acupuncture in which stones are placed in meridians on the land to activate power. The tradition called these meridians "Faery trods" or "Faery tracks." They are the roads used by the Fair Folk during the passing of seasons and should always be incorporated into the placement of the stones.

Stones may be placed singly or in groups, standing or laying, in or on the land. They may be a marker for the borderland between the worlds, a cluster of stones (usually three) forming no specific geometric pattern, or a circle of stones. Cairns or altars are often built as the focal points in Faery groves. Sometimes, they are installed by humans to tap or mark a special place of power or inner contact. Other times, they are put in place by nature herself. The stones are homes to the *dii terreni* or spirits of the earth (*The Fairy Tradition in Britain*, Spence). They are the Gaelic *Frideans* which are the most ancient beings on the planet. The Frids hold within them the history and power of both the planet and our race. Sacred stones can be used for prayer, inner contact, blessings, curses, initiations, as well as for many other purposes. If you and the *genii loci* decide that stones will be used in a grove, try to use indigenous ones. They have a stronger resonance with the land. Once in place, they will need to be fed on a regular schedule using libations. In addition, sacred stones traditionally have crystalline formations in them. This gives the stone the ability to receive and transmit spiritual forces.

In some designs, stones are placed at the four compass points, especially if a stone circle or ring cairn is used. In this type of design the four stones mediate the powers of the four Faery winds, cities, provinces (stellar, solar, lunar, and planetary), primary Faery clans, and streams of power that flow into the land. The traditional libations for the four quarter stones are: a) east receives honey, b) south receives ale, wine, mead, whiskey, rum, or some other spirit (this replaces the old offering of blood), c) west receives water, and d) the north receives milk. These libations are poured onto the stones (or into cup stones if they are used) at each turning of the seasons and whenever they are approached for favors.

Lastly, the sacred flame is used throughout the Faery practices. In fact, the mystery of the star within the stone has been a central aspect of the Faery teachings in this book. It embodies the spiritual essence in matter and the liberation of the Child of Promise. This mystical truth can be embodied in a sacred flame centered within a circle of sacred stones. In this way, it is the star that shines within the sacred stone and is the holy nemeton of the Druidic practices and the hallowed flame of traditional witchcraft.

It also embodies that holy flaming door through which comes the lords and ladies of the living flame, the Faery people. Therefore, a sacred well of flame or bonfire pit is a potent part of the outdoor grove.

WELLS AND SPRINGS

Any natural opening into the earth is a portal to the Faery realms, including caves, springs, wells, rock holes, and sink holes. But none of these figure more notably than wells and springs. These sacred waterways are featured in both Celtic religion (in the veneration of deities and saints) and folk magic including Faery lore and tutelary spirits. Today, many of these are dedicated to Catholic saints, but likely this was not always the case. Lewis Spence notes:

> Many wells and springs in Britain and France are dedicated to saints, and these fountains in ancient times, most authorities are persuaded, were regarded as resorts or dwelling-places of pagan deities or fays.

Interestingly, this phenomenon can be found all over the world in varied cultures. Sacred wells and springs as well as their waters are used for prayer, healing, cleansing, visionary work, offerings, and meditation. These holy places are usually marked by stone structures such as niches, chapels, shrines, and stone walls around or near them. The sacred waters are seen as portals where all sorts of underworld beings including ancestral, Fay and the Dreamer in the Land surface.

In Celtic tradition, water is the mystical element that links the unseen world of the spirits with humanity. It rises from the deep underworld. Therefore, it is not surprising that it would be seen as fey. Nigel Pennick illustrates this beautifully in his book *Celtic Sacred Landscapes*:

> The Celts believed that at night the sun sank beneath the waters, emerging from them again at sunrise. During the night, the illuminating and healing powers of the sun was absorbed by the waters. The tradition of incubation at holy wells, where the patient slept all night near the waters, invoked the nurturing powers of the underworld sun.

In Faery Seership, the underworld sun *is* the Lord of the Faery realms. Therefore, this practice may invoke the healing powers of the earth of light.

Feathers of Fortune

Wishes, in the form of strips of cloth, are often tied to the branches of trees growing around sacred springs and wells. These "clootie cloths" or "feathers of fortune" are tied either to leave behind sickness or woe or to ask for a blessing from the spirits, especially at the auspicious times of Hallowmas and Beltane when the hosts of the dead or the Fay rise or fall into the land and bring forth life (spring) or draw it inward (fall) to the regenerative powers of the underworld. In my tradition, there is a lovely charm spoken as these strips of cloth are tied at Beltane:

Feather of fortune, torn from a rag;
harken the maiden and hail to the hag.

Powerful Faery teachings are encoded into this simple, but profound charm. It illustrates that the power of fortune and luck is in a simple household object, an old rag. This is why a silk scarf would never be used, for it embodies greed and conceit. Rather, a simple rag cut from an old bed sheet, shirt, or blouse is the most appropriate. As the feathers are tied, the seeker chants to dismiss to the old year and decay of the Faery hag while welcoming the new possibilities embodied in the Faery maiden of the spring. It is best to use cotton material as it is biodegradable. The sacred birds then come to take your wish to the Faery Queen or tear apart your illness scattering it to the four winds of change.

TRADITIONAL OFFERINGS AND LIBATIONS

Traditions about what libations to offer to the Fair Folk and ancestral beings abound throughout the Celtic lands and in America. These practices are quite old and appear to have been problematic to the medieval church in England as noted by Keith Thomas in *Religion and the Decline of Magic*:

> The practice of setting out food and drink for the fairies had been well known in the middle ages and was inevitably condemned by the leaders of the Church, who naturally resented the propitiation of other deities. To ecclesiastics it seemed that people who left out provisions for the fairies in the hope of getting rich or gaining good fortune were virtually practicing a rival religion.

It is fortunate that, despite repeated attempts by the Church to stop this practice, it has continued into modern day on both sides of the Atlantic, in Europe and America.

There is a general consistency in what is offered to the Fay in historic folkloric practices, which include the following:

- Honey
- Water
- Milk and bread (together)
- Mead or wine
- Ale or beer
- Whiskey or rum (specifically in American Southern lore)
- Grains (such as barley, wheat, and maze in America)
- Corn or wheat dollies
- Oat cakes and butter
- Votive offerings of fire and incense (burning herbs, seeds, stems, roots, flowers, woods, and resins)
- Sacred herbs
- The first and last or best fruits of the harvest

Feeding the Fay is not only a practice to secure their favor, it also feeds and energizes the connection between humanity and the Faery people. However, the Faery and ancestral spirits do not consume the physical substance of the offering, but rather as Robert Kirk states:

> Some [Fairies] have bodies or vehicles so spongeous thin and dessicate that they are fed only by sucking into some fine spirituous liquor [essence] that appears like pure air or oil. Others feed more grossly upon the core substance of corn and liquor or on corn itself, that grows on the surface of the earth.

Dance and music are also forms of offerings acceptable to the elder race, but they cannot substitute for the aforementioned food and beverages. In fact, Faery beings are attracted by all forms of beauty, especially the arts. Wind and string instruments are particularly favored. They are also drawn to a soft melodious singing voice. However, these offerings must be given in the spirit of humility and honor. It is unwise and arrogant to match your artistic abilities with the Fair Folk. Such bad behavior will reap bad rewards.

THE MOONRIDGE PROJECT

It is important to remember that the use of groves and shrines are a very powerful part of Faery work. They play a crucial part in re-establishing a human relationship with the natural and spiritual worlds. The importance of these interface points cannot be over-stressed. If we, the seekers, are going to rejoin the sacred family of creation, we must make a place, a home, and a sanctuary for them. Only our consistent commitment and dedication will prove that our interests are not merely curiosity, hobbies, pastimes, or another attempt at spiritual or monetary exploitation. I made that commitment in the form of the Moonridge Project. For the duration of my time living on this land, Moonridge became a learning center and haven for many beings (human and other) that endeavor to recreate Eden, that garden of beauty and balance, which is the heritage of all of the Earth Mother's children.

The History

For over seven years, my home was located on a lovely twelve acre patch of land in Maryland, USA. It was the site for a nature spirit and human learning center, a sanctuary, and a testament to the power of Faery work.

This land had a history of abuse, exploitation and neglect. It was originally the site of a sand and pebble quarry. Considerable strip mining destroyed all the topsoil on about eight acres of the land, leaving it barren and badly harmed. In fact, the crest of the 25-foot ridge was once the grass line of a sloping hill. This area was blasted and dug out by machines for the harvest and sale of sand and pebbles. In ancient times, Moonridge was at the bottom of the Chesapeake Bay, which in turn was once part of the Atlantic Ocean, so it abounds with beautiful sea pebbles. The mined acreage literally looked like the surface of the moon, barren and desolate.

In the early 1980s, a lovely visionary woman named Kathy purchased the land and began its regenerative transformation. She built two geodesic dome structures that, during my stay on the land, housed an indoor temple, a training center, and my home. She also removed many of the old abandoned cars, barrels, and assorted trash that littered the land. She did some direct work with the land, but her health and age prohibited significant work. Her philosophy was "I am leaving the land to do its thing – grow and change. If the land is left alone, it will heal itself." And thus, the healing of this land began.

In the mid 1990s, I and a few other people moved to Moonridge shortly after the death of Kathy, the matron of Moonridge. By that time, Moonridge had several years to begin its healing and build on the good energies brought here by Kathy, her family, tenants, and the many people who performed sacred rites and healing practices in its ten years as a holistic retreat center. Sadly however, some of the land healed while a large area in the back was still littered, deforested, and barren. Our mission was to build on Kathy's work and then transform Moonridge into a sanctuary, living classroom, and learning center for the Faery ways. This, we all understood, would require a determined and committed co-creative partnership between those of us living and worshiping there (the humans) and the creative intelligence of Moonridge (the Faery and other nature beings).

Soon after we moved onto the land, one person visited us here and exclaimed (about the desolate mined area). "Oh, I would just leave this part of the land alone, it is trash land." This statement clearly embodied the destructive and arrogant attitude of so many of our fellow humans, especially those who harmed this land. His statement only served as further fuel for our resolve to be good neighbors to nature.

Shortly after the move, I (as the resident seer) began having clear visions about the inner workings of Moonridge, its power places, *genii loci* and areas for healing. During the early phases of this project, I became inspired as I read the works of Perelandra and Findhorn. Like Perelandra, Findhorn works with the inherent nature intelligences to guide its development. This resonated well with me, and was congruent with the mission of Moonridge and the Faery teachings as I understood them, for it inferred a partnership. Needless to say, the combination of the two was the affirmation I needed to move forward. I truly thank Ms. Wright and Perelandra, as well as the staff of Findhorn for their trail-blazing work.

Although these pioneers were definite inspirations to me, unlike Perelandra and Findhorn, I chose to build a foundation based on traditional Faery lore and techniques. The Moonridge project was destined to be unique because it focused on applying the teachings of the folkloric Faery tradition to an outcome-based learning and healing process. Indeed, the outcomes have been dramatic and inspiring.

Moonridge's mission, under guidance from the Faery realms, was to approach and regenerate the land with contemporary practices based on the foundation of historical, traditional, and folkloric Faery tradition. Part of the process involved countless hours of visionary work everyday to develop processes, techniques, and information, based on revelations received directly from the inner world, combined with traditional practices. Soon, the spirits of Moonridge revealed the three campuses (as they call them) of Moonridge: 1) the front area, which is dominated by the nature spirits, 2) the middle area, which is dominated by humans, and 3) the third area (the barren land), which is the partnership area. I found this designation of campuses as fascinating, for it demonstrated that a living community of seen and unseen beings could live in harmony and respect for each other.

The partnership campus soon became the primary focus of our work. This area, which I call the enchanted woods, became the living classroom where we humans, the Fay, and the natural world could re-acquaint ourselves, and learn about each other and how to partner. The central goal of the partnership was (and is) the regeneration of Moonridge and the refinement and dissemination of the Faery teachings. The healing excelled – truly excelled. Spiritual teachers from all over the globe began lecturing here and commenting on the power of this place. We began hearing constant comments from visitors about the spiritual presence of Moonridge and the beings and visions that are seen here. The partnership was bringing forth powerful results experienced by people even before they knew the nature of the Moonridge project.

Tirelessly we cleaned out tons of discarded tires, trash, decaying carpets, and other rubbish. We laid out leaves, chipped wood and other organic material to decay and build up the soil. We planted trees and plants. We shipped in hundreds of pounds of medium to large stones (for that was a part of what was taken from this land).

Each step was taken based on advice from the Fair Folk. This ranged from what needed to be cleaned out to what plants should be planted where and when. Each new plant became a welcomed neighbor integrated into the bio-system of Moonridge, a lovely pattern surfacing from the Earth of Light. Each week, new beings began to reveal themselves and their role at moonridge.

The power places of Moonridge also began to surface, which now includes the cairn, a stone circle, and the sacred spring, as well as smaller, more hidden sites. Along with this came the rules of the inner world of Moonridge. These power places and interface points had evolved many functions such as classrooms of study, places of pilgrimage, meditation sanctuaries, and outdoor temples. Now, seven years after our relocation to Moonridge, it stands as a living, vibrant, powerful affirmation to the potency of the alliance between humanity and the beings of nature that live on both sides of the veil. The barren land is green and growing in its vitality every year. Though we have moved from this land, the partnership changed the inner and outer landscape of Moonridge forever, leaving it as an embodiment and affirmation of the the power of inter-species partnerships for co-creation and harmony upon the sacred land.

The Moonridge Interface Points

There are many areas of great power at Moonridge, but the primary living classrooms we developed are the Faery cairn and the stone circle. Interestingly, these sacred groves are located in the areas of the enchanted forest that were in the worst shape. However, the spirits of the land were clear that they were points of great power. To this day, everyone who visits these locations concurs that they are, indeed, between the worlds.

- *The Faery Cairn* – A circular stone grove that is the primary Moonridge interface point with the unseen company. Since its construction, I have officiated the building and activation of several cairns of the same design and intent at different places around the country. Many activities occur at the cairn including meditation, vision work, magic, and inter-plane instruction. All building and land development is planned based on advice received from the Fay at the cairn. The power of this design has grown so strong that a silver amulet bearing its shape has been developed for many of the students of the Faery teachings, and you, the reader, have seen this design at the beginning of each chapter. Many sacred plants grow in or around the cairn including thyme, ground ivy, lavender, roses, apple trees, broom, mandrake, and flowering plants such as butterfly bushes to attract the hive insects. Many people have seen Faery beings in and around the cairn. It was the center of our work at Moonridge and still beats as the heart of Moonridge.

- *The Stone Circle* – It is composed of four standing stones averaging between two and three tons, each aligned to the compass directions and the pole star. They stand for the four streams of Faery magic and are the primary mediators for the stellar, solar, lunar, and planetary powers, as well as the four winds of change to the magical grove. A stone altar sits to the northeast (the place of the ever-becoming) and a cauldron for the sacred flame sat at the center. This was removed when we re-located. One pine tree was growing in the grove and was incorporated into the site. It stands for the sacred Bilé, or *axis mundi*.

Moonridge Partnership Activities

There were some ongoing activities which we integrated into all of our work at Moonridge. I believe that these added a great deal to crystallizing our partnership with the land. They involved changes in attitude and behavior in daily and spiritual life on the land. Indigenous cultures already do these practices and I advise all seekers to integrate them into their work. These practices include:

- Invite the *genii loci* into all ceremonies and spiritual rituals that you perform on your land, including holiday celebrations. The Fay should be considered as a part of your community and family.

- All planting, clearing, building, and harvesting should be done in partnership with the spirits of the land. This means that any time you perform, or intend to perform, these activities, you should approach the Fay for their input on such things as timing and placement. They will ensure that your actions are balanced with the inner and outer integrity of the ecosystem.

- Designate an area of the land that you steward (there is no such thing as a land owner), which is solely dedicated to the spirits of your land. At Moonridge, we have the nature spirit campus. All activities in this area should be focused only on the well being of the land. Human contact with it should be minimal.

- Offer libations on a regular schedule to feed the inter-plane connection. This can be done at indoor shrines or outdoor groves. Outdoor libations are always the most effective, except when working with the brownie or familial ancestral spirits.

- Open out an interface point in your home or on your land and work with it consistently. This will re-establishe a con-nection between you, the land and the unseen company.

CHAPTER 14:
THE FAERY GIFTS
AND THE FAERY LOVER

When first you came on midnight's hour, your lips were made
of flame.
A stranger passing by you said, I need not know your name.
Your cloak was soft with feathers and your eyes lit from within,
and the kisses that you gave to me I never got from kin.
No mortal man had touched me soft, nor yet come to my bed,
until the night a stranger came and took my Maidenhead.
You came to me at midnight's hour, you did not come at noon.
You wore the antler horns my love, my Horseman of the Moon.

When next you came the sun was high, you made my body sing.
Your name you would not give to me you gave instead a ring.
Your shoes were made of dragons skin, your touch was like a burn.
And you taught the art of loving to a young girl swift to learn.
No mortal man could swell my heart or cause me so much pain,
that I would leave my kith and kin to lie with him again.
You came to me at noon's high tide you beckoned me to come.
You wore a diadem of Light, my Dancer in the Sun.

The third time was at dawn glow and you cast a circle round.
You sealed it with a shouted name that echoed without sound.
You wore a shirt of Elven green, your lips they smiled at me,
and the bonny lad we got that day my world will never see.

No mortal man could give such bliss or sire me such a boy
or promise me another babe to fill my heart with joy.
You came to me at dawn glow and I followed without fear,
through the doors of destiny, My Singer of the Crystal Sphere

I came to you through gates of Stone that circle on the mound.
Your Elven name you gave to me, a secret silver sound.
Upon my feet are golden shoes I go in scarlet dressed.
My bed is where you rest your head, your mouth against my breast.
No mortal man my husband be, with him my soul I'll share.
And if so be I'm damned for this, that sorrow will I bear.
And yet I know and know full well, that love it knows no bars
and I will love for nevermore, My Walker on the Stars.

– *"The Unknown Lover," Dolores Ashcroft-Nowicki*

As we approach the closure of this treatise, you may wonder what is the end result of the Faery Seership practices? Well, there are many mystical experiences to be gleaned and revelations of wisdom in the practices of Faery Seership. They can be sought earnestly and won through devoted effort, but they cannot be seized and exploited. As the seeker masters the techniques, builds inner Faery and ancestral alliances and clears the thorn thickets that guard the way, there are certain magical gifts that are bestowed upon him or her. However, the road to these gifts is paved with challenges and ordeals as illustrated in all of the Faery tales.

The gifts do come to those who do the work. Remember, these gifts are the Faery gold which cannot be stolen, though they may be earned. Otherwise it turns to straw when brought to the surface world or brings ancestral curses upon the thief. The bonnie road to Faeryland requires an abiding inner silence from the seeker if they are to hear its teaching and guiding voices. It is the voice of our fear and longing that initially speaks the loudest. Then, the voices of the ancestors cry out for redemption, challenging the seeker on the silent road to the throne. This may be one of the greatest of challenges, for the path to the throne of dominion leads through the Cave of Voices and these ancestral voices will, and must, be heard. They are embedded in the River of Blood, which flows through every seeker. The moment we enter into the other world, we begin wading through the River of Blood. Know this: we are all stained with the passions of our ancestry. We are all born to redeem them.

The Faery magic will not be released to us without the "heart of innocence" that comes when we work to redeem ourselves and our ancestors. This redemption begins the process of deep, abiding healing. For true spiritual development involves recognition that our destinies are intertwined with other beings and our ancestors. There are simply no short cuts or ways around this. *If you want a less intense path, do not tread the enchanted ways of Faery.*

The Faery realms operate very differently from our own. We do not set the rules, though we do set our own challenges. The first rule is that the natural world is its outer temple and the seeker's mind is the key. If the seeker has no respect for the natural world, then their every effort will be thwarted. Use of this mind key can be tricky, as humans tend to know less about what resides within them and more about what appears around them. This key opens the flaming door to the heart, wherein dwells our deepest treasures. However, there can be no delusion in the quest for this key or it will slip out of the seeker's hands as illusive as the wind, always just out of reach. For this key is one and the same as the golden cord that connects all things. Our minds and hearts are the hands that grasp it. The seeker must be honest in all thoughts, words and deeds, for integrity is a must for in the Faery world and the seeker's, word is their bond.

Though this path is ancient and well worn by the footprints of the wise, it is also fraught with guardians and riddles. Our own minds create these guardians of the threshold. Only those persons who seek to return the crown to the Queen and free the Child of Promise trapped in the secret tower will have the unstained heart of a child that knows the simple answers to the riddles and the faith to see the beauty hidden behind an ugly face. These are statements directly from the Faery teachings and major keys to the hidden ways.

So what are the gifts that come to the true seeker? The beautiful poem at the beginning of this chapter tells of the most coveted of treasures, the Faery lover. The Faery lover often leads to the Faery marriage, an eternal symbiosis between the seeker and their Faery lover. As this enchanting and beautiful poem illustrates, this is not a normal love affair. It is a completion of the soul and no human lover can ever quite match the power of the romantic unseen hand. In addition to the Faery lover, which is perhaps the most intense of all the gifts, there are others. Each of these gifts brings potent skills in varying levels to the evolved seer. Although there are other gifts, these are primary:

- *Cousins and Co-walkers* – The inner world allies that become a part of an inter-plane team between the seer and the Faery beings and ancestors.

- *The Second Sight* – Enhanced psychic ability and the ability to perceive and understand the spirit world, which includes the spirit tongue. The spirit tongue is often discussed in folklore as the gift of two tongues or voices, one for humanity and the other for the ancestral and Faery spirits as well as deities.

- *The Tongue That Cannot Lie* – Prophetic ability as well as the "anointed tongue," which speaks words of great power in the form of poetry, invocations, chants, songs, and other inspired orations.

- *The Faery Breath* – Also called "the Breath of the Land," the ability to be the voice for the land, the Fay and the ancestors, and the ability to mediate power from the Faery world to the surface world through the breath. This gift allows the seer to stand in for the land and speak for it as its human tongue.

- *Turning* – The Faery term for magic, including the ability to curse, cure and bless. Glamour, the ability to enchant others through a type of otherworldly charisma, is also a part of the skills of turning.

- *The Faery Touch* – The ability to mediate contact from the Faery realms to the surface world. Often, the Faery touch gives the seer the ability to heal. It also allows the seer to transmit inner contact outward and link another human into a chain of Faery contact. This brings about what can be best described as initiation. In order for a seer to initiate through the touch, they themselves must have been touched and brought into the inner clan.

- *Shape Shifting and Flying* – Skills associated with transformation and movement through many worlds, planes and experiences. The more enchanted the seer becomes, the more these skills evolve.

- *The Acquisition of Enchanted Tools* – Physical implements that come to the seer through Faery magic. Lore tells of such things as enchanted hats, rods, stones, kettles, ovens, necklaces and rings which have some magical ability granted to it by Faery beings. Most seers have a collection of these that come over years and are passed to their heir.

- *The Faery Lover / Marriage* – Marks the latter stages in a Faery seer's development. A Faery being, traditionally of the opposite gender, often presents itself as a cousin, ally and co-walker and eventually a full partner. If the relationship evolves toward a full symbiosis of the human and Faery partners, then the marriage takes place. There are rigid traditions about this. It is not a practice taken lightly. When the marriage occurs, it is for eternity.

THE MYSTERIES OF THE FAERY LOVER

Perhaps one of the most prevalent but most misunderstood and trivialized gifts in the Faery practices is the concept of the Faery lover or Faery marriage. Far from being a mere erotic fantasy regarding sexual exchange with a spirit, this concept embodies a very powerful and sacred aspect of Faery Seership practices and associated spiritual practices.

The Faery marriage involves a merging of human and Faery intelligence into a symbiotic relationship that heals the fractured nature of both beings, brings them into direct communion with the unfolding vision of the universe, and fulfills the destiny of humanity to bring its free will into oneness with the will of the planet earth and, consequentially, the stars. In this way, humanity brings heaven to earth and returns it back again. I receive many calls from people who have encountered a spirit being that they identify as "Fay," felt the enchantment of the connection (as well as the sensuality) and immediately feel that they should marry this being. Clearly, though well meaning, these people do not understand the meaning of a Faery marriage nor the implications. For this reason, I have detailed the process that leads to the Faery marriage. *Very few students of Faery Seership ever make it to this level of exchange with the Fay.*

The true Faery marriage requires immense inner work and transformation of the self on every level and usually takes seven to nine years at a minimum to achieve. This level of exchange can produce initial unsettling and difficult changes in the human seeker. Most seekers are not suited to this level of exchange. The Faery gifts detailed above are a direct result of a process of engagement, exchange and symbiosis between the human seeker and the Faery contact. This process is best described as levels or phases of contact and exchange with predictable elements or symptoms related to each phase. Below, I have provided a detailed review of this process, so the reader can understand that the Faery marriage is not a trivialized spirit romance. It is the rare product of two beings sharing knowledge, power, essence and destiny. It is also connected to an ancient alliance between two species. In the end, the marriage is what makes a seer and gives them the ability to open out and fuse contacts between other humans and Faery beings as a mediator and bridge for both species. Understanding these levels will greatly enhance the student of Faery Seership's ability to understand their relationships with the Fay.

The levels of contact and exchange with a Faery being are as follows:

1st Stage: The Contact

During this phase of exchange, the human seeker and the Faery being encounter each other for the first time. Most often this occurs during visionary or magical processes aimed at opening inner contact outward into this world (i.e., "thinning space," opening the way" or "opening the well" techniques), or sending outer perception inward through meditative techniques (i.e., "flying," "traveling" or "journeying"). Occasionally, this encounter happens during near-death experiences or disturbingly at haunted places such as forests, lakes, sea-shores, ancient sites and other places that are "betwixt and between," At this point both entities (human and Fay) experience recognition and resonance with each other which causes initial shifts in energetic patterns and perception. A human seeker will make many contacts in the course of their Seership work.

2nd Stage: The Cousin

During this phase of exchange, contact has already been made (as discussed above) and begins to develop a deeper affinity or familiarity. The human begins to notice a resonance with the Faery being and communication becomes more consistent, personal and impacting on both beings. The cousin will begin to appear in nearly every meditation or visionary technique employed by the human that allows interchange between the surface and under worlds. At this level, the contact has moved from mere recognition into a level of exchange that may feel to the human like a friendship. Humans often report that they feel a kindredship with their cousin that feels familial.

3rd Stage: The Co-Walker

During this level of exchange, the cousin becomes so much a constant in the life of the human (and vice versa) that the two seem to walk together through both levels of life. Thus, the name "co-walker" is used to describe this phase. Most contacts that move beyond the cousin phase to co-walker never move beyond this phase. In fact, if a human seeker develops a relationship with a co-walker, they will receive many of the Faery gifts. The co-walker is an ally and familiar spirit in the work of the human. The human is also an ally and familiar spirit to the Fay. Often, the co-walker appears as a miniature or modified image of the human seeker because they (the Fay) are reflected through the magnetic virtues of the dream walker. This occurs for two reasons: 1) sometimes the encounter is not Faery, but is indeed an encounter between the surface walker and the dream walker of the human seeker; or 2) the Faery being is making contact at a deeper level with the human seeker through impacting the dream walker as an interface and incorporating some of the dream walker's imagery into its projections. This aspect will shift after a while and the Fay will take on an image of its own based on the images stored in the central nervous system of the human seeker or on other resources such as those within the River of Blood, those inherited from previous ancestors in the human's lineage or elements found in the larger human psychic pool. Often, the human will experience major emotional and sensual experiences in this phase due to the intimate levels of exchange and contact between the two beings. These feelings can be misinterpreted as erotic and sensual, which is not the intention of the Fay. These feelings are just a manner in which the human is experiencing the exchange of energy and deep contact. The human seeker is advised to raise their awareness to a more refined level that allows them to move beyond a procreative reaction to a spiritual exchange and communion of light.

4th Stage: The Companion (The Lover) and the Ring of Light

During this level of exchange, the cousin and human become even more constant in each other's lives. A deeper affinity grows between both beings as they share the surface and underworld lives and cultures of both the human and Faery worlds. Powerful energetic shifts begin to happen to the human seeker that are experienced as sensual feelings, hot flashes, major shifts in sensory perception, synesthesia (the mixing of senses), sudden flashes of awareness without apparent traceable sources and the feeling of deep companionship. At this level, the human experiences major readjustments to their energetic bodies, which allow for a clarification of imprinting and other forms of communication from the Faery companion. Visions tend to come spontaneously to the human as the Fay opens energetic pathways to the human that previously were closed. There will be nearly daily contacts sessions for the exchange of information about both species and the human and Fay initialize a symbiotic life with each other. During visionary processes, imprinting sessions, journey work and dream sessions, the human being may begin to see or sense the presence of a ring of light that is passing around, through and even touching both the human and Fay. Often, this is experienced in both the dream walker (in visions, dreams, etc.) and the surface walker in energetic sensations and actual visual sightings of a stream of light passing from the other world into the body of the human seeker. In Seership tradition, this experience is called "the Ring of Light" and is the energetic wedding band of the two beings beginning to emerge. The ring of light denotes serious shifts in both beings that often may herald the beginning of the marriage level of contact and exchange.

5th Stage: The Consort (or Marriage)

During this phase of exchange, the folk rite of Faery marriage occurs. This simple rite mediates the essence and existence of the Ring of Light through and into the bodies of the human and Fay and completes the symbiosis that transforms both the human and the Fay into "other" (see below). In some older witchcraft traditions, this brings through the Faery blood that transforms a human seeker into a witch. Traditionally speaking, the rite must be performed by a contacted seer who is already in-dwelled by a Faery or otherworld being. It requires a full overshadowing of the Fay contact in the body of an opposite gender human host. This part of the rite is essential for the merging of the energetic bodies of the human and the Fay to occur in this world as well as the other. The marriage is not a spontaneous event that suddenly occurs in the life of a human seeker. Many students contact me saying it occurred in their dreams and now they are married. It is doubtful, if not impossible, that the full marriage is occurring in these reports. Likely, the human is perceiving the changing and more intimate patterns of their contact in their dreams or they are simply projecting their wishes, fantasies or pathologies into the dream world and incorporating a Fay image into the internal fantasy-scape. The marriage does not "just happen". The Fay will not and cannot force a human into this level of partnership and a human cannot force it upon a Fay. This phase occurs as a natural part of an unfolding process. When it is time for the marriage to occur, the would-be seer will have consistent contact from the Fay and a host for the marriage will be available. In other words, the spirit world will ensure that all is in place for the blessed event to occur.

6th Stage: The Co-creation of "Other"

This is not the final phase of exchange, but the opening of a new horizon of spiritual growth and power for the human seeker and the Faery contact. Once the marriage has truly occurred, the full transformation of the human seeker into seer begins. Phases 1-5 clarified and strengthened the connections between the human seeker and the Fay and energized a transformation in both. The result is the birthing of a new type of being that is not fully human nor fully Fay, and the human mediates this being through their incarnate lives into the surface world while the Fay mediates it into non-carnate life into the underworld. In many ways, the human has now become one of the "enchanted ones," a term used to describe a host of magical beings. The "other" is a living bridge for the Faery and human races, gifted with deep running spiritual wisdom and magical skill. They are also uncanny in their nature and definitely otherworldly. There are few of these beings. Many would describe an "other" as one with one foot in both worlds. As I describe my Faery marriage to my students, "when I close my eyes, I see into her world; when I open them, she (my Faery Queen) sees into mine."

THE TREE OF ENCHANTMENTS

Opening the hidden gates that lie between this world and the Faery realm begins a powerful and sometimes disturbing spiritual adventure and transformational process. Many spirit encounters happen along this path before and after the Faery marriage. The journey to open the sacred well, which is the portal to the realms of enchantment, begins by encountering the mysterious forces of nature and her spiritual beings and the human ancestral wisdom in our blood. When the spiritual forces of nature and ancestry come together within us, they open the portal to the underworld, a great enchanted well. Once this sacred well opens to the seeker, a process is initiated that allows them to perceive a level of spiritual life heretofore unknown or hidden just beyond view. There are many beings that reside at the threshold between the worlds and in the star and sea realms and they are encountered along the way. These beings shape our destinies and hold many keys to the doors of our potentials as human and spirit beings. In the Faery Seership practices, the process of the journey, beings encountered at the three levels of life, and a mass of other lore associated with the journey and the attunement processes are detailed in what I term as "the Tree of Enchantments."

Working with the Tree of Enchantments attunes us to the sacred tree that aligns the three worlds. Initially the tree is inverted in the journey into the underworld. It goes upright when the seeker brings their three walkers into unity and marries the dream walker with one of the "angels in the land." The information in this chapter gives a brief introduction to some of the vast beings on the Tree of Enchantment. Work with the inner contacts of the Tree of Enchantments, and most specifically, the Faery beings, transforms the seeker and makes them ready for a potential Faery marriage. Regardless of the whether the marriage occurs in this life or another, the human is always transformed by the encountering the forces of this sacred tree. As we say in the Faery Seership tradition, we first bit the apple from the tree of wisdom and gained free will, now the second one brings wisdom. But, we must return to the edenic paradise of Faery for that sacred apple, which grows on the Tree of Enchantments. What and who will we encounter in the journey? Well, that depends on the nature of the seeker and the depth of their venture. However, no matter what level or where the seeker journeys in the three worlds of the tree, they will encounter the forces and forms associated with what we call "the vision keys."

The collective beings and portals on the tree of enchantments are called "vision keys" and they embody the major contacts and transition points (or portals) in Faery Seership. There are many types of beings associated with these keys but that is the subject of a future discourse. As this book is an introduction to the Faery teachings and the practices of Faery Seership, I will provide some basic understanding of these keys and the portals to them for they will be encountered in any journey through the worlds. The exercises provided earlier in this book will begin the journey into the Tree of Enchantments and with practice, will bring about encounters with the vision keys or their attending beings. However, it in important that the reader understand that these exercises and the other material in this book are only the beginning of a long and beautiful road leading to many spiritual truths.

THE VISION KEYS AND THE THRESHOLDS

There are many inner contacts in each of the three realms of the Tree of Enchantments. Each one is both a guardian and a guide in that they preserve as well as transmit major wells of wisdom, powers and universal intelligence. Each plays a vital part in the creative process and unfolding vision of the Ancient One. It would be impossible to identify all of the beings at all levels that are involved in moving universal intelligence through its myriad forms and experiences, but there are some primary ones. These major beings could be termed as grand mediators of divine power or even as architects of universal creation. They are vast in their power and function. As mentioned in earlier chapters, Faery seers give honor to and partner with these beings, but do not worship them. Some of these contacts have been presented in detail in previous chapters, some have not. We can spend an entire lifetime approaching an understanding of these beings.

Though the Fay are not immortal, there are vast beings in the world of enchantment that live beyond the cycles of change. They are the engineers of creation and its tides and they are the vision keys. The Faery teachings often bring us into contact with these beings. They are so vast that they could be termed as gods and goddesses, but not in the classic sense. They are pre-human beings that embody universal principals and effect broad universal and planetary dynamics. These creation forces are not worshiped; they are contacted, approached and engaged. In fact, they are active throughout all of creation, including within you and me. This action is constant and written into the

246 THE FAERY TEACHINGS

secret laws of nature. Through visionary work, the seeker may contact them and unfold their vast mysteries within themselves and in the world around them. Inner pathways to contact are encoded into the visionary processes of the Faery Seership practices. Oral lore tells of the ancient origins of these images. Each of the images and the names of the keys were described to me through oral tradition and inner work.

The vision keys are:

- *The Utterer* – a feminine being which breathed forth life and motion and is the timeless ocean of outer space

- *The Star Father* – a masculine being who was first begotten of the void and giver of light

- *The Divine Ancestor* – the androgynous parent of all humanity, which embodies the collective wisdom of our species

- *The Guardian of Nature* – a masculine being that is stands at the threshold of the underworld, with the sacred horns and is the father of the natural world

- *The Child of Promise* (also known as *the Dreamer* in the Land) – the sun/son of the star father and the utterer, which is embodied in all of us and yet lies sleeping and dreaming in the deepest levels of the underworld

- *The Weaver* – an androgynous being and the weaver of the patterns of life, death and fate

Some of these beings dwell at the borderline of the seen and unseen. An example of this is the Guardian of Nature, whose presence is seen in the untamed power of the natural world and felt when we are alone, immerse in nature and feel the eyes of wildness peering upon us. Another example is the Divine Ancestor, whose presence is felt moving through the ancient blood of our Elders when we are in their presence in life or at the graveyard. These beings are always present to us because nature and our blood are always physically present. The other beings are deeper in the strata of life in the underworld or in the "inflowing" nature of the celestial world that appears to beam down upon and into our receptive planet. These beings make themselves obvious to us when we look deep into the processes of life or are swept into the current of change by forces we cannot see, but can sense. All of these primary contacts or "keys" open vast forces attended to by other beings that act as cells in the bodies of the primary beings. For example, the Faery are the mediators of the powers of the Child of Promise that sleeps at the center of our planet dreaming the world into being. This Dreamer is often identified as Lucifer, or the Lord of Light, which is the molten core of our planet. This core is the inner star of our world that gives forth life and vitality to all of life. Our red, pulsing, beating hearts contain the embodiment of the Dreamer in our physical bodies.

There are also primary entry and exit points to these beings and their worlds. Aspects of these portals have been presented throughout this book, especially in the visionary constructs. Though the practices of the Faery seer are almost exclusively focused on the underworld, it is important for the seeker to have a good grasp of each of the worlds and how they interface. For in truth, there is only one world with many patterns and functions. The three worlds are really vast dynamics of one living being. The three worlds are like the cogs within a clock. There are many parts driving the activities of one clock and they can be likened to major energetic processes and systems in our own bodies. Each being and cluster are like cells and organs that maintain the structural integrity of the whole organism.

The three primary portals to the vision keys are the called "the Holy and Formless Fire" (from the upper world to the underworld), "the Well of Enchantment" (from the surface world to the underworld), and "the Star Within the Stone" (from the underworld to the upper world). These portals are thresholds that are living dynamics within themselves where the realms bleed into each other. They are hidden paths in a grander scheme. They are also border areas where the keys unlock changes in the creative life force as it incarnates or dis-carnates and changes form, structure and dynamic activity. All of the exercises in this book and in all Faery Seership training are focused on encountering the keys and the beings that mediate their power. The Faery beings will assist us in this journey as their contact is made. The Opening of the Well exercise provided earlier in this book starts the seeker on opening the well. The Star Within the Stone requires much deeper work for it is the pivot Stone of Destiny that reveals purpose. The Holy and Formless Fire is only revealed when we step beyond all form into pure essence and thus is the end of our journey through form.

Encounters with the vision keys work like the tumblers in a lock. As each is encountered, they open doors to the unseen world. What lies beyond these doors can be enlightening and disturbing, but is never harmful unless they are exploited. Who knows what great gifts await you in the land of enchantment? Only the Faery people know. Seek, find, share and keep seeking. This is the Faery way. The ultimate guide to these hidden paths is in the secrets of Nature herself for ultimately she is the Weaver of Destiny. This mystery is reflected in a wonderful poem written by Ralph Waldo Trine and published in his book entitled *What All The World's A-Seeking*, which speaks beautifully to the laws of nature (which are the laws of spirit):

Would you find that wonderful life supernal,
That life so abounding, rich and so free?

Seek then the laws of the Spirit Eternal,
With them bring your life into harmony.

Never forget that Nature is the grand grimoire of the creator's magic – regardless of religion or practice. Read it well. Understand and apply its teachings and you will be truly wise.

CHAPTER 15:
REFLECTIONS OF A FAERY SEER

Lay me to sleep in the sheltering flame,
O Master of the hidden fire!
Wash pure my heart, and cleanse for me
My soul's desire.

In flame of sunrise bathe my mind,
O Master of the hidden fire,
That, when I wake, clear eyed may be
My soul's desire.

— *"The Mystic's Prayer," Fiona Macleod*

THE ROAD TO ENCHANTMENT

Over the many years of living and sharing the Faery teachings, several occultists, teachers and wisdom keepers have asked me to write about my journey to becoming a Faery seer. Or, as one noted occultist and author asked, "I want to know how Orion got this way, what shaped him." Truly, I am not finished becoming a Faery seer. In fact, I am not sure one can ever be finished because the road of Seership leads into and through a discovery of the many hidden treasures in the vast world of the spirits and spiritual forces not to mention the unfathomable depths of our souls.

I have reflected on this question for three years now since the first release of the *The Faery Teachings,* when it was voiced by a dear friend of mine. My inner response to this question, more important than my journey as one seer, is this question: What shapes the journey of any person seeking the hidden ways, opening these roads into themselves and becoming a seer? Therefore, the few elements that I share about my journey and experiences are less about me. More, they are about the sculpting hands of the spirit world changing the shape of my inner and outer life so that I may be able to see into that other world, speak of what I see, lead others to a discovery of the underworld and be a voice for the spirit world. In the end, these are the true achievements of a Faery Seer. This chapter will reflect on some of those specific elements of my life, but the primary focus will be on significant events, insights, challenges and opportunities that have shaped the life of this seer and likely will shape any reader who seriously pursues this path. Hopefully, the contents of this chapter will aide the seeker in their search for meaning and truth and the secret ways of Faery.

THE AWAKENING

As I have noted in previous chapters of this book, I grew up in a family and community heavily influenced by southern and Appalachian culture. Elements of old Irish, Scottish and English tradition coupled with major African influences from the slave trade shaped my spiritual landscape. Spirits, healings, conjure and the second sight were a constant presence throughout my life as a child living in the Shenandoah Valley in Virginia, though a great deal of my early years were also spent in the mountains of West Virginia. In this culture, spirits are a constant presence around every corner, in haunted houses, shadow roads (haunted roads), spooked woods, spirited bridges, live graves and in dreams and visions as forbearers of any significant event. In short, the human world and the spirit world are constantly overlapping and influencing each other.

In my culture, "*the spirits are, indeed, your closest neighbors living just next door to your breath*," as my mother often advised. It would be unimaginable to consider not believing in them. To do so would conflict with common sense and common experience. After all, our sciences have not proven that they do not exist, and what about the countless centuries of reported experiences with spirits? Are all of these experiences simply imaginary because our sciences lack the technology to confirm them? I think not!

My family has always been known for the presence of the "veil," a placental sheath that falls over the eyes of the newborn that indicates that the child will have "the gift" or "the blessing" of the second sight. This "blessing" indicates that the child will be able to see into the other world of the spirits and they (the spirits) will be able to speak to the human and give them pre-vision, or the ability to see what may occur in the future. This aspect of the veil is the one most talked about. The ability is usually presented through "tokens" or signs given to the gifted one. However, in rare cases such as mine, the gift goes much further. My veil granted me the ability to not only receive tokens, which are the intermediary influences of the spirits, but to contact and be contacted by the spirits directly. This gift may sound like fun to the morbid thrill seeker, but was terrifying to a child being contacted by a murdered loved one, or a teenager who just died in a car crash, or a tortured slave spirit. The early years of the awakening of the gift were not fun at all. They were troubling, indeed. This is one of the reasons why I have chosen to teach information that provides a sound mapping of the inscape of the spirit world: to aid others who have some level of the gift and especially those in the early phases of its awakening.

The reader must understand that it is not necessary that one be born with the veil to have the gift. Many people born without it are quite gifted. However, those born with the veil have a broader range of gifts and have no choice in its awakening. It will awaken usually beginning at puberty and continuing to mature into the mid-thirties. So, my gift, my culture and my mother form the foundational roots of my path in Seership. From these great roots grows a vast tree of experiences with witches, voodoos, hoodoos, conjurers, faith healers, seers and other traditional magic workers and walkers between the worlds. Always, however, the fuel for this quest was my desire to understand the realms of spirit and the role of humanity (including, but not specific to, myself). I could have never predicted that this quest would lead me to the dark edges of life and death, night and day, human and other, hope and despair, miraculous and the morbid. You see, in order to teach these ways, one must become the embodiment of these ways. Faery Seership truly challenges the seeker to look beyond human conceptions and culture, outside of our comfortable dogmas and rules, and into the living world of Faery ... the world of enchantment and of the hidden ... the astoundingly powerful and wise face of nature, ancestry and universal consciousness on its terms. In doing so, our individual purpose in the context of greater life emerges and Eden unfolds within us.

WHO SETS ABOVE YOU?

Often, when people would come to my mother for advice, one of the first things she would say to them is "let's see who sits above you." I had also heard other gifted ones and conjurers say this to clients or those seeking their assistance. Of course, as a child I just thought these people were kind of weird and didn't pay too much care since it seemed normal to them. This changed as I began to "see what (or who) sits above people."

This statement was, in fact, a form of diagnosis; a way of looking at a person and seeing what spirits or spiritual forces were working upon the individual. These spirits form a sort of guiding and guarding family for each surface walker. We have a team whether we know them or not; whether we allow their influences to flow to us unhindered or not. Another interesting comment I heard from an old Granny Woman (a conjure woman) was "that if a person ain't got no spirits, they ain't got no chance in life." It is important for the reader to understand both of these concepts in their quest for understanding the spirit world and its influence on our lives. The bottom line is this; if we seek to be spiritual, we must understand our place in the spiritual worlds and the beings that share symbiotic life with us.

We walk this surface world in search of experiences, meaning, fulfillment, happiness and the many treasures we seek as humans. We must not be deluded into thinking that we walk alone and only for ourselves. The Faery teachings are clear that we walk this world on behalf of our incarnate selves (the surface walker), our soul purpose (the dream walker), our spiritual core (star walker), the ancestral spirits, the vision of the planet (the Dreamer), her attending spirits and a higher power, which we may call God, Goddess, the Ancient One or a host of other names. Without contact with these forces, we lack vision, purpose, inner communion, clarity, protection, guidance and context; all of which are crucial for surviving the elemental storm of the surface world and attaining the purpose of our existence. These are the spirits that "sit above you" as guiding forces. To take this teaching further, I recall times when my mother said to a client, "Why dear, nothing sits above you; you've lost your faith and closed the doors. You have to go and pray every day to open the doors and build the bridge of faith that allows God (or the spirits) to reach you." In other words, we must invite the spirit world into our lives for a healthy relationship with them. Otherwise, their influence will come to us in shocking and often disturbing ways when we are in crisis or caught "betwixt and between" life and death, sleep and awake, dreaming and thinking. Our belief in them is an aid but does not even in the slightest way define their existence.

This concept is core to the world of the seer. There must be a constant and organic relationship with the spirit world filled with prayer and meditations. These two practices are the pillars of the temple to the spirit world, whether it is the upper or underworld. With prayer, you reach out to the unseen forces and speak and communicate with them. With meditation, you listen to the guidance of the spirits. Both of these form the active relationship crucial to the seer's abilities. Without these in place, the gifted ones are often plagued by the influences of the human and elemental world. In my experience, imbalance, distraction and fear come into our consciousness and take root when these disciplines lack. Our inner/underworld and our surface world are shaped by elemental forces that, though powerful, sacred and necessary, also affect our passions, fears, cravings and whims. Without contact with our core essence and rarefied spiritual forces, we can easily be lead astray and lose contact with these guiding forces. In short, not all of nature is kind, and not all of humanity is human. The spark for the fires of inquiry for the student seer should be fueled by this under-standing, coupled with an unquenchable thirst for knowledge and wisdom.

It is so easy to be distracted from the spiritual voices that guide us. These distractions are primarily human creations. I share with you this prayer which I wrote as a result of my understanding of this process and my desire to stay plugged in to that still, quiet voice that utters from the depths of the cave of my being and helps me stay upon my path of discovery and fulfillment. I hope that this prayer proves useful to you as well. Though I call it "A Witch's Prayer," it can be used by any spiritual person by adding the name of their deity in the first line. The prayer reads as follows:

Great Mother ... Great Father, let me be open to and guided by the highest and most noble inspirations and aspirations.

Let me not falter nor let my feet stray from this guidance.

Grant me inner stillness and the joy that comes when thee and me are as one.

Let neither the winds of change nor the whim of humanity, nor the tides of form, distract me from the still voice.

*And, should I be distracted, lovingly and swiftly place my feet
and mind back on the path of true wisdom.*

So be it!

It has been my experience that we are most in crisis when
that still voice that utters through our walkers is hushed by the
distractions of our world. I cannot advise the seeker enough of
the irreplaceable roles of meditation and prayer in the spiritual
quest. These practices greatly assist the threefold life of the
walkers to come into alignment and allow the inflowing tides of
divinity and "those who sit above you" to offer guidance and
directions.

MANY SPIRITS, MANY TONGUES

As I have grown in the Faery ways, I have come to understand
that the spirits speak to us in many ways, nearly all of the time.
As we move through our surface life on this planet, the spirits
offer insights to use in a myriad of ways and manners from the
most subtle to the most overt. This leads me back to a saying my
mother often shared, "You never know who the angels are." As
I have walked the grey roads between the worlds, I have found
this to be true over and over again.

The spirits can speak to us through persons, places and
things. They can speak through homeless strangers on the road.
They can speak to us in dreams and inspirations. They can speak
to us through circumstances and situations that form strange
patterns that reveal things. They often speak to us at the height
of delight or the depths of despair when we are not so firmly
footed on our convictions and possibility can leak through the
cracks of our consciousness. Their (the spirits') church is the
universe and they are not confined to a specific day each week
in a particular building. In fact, no spirit being is confined in
such a way. They often speak to us when our death-grip hold on
reality is shaken loose.

Initially, the influences of the spirit world (Faery and other) can be quite unsettling because their influences are filtered through our fears, distractions, belief systems and paradigms. The early influences of the spirits may frighten the seeker because they are so fluid, yet real. The spirits often require adjustments in our own perceptions and lifestyles. I found that the more our lives are lived consciously in a spiritual and in-spirited way, the more we cannot ignore the spirit influences in our lives and those around us. Once the communication opens up, it never closes down again. To do so would be like learning English, speaking it for years in a living context, then trying through mere determination to pretend that you do not understand what people are saying when they are speaking English. Too late – the language and the understanding are within you.

In the early phases of growth as a student of Seership, the seeker will need to "clean out the closet" of their minds. As I noted earlier, the contact with the spirit world has to flow through your preconceived notions and fears. This taints the communication and causes the most anointed of contact to become debased and frightening, which is not the intent of the spirits. This is especially true for the ancestral spirits, which challenge our concepts of life, death and the afterlife, and the Faery spirits, which challenge our concepts of nature spirits, angelic forces and other forms of life otherwise hidden from the eyes of humanity. The seeker will need to look closely at their beliefs, their fears, their hopes, their passions, their driving forces (i.e. what truly grips the steering wheel of your life) and refine these elements so that the spirit contact has good wiring to flow through.

WHAT DRIVES THE SEEKER TO SEEK?

There are many forces that cause a human to seek for the hidden paths into the spirit world. Some of these forces come from inner or underworld forces. Some of them come from stellar or upper world sources. We must all remember that though we seem to exist as individuals with our personal quests and visions, this individuality exists as one string in a greater fabric, one role in a greater society of spiritual life, human and non-human. Therefore, the drive for seeking comes from our inner human life (i.e. curiosity, boredom, depression, dissatisfaction with life, crisis, a spirit visitation, etc.), our life in the human society (the death of a loved one, exposure to an anointed person or sacred place, contact with information or material) and more importantly, the roles(s) of ourselves within a greater context in symbiosis with other forms of life (i.e. the human or spirit world places us in a situation where we must evolve spiritually or enter into crisis or personal destruction). The initial spark for our quest is what I term "divine discontent or restlessness." This is an inborn spiritual dynamic that ensures that all of creation fulfills their role in the unfolding vision of the Ancient One. I have found that there are three elements that cause the seeking nature to awaken. When any of these three or all of these three enters into the life of a seeker, the quest begins to unfold. The three elements are as follows:

- *Discontent* – This form of restlessness may feel like a lack of fulfillment, intense curiosity or an overwhelming "need to know" for the seeker. Discontent will not be relieved or lessened until it is addressed. In fact, it never really leaves us. It only goes into remission until the three walkers become activated by spiritual atrophy or the other two elements indicated below. The seeker must understand that discontent is a force to be reckoned with. It cannot be ignored. It cannot be medicated away. It can only be addressed though a spiritual quest. Again, meditation and prayer will help clarify the needs and intentions of this dynamic as it moves through you.

- *Necessity* – This form of restlessness is caused by need or a void that needs to be filled at the individual or collective levels. For the individual, the need may be caused by a crisis of some type that causes the seeker to question life, spirit and their role and destiny in life. This questioning can act like fire to a powder keg and cause a whole series of questions and impulses to rise from the underworld as it sends out a beacon to the spirits that the wall of rationalization is down and the seeker needs guidance and help.

• *Opportunity* – This form of restlessness is prompted by the availability of spiritual beings, information and guidance in the life of the seeker. When discontent and necessity meet the necessary resources to initiate the quest, it becomes hard for the seeker to ignore and block the process. Many times opportunity is described to me by my students as a door that suddenly opened to them even before they knocked. When the spirits present opportunity, the seeker is wise to take it.

These three elements act like tumblers in a lock. When they come into alignment with each other, a major life transformation is at hand and much wisdom will be revealed. I need to point out that though I am primarily talking about these elements on an individualized level, the individual exists in context within a greater collective in the world of the spirits. The spirit or Nar of our species and the great ancestral being of humanity also experiences discontent, which causes necessity and draws opportunity into our individual lives and this can cause the quest to begin.

COMING BACK TO THE MOTHER LAND

At this time in human life, we find ourselves feeling isolated from much of the living world. The conveniences of electricity, the demands of human social life, changing political climates and other human life often takes us further away from the natural world and the spiritual natures of our very existence. However, no matter how distracted we as humans become, nature and her attending spirit beings are always on track, attuned and aware of where this planet and its inhabitants are going and how to get there. For this reason, it is crucial that all seekers have some land-base as a point of contact with the natural, non-human world. We must never forget that the land – the motherland – is what provides us context outside of the delusions of humanity and "humanocentric" life. All seekers need this home-base, whether it is in a park, excursions to the woods, or their own home-based land. This point of contact with the collective powers of nature is pivotal in the growth of the seer. Many opportunities arise in the relationship between the human and the land for the seeker to understand the inner workings of creation and vision unfoldment from the perspective of the spirit world.

I was born and raised on a lot of land that was a mix of wild woods and farmed fields. Both of these points of contact with nature allowed me to "plug in" to the undaunted currents of nature and to make contact with Faery and other spirit beings. Most of my early life was spent in the woods, following the winding ways of streams into haunted glens and ancient fossil beds. This shaped my intimate relationship with nature. Later in life, I moved to the Moonridge sanctuary and learned more directly about the inner processes of the spirit world through application of the Faery teachings. This contact with the land acted (and still acts) as a detoxification of the human life imprints on my spirit and allows me to look closer into the original plan held in the nature of the Faery world in all its primal power and beauty.

Students often ask me what has changed in my paradigm since I left the physical presence of my beloved Moonridge. Well, I share this for all seekers who read my work to ponder and apply to their lives. Ultimately, physical land is an outer form of an inner dynamic. It is a place where the underworld surfaces in a particular pattern. The more that pattern is either undisturbed by humanity or cultivated in partnership with the spirits of nature, the more that pattern is a living being that can introduce and initiate human seekers back into the oneness – the family of the living earth. But truly, the land is us and we are the land. Our bodies are made of the substance of this living planet and as long as we have our bodies, we have the land – "for in truth they are one."

Moonridge allowed me that opportunity to re-connect with the living earth of light. It allowed me to intimately explore the inner life of our beautiful, miraculous planet. She taught me how creation, destruction and regeneration work in its service to a great and powerful planetary vision. She also showed me how this is reflected in my walkers on every level. So, how did it change me? Well, I have taken the lessons of this awesome teacher named Moonridge and integrated them into my being. I now know, without a shadow of doubt, that the sacred land emerges everywhere we are. We only need to turn our hearts inward to the soul of the world and draw out the paradise therein. For me, my journey has moved me from a specific sacred place to making all places sacred. It has moved me from just the mysteries of the soiled land to the mysteries of blood, bone and flesh, for they are also of the sacred soil. Indeed, Moonridge gifted me with her voice so I may speak to the land beneath our feet and the land that houses our spirits (our bodies) whenever discontent, necessity and opportunity will it so. In doing so, I serve the sacred land and Dreaming Child of Promise within the land, within you, within me and ultimately within the stars!

In Closure

We are all blessed that so many of the rich traditions associated with the Faery ways have survived through folklore and ballads and have been resurfaced through research, both academic and intuitive. These ways offer deep insights into the natural and spiritual worlds that may lead us out of the way of ecological disaster and into our spiritual destinies to be at one with the creator. I truly believe that these teachings, and others like them, will play a pivotal role in saving humanity from itself. I am hopeful that enough human seekers will hear the call of enchantment and resume their place upon the sacred land. Then, and only then, will our ancestors and ourselves be redeemed. Then the vision of the Dreamer will be fulfilled and the Garden of Eden will flourish. I bid you blessings on your path and may the hands of the People of Peace guide you always.

With this, I leave you to your discoveries.

BIBLIOGRAPHY

BOOKS

Briggs, Katherine (1976). *An Encyclopedia of Fairies, Hobgoblins, Brownies, Bogies and Other Supernatural Creatures*. New York: Pantheon Books.

Briggs, Katherine (1978). *The Vanishing People: Fairy Lore and Legends*. New York: Pantheon Books.

Campbell, J. F.(1893). *Popular Tales of the West Highlands* (republished in March, 1999). Chester Springs: Dufour Editions.

Cooper, J.C. (1983). *Fairy Tales: Allegories of Inner Life*. Wellingborough, Northhamptonshire: Aquarian Press Ltd.

Emerson, Ralph Waldo (1994). *Nature and Other Writings*, ed: Peter Turner. Boston and London: Shambhala.

Hartman, Franz (1884). *Magic: White and Black*. Montana: reprinted by Kessinger Publishing Company.

Kipling, Rudyard (1910). *Rewards and Fairies*. Garden City: Doubleday, Page and Co.

Keightley, Thomas (1880). *The World Guide to Gnomes, Fairies and Elves*. New York: Avenel Books.

Macleod, Fiona (1907). *From the Hills of Dream*. London: William Heinemann.

Macleod, Fiona (1911). *The Silence of Amore: Where the Forrest Murmurs*. New York: Fox Duffield and Co.

Macleod, Fiona (1906). *The Washer of the Ford: Legendary Moralities and Barbaric Tales*. New York: Fox Duffield and Co.

McNeill, Marian F. (1956). *The Silver Bough: Vol. One*. Edinburgh: Cannongate Classics.

Pennick, Nigel (1996): *Celtic Sacred Landscapes*. New York: Thames and Hudson.

Rhys, John (1901, republished 1972). *Celtic Folklore: Welsh and Manx.* New York: Benjamin Blom, Inc.

Ross, Anne (1976). *The Folklore of the Scottish Highlands.* New York: Barnes and Noble.

Spence, Lewis (1946). *British Fairy Origins.* Wellingborough, Northhamptonshire: Aquarian Press Ltd.

Spence, Lewis (1948). *The Fairy Tradition in Britain.* Montana: Rider and Co.

Spence, Lewis (1951). *Second Sight: Its History and Origins.* London: Rider and Co.

Stewart, Grant W. (1823). *The Popular Superstitions of the Highlanders of Scotland.* Archibald Constable (Ward Lock, reprinted London 1970).

Stewart, R.J. (1985). *The Underworld Initiation.* Wellingborough, Northhamptonshire: Aquarian Press Ltd.

Stewart, R.J. (1990). *Robert Kirk: Walker Between the Worlds, a new version of The Secret Commonwealth of Elves, Fauns and Faeries in modern English with commentary.* UK: Element Books.

Stewart, R.J. (1995). *The Living World of Faery.* Somerset: Gothic Image Publications.

Thomas, Keith (1971). *Religion and the Decline of Magic.* New York: Charles Scribner's Sons.

Trine, Ralph Waldo (1896). *What All The World's A-Seeking.* New York: Thomas Y. Crowell & Co.

Evans-Wentz, W.Y. (1911). *The Fairy Faith in Celtic Countries.* New York: Citadel Press/ Carol Publishing Group.

Wright Small, Machaelle (1997). *Co-Creative Science.* Jeffersonton: Perelandra.

Yearsley, Macleod (1924). *The Folklore of Fairy Tale.* London: Watts and Co.

Yeats, W.B. (1918). *Irish Fairy and Folk Tales.* New York: Boni and Leveright, Inc.

Wilde, Lady (1887). *Ancient Legends, Mystic Charms and Superstitions of Ireland.* UK: Chatto and Windos

MUSIC

'We Do Not Die' (Lynda Millard, copyright 1996, Glass Umbrella Music/ASCAP; Lyrics: Lynda Millard Music: Lynda Millard & Ginger Doss, Dreamtrybe)

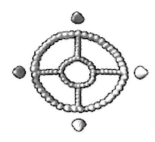

Pronunciation Guide

Alraun	Al'rune	Deosil	jesh'al
Ankou	ankh'koo	dii terreni	dee-ee' tareenee
Annwn	Ah'noon	dynion hysbys	din'eon hisbis
axis mundi	ak'sis mun'di	eddy of wights	edi uv wites
Banshee	ban'shee	Gaelic	gay'lik
Bawm	balm	genii loci	jee'ni loekee
Beltane	bel'tane	glaistig	glas'stig
Bilé	bee'lay	Gwynfyd	gwin'vid
Brownie	broo'nie	kain or teind	kane, tane
Brunaidh	brun'ayith	Prudwyn	prud'oon
Bucca	boo'ka	Sain	sane
Bucolauns	boo'kalawns	Samhain	sow'en
Clach na Glaistg	clock na glasstig	Toradh	toe'rath
Daione Sidhe	Doon she	Tuathal	too'ahtall
Ddaer	thay'er	Tylwyth Teg	tull'with teg

About the Artists

Martin Bridge

Martin Bridge is a teacher and artist in both
Theatrical and Fine Arts. His work includes a wide
variety of media. Masks are among his favorite subjects
and he teaches workshops in their creation and use in
Magic and Ritual. For more information and to view
some of his work visit www.martin.ritualarts.org

Andrew Goldys

Andrew Goldys is a freelance artist. His finds his influence
in surrealism, Tibetan Buddhism, shamanism, Jungian and
Grof psychology. His interests lay in working with sound and
vision. Most of his inspiration comes from nature itself: in
the trees, waters, leaves and rocks. To contact Andrew, email
werd_na_syd_log@aol.com or write to Muse Press.

FOR FURTHER EXPLORATION, PLEASE CONTACT

FAERY SEERSHIP

Orion Foxwood
P.O. Box 5128, Laurel, MD 20726
L.Orion@foxwood-temple.net

R.J. Stewart
www.dreampower.com

Dolores Ashcroft-Nowicki
http://dolores.ashcroft-nowicki.com

ARTWORK AND ILLUSTRATION

Martin Bridge
www.martin.ritualarts.org

Andrew Goldys
werd_na_syd_log@aol.com

EDITING, TYPESETTING AND PUBLICATION DESIGN

Jenny Stracke
P.O. Box 7803, Roanoke, VA 24019
willowdfox@cox.net

Recent titles from R J Stewart Books

R.J. Stewart Books

Online retail and wholesale ordering: www.rjstewart.net
Our new books are also distributed to the book trade
by Ingrams and Baker and Taylor in the USA and UK.

FORTY YEARS WITH THE FAIRIES
Daphne Charters   978-0-9791402-9-7
A remarkable account of communion with the realms of fairy and nature
spirits by the late British seeress Daphne Charters, from her collected
manuscripts written in the 1950's.

THE SPHERE OF ART
R.J. Stewart   978-0-9791402-6-6
The Sphere of Art embodies the most advanced work in R.J. Stewart's
Inner Temple Traditions Inner Convocation program, taught internation-
ally from 1988 to the present day. It is a direct method of magical transformation handed down through both an inner spiritual and outer historical lineage of teaching and practice.

STEWART FARRAR: WRITER ON A BROOKSTICK
Elizabeth Guerra with Janet Farrar   978-0-9791402-7-3
Stewart Farrar found Witchcraft by accident but devoted the rest of his
life to the subject by educating others. He became one of the most pro-
lific and much loved writers on the subject, and in doing so, helped to
make Wicca a viable and accessible path for many.

THE WELL OF LIGHT:
FROM FAERY HEALING TO EARTH HEALING
R.J. Stewart   978-0-9791402-1-1
Faery healing is a form of spiritual healing known in folkloric tradition
and implies a working relationship between humans and the spiritual forces
of the land and region in which they live. This book contains a wealth of
med-itations, visions and ceremonies on earth-based spirituality, including unique material never before published, such as working with the
Well of Light, communion through Go-Betweens and the Mystery of the
Double Rose.

THE SPIRIT CORD
R.J. Stewart   978-0-9791402-0-4
Explore insights and practical methods of Cord meditation, empowered
vision and spiritual magic using a physical cord in a set of simple and
powerful practices which range from the mystical and ancestral traditions of the ancient world to a unique set of contemporary methods for
transforming consciousness. The contemporary forms are the result of
more than thirty years of work by R. J. Stewart and have been developed
and tested in on-going groups in the USA and Britain.

And new editions of these classic works

ADVANCED MAGICAL ARTS
R.J. Stewart   978-0-9791402-3-5
R.J. Stewart draws upon the coherent, mature and enduring systems of
magic, long preserved in our Western culture. With beautiful illustrations by Miranda Gray, he offers a series of fundamental aspects of the
magical arts, which he supports with practical examples.

ROBERT KIRK: WALKER BETWEEN THE WORLDS
R.J. Stewart   978-0-9791402-4-2
This is R.J. Stewart's definitive annotated edition of the famous note-
book on Scottish folkloric faery tradtition from 1692 entitled "The Se-
cret Commonwealth of Elves, Fauns and Fairies," written by the Rev.
Robert Kirk not long before his death.

WITCHES WERE FOR HANGING
Patricia Crowther   978-0-9791402-5-9
In 1645, the infamous Matthew Hopkins, self-styled Witchfinder Gen-
eral, is sweeping though Essex leaving a trail of torture and death behind
him. The Nokes family are real witches and their attempts to outwit
Hopkins leads them into many terrifying situations.

*You can order these titles plus CDs of music, meditations and
guided visualizations from:*

R.J. Stewart Books
P.O. Box 802, Arcata, CA 95518
Online: www.rjstewart.net

Additional titles include:

EARTH LIGHT: THE ANCIENT PATH TO TRANSFORMATION
R.J. Stewart   1-892137-01-1

LIVING WORLD OF FAERY
R.J. Stewart   1-892137-09-7

MAGICAL TALES: THE STORY-TELLING TRADITION
R.J. Stewart   1-892137-02-X

THE MIRACLE TREE: DEMYSTIFYING THE QABALAH
R.J. Stewart   1-56414-650-2

THE POWER WITHIN THE LAND
R.J. Stewart   1-892137-00-3

THE SPIRITUAL DIMENSION OF MUSIC
R.J. Stewart   0-89281-312-1

UNDERWORLD INITIATION
R.J. Stewart   1-892137-03-8

WHERE IS ST. GEORGE? (30TH ANNIVERSARY EDITION)
R.J. Stewart   978-0-9791700-0-3

CPSIA information can be obtained
at www.ICGtesting.com
Printed in the USA
FSOW01n0855040316
17694FS

9 780979 140228